THE A

THE AENEID

SECOND EDITION

R.D. Williams

Foreword by James Morwood

Bristol Classical Press

Second edition published in 2009 by
Bristol Classical Press
an imprint of
Gerald Duckworth & Co. Ltd.
90-93 Cowcross Street, London EC1M 6BF
Tel: 020 7490 7300
Fax: 020 7490 0080
info@duckworth-publishers.co.uk
www.ducknet.co.uk

First edition published by Allen & Unwin in 1987

A catalogue record for this book is available
from the British Library

ISBN 978 1 85399 714 3

Printed and bound by CPI Group (UK) Ltd, Croydon, CR0 4YY

MIX
Paper from
responsible sources
FSC
www.fsc.org   FSC® C013604

CONTENTS

FOREWORD

English-speaking readers of the *Aeneid* are very fortunate to have two admirable guidebooks to the poem. One of them, W.A. Camps' *An Introduction to Virgil's Aeneid*, appeared in 1969. As the great Virgilian R.G. Austin wrote in the *Journal of Roman Studies*, it is a book which 'should be in the hands of all students of Virgil, of whatever age'.[1] The other is the present volume, the posthumous work of R.D. Williams, which was seen through to publication in 1987 by Fred Robertson, his colleague at Reading University where he spent his entire academic career (1945-83).[2] Comparisons between two books of such quality would be invidious. It remains true, however, that, while Camps had a broader scholarly range, writing a parallel (though shorter) introduction to Homer as well as editing the four books of Propertius, Williams, his interest in Statius notwithstanding,[3] was essentially a one-author man.[4] He lived and breathed Virgil, and this book was the summation of a lifetime's study and love. I once heard him say that he read the *Aeneid* once every year, adding characteristically that he found himself wondering each time whether Aeneas was going to make it.[5] His total immersion in the poet's work is evident on every page of his final book.

In addition, it is clear that here we have a man with a mission. He was eager to reach out to his readers and to leave them in no doubt about the greatness of Virgil's achievement. This evangelistic ambition was a feature of his whole career. He produced scholarly editions of Books 3 and 5 of the *Aeneid* in 1962 and 1960 respectively (Oxford, reprinted by Bristol

[1] W.A. Camps, *An Introduction to Virgil's Aeneid* (Oxford, 1969); review *JRS* 60 (1970) 261-2.

[2] Jasper Griffin's *Virgil* (Oxford, 1986) in the Past Masters series had appeared the year before. It is an elegant and perceptive book, but since it deals with the poet's whole oeuvre and devotes only fifty well-spaced pages to the *Aeneid*, it is not comparable with the Camps and Williams works. K.W. Gransden's *Virgil, The Aeneid* first appeared in 1990 in the Cambridge 'Landmarks of World Literature' series and a second edition by S.J. Harrison was published as a 'Student Guide' by Cambridge in 2004. It is a helpful vade-mecum, but it is written on a more modest scale than the Camps and Williams books.

[3] His first scholarly interest was the Silver Age, particularly Statius, and this led to his *Statius, Thebaid 10, Mnemosyne* suppl. vol. 22 (Leiden, 1972), 'a sensible and useful edition' (H.MacL. Currie, *Vergilius* 32 (1986) 6).

[4] The catalogue of the libraries of Oxford University credits him with the editorship of the *Crop Protection Handbook*, a splendidly apt subject for an editor of the *Georgics*. Alas, the attribution proves to be a false one.

[5] He writes with supreme insight of Aeneas' dilemma in his relationship with Dido on pp. 86-9 of the present volume.

Classical Press) and published a two-volume edition of the whole poem in 1972 and 1973 (Macmillan, reprinted by Bristol Classical Press). This was conceived as a replacement for T.E. Page's edition of 1894 and 1900, and remains a masterpiece of concision and clarity as well as locating the poem in the scholarship of his time. It glitters with insights and glows with a love of literature. In 1967 he produced his *Virgil*, the first of the important *Greece and Rome* New Surveys, for an adult audience. But then in 1973 came his *Aeneas and the Roman Hero* (Macmillan, reprinted by Bristol Classical Press) aimed at O-level (now GCSE) students, to be followed in 1985 by his *The Aeneid of Virgil: A Companion to the Translation of C. Day Lewis* (Bristol Classical Press), designed largely for A-level candidates. Neither book assumes any knowledge of Latin. Writing *con amore* and with splendid clarity and a total absence of condescension, Williams targeted his book at young students studying classical civilization, which was fast on its way to becoming the major growth area in school classics.

The present book was written for the Unwin Critical Library. Claude Rawson, the general editor of the series, summed up its aims in his Preface. It was intended 'for serious students and teachers of literature, and for knowledgeable non-academic readers'. One of the objectives was to provide the latter 'with reliable and stimulating works of reference and guidance, embodying the present state of knowledge and opinion in a conveniently accessible form'. Thus in Williams' volume quotations are almost always translated, though a certain basic knowledge of Latin is assumed. The democratizing aims of the book perhaps contributed to the fact that it flew below much of the radar as far as reviews were concerned. It was given short 'notices' in the *Journal of Roman Studies* (by Philip Hardie, positive if a tad lukewarm) and the *Classical Review* (by Nicholas Horsfall, decidedly *de haut en bas*).[6] And, rather strangely, the writer of the entry on Williams in the 2004 *Dictionary of British Classicists* fails to mention the book in his text and does not trouble to give the place of publication in his bibliography.[7] The muted response which it encountered in 1987 has led to its being far less well known than it should be, and it is splendid that Bristol Classical Press has elected to give it a new lease of life.

Though Williams had so often traversed this terrain, his message comes across with a remarkable freshness. His sensitive understanding of the vast range of Latin literature enables him to set the poem in its context. He was sympathetic to the so-called 'Harvard School' of Virgil scholars in the

---

[6] *JRS* 80 (1990) 268; *CR* 38-2 (1988) 410-11. Horsfall acidly comments that 'scholarly recognition at the highest level [Williams] neither expected nor won, yet the volume and persistence of his output created an impression that he was a truly significant Virgil scholar'.

[7] Rather less trivial omissions from this bibliography are Williams' brilliant essay on reception, 'Changing attitudes to Virgil', in D.R. Dudley (ed.), *Virgil* (Routledge and Kegan Paul, 1969) 119-38, and his chapter on the *Aeneid* in E.J. Kenney and W.V. Clausen (eds), *The Cambridge History of Classical Literature*, vol. 2: *Latin Literature* (Cambridge, 1982) 333-69.

USA in the 1950s and 60s[8] who felt that the poem had two voices, 'a public voice of triumph and a private voice of regret'.[9] The optimism attendant on the Roman mission is offset, perhaps overwhelmed – the Harvard School was deeply inclined to pessimism – by the poem's acknowledgement of the horror and suffering which it caused. His responsiveness to the influential work of the American Brooks Otis,[10] who took an essentially optimistic view of the poem and was, one suspects, the contemporary scholar who spoke most directly to him, led him to avoid the extremes of Harvard School pessimism.[11] If the two voices approach has become standard in the English-speaking world, Williams was one of the scholars who made it so.

He is first-class – and atypical – on Virgil's excellence as a war poet.[12] And he gives due weight to the second half of the poem, including for example a splendid summary of the altercation between Drances and Turnus in Book 11 (p. 75).[13] A creature of his time, he conducts discussions of passages using the methodology of the 'new criticism'. They still illuminate and enrich. His commentary on Dido's great speech at 4.584-629 is a classic of its kind (pp. 112-17).[14] Above all, Williams sees the poem as a *whole*. The individual sections, for example the especially memorable chapter on religion and the gods, are subsumed into a unified, though far from unproblematic vision of Virgil's mighty structure.

[8] Representative figures were Adam Parry, Wendell Clausen and Michael Putnam.

[9] A. Parry, 'The two voices of Virgil's *Aeneid*', *Arion* 2-4 (1963) 66-80; quotation p. 79.

[10] B. Otis, *Virgil, A Study in Civilized Poetry* (Oxford, 1964).

[11] The issue is dealt with in Chapter 5 of the present book. In his discussion in the Introduction to his edition of the poem, Williams makes use of the terms 'public voice' and 'private voice' and remarks that 'there is a powerful tension between the primary subject of the poem, Rome's greatness, and the pathos of human suffering which exists in spite of, or even because of, Rome's greatness. The element of pathos is so obvious to all readers of Virgil, and has been so strongly stressed in the last hundred years of Virgil criticism, that it is necessary to emphasize the other polarity, the optimistic note of Rome's greatness. The poem is first and foremost about Rome's mission, about the restoration of the Golden Age which can be achieved under Augustus. This was what the ancient critics thought the poem was about, and so did the English eighteenth century, and they were not wrong.' Williams goes on to do justice to 'the private voice', acknowledging 'the sacrifice of Dido and the destruction of Turnus and countless other warriors' as well as 'the opposition of Juno and all the suffering which she can cause' (*The Aeneid of Virgil, Books 1-6*, xx-xxii).

[12] For characteristic denigration of this aspect of the poet's work, see e.g. R. Jenkyns, *Virgil's Experience* (Oxford, 1998) 10: 'In the books of warfare Virgil has some difficulty in maintaining variety of narrative and force of feeling: we detect signs of strain from time to time.'

[13] In 1817 Byron avoided a visit to Mantua since it was the 'birthplace of that harmonious plagiary [i.e. plagiarist] and miserable flatterer, whose cursed hexameters were drilled into me at Harrow'. Yet it was at Harrow that he was given the stimulation of performing in the Drances/Turnus episode, at Speeches in 1804. Because of his club foot, he chose to play the sedentary part of Latinus, while Robert Peel, the future prime minister, enacted Turnus (Christopher Tyerman, *A History of Harrow School* (Oxford, 2000) 157-8).

[14] Is the new criticism making a come-back? *The Cambridge Companion to Lucretius* of 2007 contains a newly written chapter by E.J. Kenney ('Lucretian texture: style, metre and rhetoric in the *De rerum natura*') which includes two particularly valuable examples.

There are some odd gaps. Perhaps feeling that they would prove alienating for the non-academic reader, Williams includes no detailed discussion of metrical matters. One will have to go to pp. 42-5 of his New Survey to see what he has to say about these. And disappointingly, we encounter in these pages no serious appreciation of Virgil's mastery at bringing a scene to life. One need only turn to Williams' edition of Book 5 to sample his fine responsiveness to Virgil's evocative genius in his description of the aftermath of the foot race (p. 113 on 340-61):

> Virgil's brief description gives a lively picture of the chief persons involved in the dispute – Salius filled with excited indignation, and loudly protesting; Euryalus silent, winning people's sympathy by his evident fear of the protest being upheld; Diores vehemently opposing Salius' objection, in case he should lose his third prize; Aeneas benevolent and tactful, meeting the situation by awarding an extra prize to Salius; finally Nisus, covered with mud, urging with a theatrical gesture his own very doubtful claim, and Aeneas smilingly accepting it.

The vitality of Williams' note at this point is but one of many features of his work that make it clear why he proves so rewarding a guide to the poem.

As Williams was working on the present book, approaches in Virgil criticism were changing fast. Writing a New Survey on the poet in 1998 to replace Williams' pioneering book of thirty years before, Philip Hardie pointed out how 'the terrain has been very considerably reshaped by the undiminishing flood of new critical studies, particularly in the areas of poetics, allusion, narrative, and politics and ideology'.[15] Indeed, Hardie's book gives us an admirable account of where Virgil scholarship stood at the end of the twentieth century. Williams writes well of the deaths of Nisus and Euryalus (p. 63), but Hardie's edition of Book 9, dating from seven years later,[16] speaks an entirely different language. He remarks that

> despite their bravery and strength of arm [Nisus and Euryalus] are destroyed on the threshold of adult manhood because of a lingering immaturity. The night in which [they] run amok and then die may also symbolize their failure to emerge into the full daylight of the adult male hero (real men fight during the day).

Hardie's sense of how the two young heroes have failed to undergo a rite of passage to adulthood and his alertness to the possible symbolism of

---

[15] Philip Hardie, *Virgil*, New Surveys in the Classics 28 (Oxford, 1998) iii. S.J. Harrison gives a valuable account of the movements in twentieth-century Virgil criticism in S.J. Harrison (ed.), *Oxford Readings in Vergil's Aeneid* (Oxford and New York, 1990) 1-20.

[16] (Cambridge, 1994) 16.

their final night are characteristic of the critical sea change:[17] this is not the way that Williams thought or wrote. Yet the more recent critic referred to Williams' New Survey as 'elegant and human'. His voice may not have the precision, stylishness and distinction of R.G. Austin, a Virgil scholar whom he much admired, but it still has much to say to us. It has not seriously dated.

One of Williams' major areas of strength throughout his career was his mastery of the field of what we now refer to as reception. One of the delights of his editions of Virgil is provided by constant encounters with quotations from English literature invoked as parallels. On the 'marriage' in the cave on Book 4 (166ff.) which begins with Earth giving the sign, he quotes Milton's verses at the cataclysmic moment when Adam eats the apple and brings Sin and Death into the world:

> Earth felt the wound, and Nature from her seate
> Sighing through all her Works gave signs of woe,
> That all was lost. (*Paradise Lost* 9.782-4)

The cosmic power unleashed in both passages sets Virgil and Milton in a mutually illuminating symbiosis. Chapter 8 of the present book, entitled 'The Influence of the *Aeneid*', is hugely enjoyable and highlights Williams' role as a pioneer in this ever-expanding sphere. Almost at the very end, he quotes Tennyson's poem 'To Virgil', written at the request of the Mantuans to commemorate the nineteenth centenary of the poet's death. I have always had problems with the final stanza:

> I salute thee, Mantovano,
>   I that loved thee since my day began,
> Wielder of the stateliest measure
>   Ever moulded by the lips of man.

The hexameter may well be capable of expressing great stateliness but it is not a quality that I for one often find in Virgil. When he becomes stately, we should be on our guard: subversion is almost certain to lie in wait. 'Mantovano', Tennyson's embarrassingly orotund appellation for Virgil (it means 'the man from Mantua'), makes me think of the soupy band-leader Mantovani, a slightly earlier contemporary of Williams famous for his swooning strings. This 'mnemonic irrelevance' – the term is I.A. Richards'

[17] As Hardie remarks (16, n. 24), 'we are close to the symbolic structures of the Greek *ephebeia*, in which hunting and the night are associated with the passage of the adolescent to the status of male hoplite'. He refers to the classic discussion by P. Vidal-Naquet, 'The Black Hunter and the origin of the Athenian *ephebeia*', in R.L. Gordon (ed.), *Myth, Religion and Society* (Cambridge, 1981) 147-62.

– may in fact be less irrelevant to what Tennyson seems to be saying than it at first appears. The thought of the one-dimensional appeal of the musician may throw into relief that complexity in Virgil which denies us lasting acquiescence in anything as straightforward as stateliness. However, even if Tennyson has got it wrong in this concluding verse – and many Virgilians will feel strongly that he hasn't –, he is supremely insightful everywhere else, and Williams is spot on in his view that the poem 'not only expresses a most sincere and heart-felt admiration for the greatest of Mantua's sons but contains phrases which superbly describe the most essential qualities of Virgil's work: the mysterious spell of his diction and versification, and the basic conflict in the *Aeneid* between pathos ("sadness at the doubtful doom of human kind") and patriotic optimism ("sound for ever of Imperial Rome")'. The Victorian bard and the insightful scholar here shake hands in their appreciation of the greatest of the Roman poets.

James Morwood
Wadham College, Oxford

Bibliographical Note

R.D. Williams (1917-86)
For appreciation of his life and work, see Anon., *The Times*, 15 July 1986, 18; Anon., *The University of Reading Bulletin* no. 195 (1986); H. MacL. Currie and Robert B. Lloyd, *Vergilius* 32 (1986) 5-6: Roger Rees in R.B. Todd (ed.), *The Dictionary of British Classicists* (Bristol: Thoemmes Continuum).

Select Virgil bibliography
A selection from the vast number of books and articles on Virgil and the *Aeneid* published in English since 1980.

The recommended prose translation is that by D.A. West (Penguin, 1991).

F. Cairns, *Virgil's Augustan Epic* (Cambridge, 1989).
W. Clausen, *Virgil's Aeneid and the Tradition of Hellenistic Poetry* (California, 1987).
G.B. Conte, *The Rhetoric of Imitation: Genre and Poetic Memory in Virgil and Other Latin Poets* (Ithaca, 1986).
D.C. Feeney, *The Gods in Epic* (Oxford, 1991) chs 3-4.
K.W. Gransden, *Virgil's Iliad: An Essay on Epic Narrative* (Cambridge, 1984).
K.W. Gransden, *Virgil, The Aeneid* (2nd edn by S.J. Harrison) (Cambridge, 2004).
J. Griffin, 'The creation of characters in the Aeneid', in B.K. Gold (ed.), *Literature and Artistic Patronage in Ancient Rome* (Texas, 1982) 118-34, or in his *Latin Poetry and Roman Life* (Duckworth, 1986).
J. Griffin, *Virgil* (Oxford, 1986).
P. Hardie, *Virgil* (Greece and Rome, New Surveys 28, Oxford 1998).
P. Hardie, *Virgil's Aeneid: Cosmos and Imperium* (Oxford, 1986): see review by J. Griffin, *JRS* 78 (1988).

P. Hardie (ed.), *Virgil: Critical Assessments of Classical Authors*, 4 vols (London, 1999).

S.J. Harrison (ed.), *Oxford Readings in Vergil's Aeneid* (Oxford, 1990).

R. Heinze, *Virgil's Epic Technique* (originally published in German, 1903; Eng. tr. Bristol, 1993).

N.M. Horsfall (ed.), *A Companion to the Study of Virgil* (Leiden, 1995).

R.H.A. Jenkyns, *Classical Epic: Homer and Virgil* (Bristol Classical Press, 1992).

R.H.A. Jenkyns, *Virgil's Experience: Nature and History, Names, and Places* (Oxford, 1998).

R.O.A.M. Lyne, *Further Voices in Virgil's Aeneid* (Oxford, 1987).

R.O.A.M. Lyne, *Words and the Poet* (Oxford, 1989).

C.A. Martindale (ed.), *The Cambridge Companion to Virgil* (Cambridge, 1997).

I. McAuslan and P. Walcot (eds), *Virgil* (Oxford, 1990).

J.J. O'Hara, *Death and the Optimistic Prophecy in Vergil's Aeneid* (Princeton, 1990).

A. Rossi, *Contexts of War: Manipulation of Genre in Virgilian Battle Narrative* (Ann Arbor, 2003); see review in *BMCR* 2004 (11).

W.J.N. Rudd, 'The idea of empire in the *Aeneid*', *Hermathena* 134 (1983) 33-50.

H.-P. Stahl (ed.), *Virgil's Aeneid: Augustan Epic and Political Context* (Leiden, 1998).

G. Williams, *Technique and Ideas in the Aeneid* (Yale, 1983).

PREFACE

The intention of this book is first to analyse the *Aeneid*'s exploration of the issues confronting Aeneas and so by implication confronting Virgil's contemporaries, issues of human behaviour in triumph and disaster which continue to be the concern of modern society. Secondly I have tried to analyse the poetic techniques in which Virgil shows such surpassing mastery. I have aimed to present a broad picture of the historical and literary background which conditioned his writing, while at the same time surveying the timeless and universal nature of the achievement which has made the *Aeneid* so widely influential throughout the 2,000 years of its life so far.

I hope that the book will be of use both for professional scholars and for students of the *Aeneid* in universities and elsewhere, and also for the wider public of those to whom great literature provides fascination for its own sake.

I am much indebted to the Leverhulme Trust for the award of an Emeritus Research Fellowship to provide financial assistance for the completion of this book, and to my colleague at Reading University Mr F. Robertson, who has read through the whole work and assisted me with his comments and suggestions. My debt to earlier Virgilian scholars is too extensive to be listed, but I cannot let this opportunity pass without indicating my gratitude to Dr T. R. Glover, who taught me at Cambridge to love Virgil, and to Professor R. G. Austin, whose many commentaries on Virgil have been a constant source of inspiration.

The text I have used in quoting Virgil is basically Mynors's text, in the Oxford Classical Texts series, with minor modifications. The translations, except those specifically attributed to others, are my own.

R. D. Williams
1986

THE AENEID

CHAPTER 1

Virgil's Life and Works

A great national poet is likely to be both a product of his times and an individual genius with insights extending far beyond those of his contemporaries. This is to say that he must be influenced, perhaps positively, perhaps negatively, by the social and political environment in which he lives; but he must also step outside the ordinary run of opinion and counter-opinion and see his own times *sub specie aeternitatis*. He must have the ability of expressing memorably and movingly aspects of human experience which 'find an echo in every heart', but he must also illuminate areas which have not been previously seen for what they are. More perhaps than in most literature the Roman poets were influenced by tradition, and Virgil most certainly was; but he could also view this tradition and its implications in a new and more penetrating way, and this indeed he did in his *Aeneid*.

Publius Vergilius Maro (70–19 BC) was born in northern Italy, in a village not far from Mantua, an area which at the time of his birth had not yet received full Roman citizenship. Thus his formative years, like those of Catullus, were spent in a region racially and culturally distinct from the central area around Rome (which later on he got to know well), and from the rich southern region of Campania, where he spent most of his later life. He knew poverty and hardship in his early years before achieving the leisure and fame and friendship with the leading figures of Rome which his poetry brought him. It is important to realize that there was this variety of social experience in his life, because it was through this that he was able to use his literary heritage in a way related to real life as he knew it.

His parents were both of humble origin and his father seems to have been a small peasant farmer. He was able, however, to give Virgil a good education, first locally, then at Milan and finally in Rome. Virgil is said to have been of delicate health, and very shy and self-effacing in demeanour; we are told that he pleaded just one case in court, at which he spoke most unimpressively. He clearly was not a man of affairs, though ironically most of his life was spent in close touch with the leading politicians of Rome. He was never married, and is said to have had the nickname Parthenias, 'the maiden'. It seems quite clear that he lived a retiring life as a scholar and poet who moved most easily in his own world of creative imagination; yet in the *Aeneid* his subject is the past, present and future of Rome and its great leaders.

In his twenties he rapidly became very well known through his poetry. There exist a number of minor poems commonly attributed to him in antiquity, and nowadays called the *Appendix Vergiliana*; it is highly unlikely that he was in fact the author of these (with one or two possible minor exceptions), and it was evidently the *Eclogues* which brought him fame. These were pastoral poems written at intervals between about 42 BC and 37 BC (or perhaps 35 BC) and published as a collection of ten in 37 or 35 BC. But the individual poems became well known before the collection was published, and they indicate that at this early stage Virgil knew well many of the leading figures of Rome. Most of the poems, especially the earlier ones, are closely modelled on the pastoral poems of the Greek Theocritus, but there are many literary allusions to contemporary Roman poets: Maevius, Bavius and Pollio in *Eclogues* 3, Gallus in 6 and 10, Varius and Cinna in 9. Of these Pollio and Gallus were also prominent statesmen: Pollio was consul in 40 BC and Gallus became the first prefect of Egypt. There are references too (*Ecl.* 6 and 9) to Varus, a prominent soldier and administrator, and to Octavian himself in *Eclogues* 1 (not named but obviously referred to). It is generally considered, probably correctly, from evidence based on *Eclogues* 1 and 9 that Virgil's friendship with these prominent men led to the restoration of the family farm after its confiscation during the settlement of veteran soldiers after the Battle of Philippi in 42 BC.

The *Ecologues* are delicate poems in a minor key, written very much under the Hellenistic influence which at that time was extremely dominant in Latin literary circles. They are obviously very unlike the *Aeneid*, both in tone and in diction and metrical movement; but already we see indications of some of the major features of the *Aeneid*, especially the note of pathos for unhappy love or early death and in particular sympathy for the lonely individual whose life is violated by the march of great political events over which he has no control.

From 37 to 30 BC Virgil was occupied with the four books of *Georgics*, often referred to as the most perfectly finished work of Latin literature (along perhaps with Horace's *Odes*). He composed at a rate which works out at less than a line a day, and was said 'to have wittily remarked that he fashioned his poetry as a she-bear her cubs, gradually licking it into shape' (Donatus, *Vita Vergilii*, 22). The poem is ostensibly a didactic work on farming, giving instruction on how to care for the land and its animals; but in reality it aims to use the didactic framework in order to express and communicate to others a deep love for Nature and the countryside. Seneca was exactly right when he commented that Virgil wrote his *Georgics* not to instruct farmers but to delight readers. Compared with the *Eclogues* the hexameter movement is more varied, the descriptive writing richer. The poet shows a brilliant ability to construct material on a large scale in such a way as to produce symmetries and contrasts that are highly effective. This ability, already evident in the short *Eclogues*, was to be vital for the poetic architecture of the *Aeneid*. The fourth book of *Georgics* ends with an epyllion, a short narrative poem of the kind beloved by the Hellenistic writers, about Aristaeus and the loss and restoration of his bees, with an inset story of Orpheus and Eurydice. This was Virgil's first published attempt at narrative poetry, and though on a small scale was an indication that his future poetic plans were to be based on narrative poetry.

We have evidence from the ancient commentators that during this time Virgil was planning an epic poem, as well as his own testimony at the beginning of *Georgics* 3 (see Chapter 4). The rest of his life was occupied in writing the *Aeneid*, which he sketched first in prose, then wrote in separate sections as the mood took him. In the year 19 BC, when he was planning to spend another three years on the revision of the poem, he undertook a journey to Greece (probably to get local colour for the part of the *Aeneid* concerned with that area, *Aeneid* 3 in particular), but in Greece he fell ill of a fever, and died on his return to Italy at Brundisium. On his deathbed he asked that the *Aeneid* should be burned, but his request was refused and he left the poem with Varius and Tucca, with instructions that they should not publish anything which he himself would not have published. At the insistence of Augustus the poem was published with hardly any alterations (*summatim emendata*); one indication of its lack of final finish is the presence of some fifty half-lines, and there are certain minor inconsistencies and passages which look like stop-gaps. But it should be firmly understood that the poem is finished and complete except for minor details, and there are no sufficient grounds for thinking that Virgil wanted the poem burned because he was essentially dissatisfied with it. The unresolved conflicts and dilemmas of the poem are inherent in its whole nature from start to finish, and indeed are an essential part of its claim to greatness.

CHAPTER 2

The Political and Literary Background of Virgil's Times

The *Aeneid* was written in the golden age of Latin literature, during the first dozen years of Augustus' supremacy, at a time when at long last stability had returned to the Roman world and the prospects seemed bright and exciting. It was a time of celebration, and patronage of literature, directed by Maecenas and Messalla and many others, was in a flourishing condition (in contrast with the complaints of poverty and lack of patronage several generations later by Juvenal and Martial). Highly talented contemporaries of Virgil were Horace, Livy, Propertius and Tibullus, as well as Gallus and many others whose works are lost.

Virgil's youth and early manhood had been spent during the period of constant unrest and civil war which marked the last years of the Roman republic. Following the Social War against the Italians and the civil war between Marius and Sulla near the beginning of the century there had been the slave rising under Spartacus in 73 BC, the conspiracy of Catiline in 63 BC and the long struggle for supreme power between Pompey and Julius Caesar which culminated in the defeat and death of Pompey and the sole rule of Caesar. Staunch Republicans, led by Brutus and Cassius, ended what they regarded as dictatorship, or kingship under another name, by assassinating Caesar in 44 BC. They were opposed by Caesar's right-hand man Marcus Antonius, who was eventually joined by the young Octavian, the future emperor. He was the son of Atia, Caesar's niece, and in Caesar's will was adopted as his son. Together with Lepidus they formed a triumvirate, and were successful in defeating Brutus and Cassius at Philippi in 42 BC. There followed executions by proscription of the leading Republicans, including Cicero. But this was far from the end of civil strife: Sextus Pompeius continued a guerilla warfare on behalf of the Republicans, and Antony and Octavian became obvious competitors for sole power, despite the *mariage de convenance* of Antony to Octavian's sister.

This extremely condensed account of the events during Virgil's first thirty-five years gives some idea of the horrors experienced during this time, and they are reflected in his poetry. *Eclogues* 1 and 9 are about the pathetic plight of the small farmer evicted from his land by the military; and *Georgics* 1 ends with a vivid account of the terrible portents after the assassination of Julius Caesar, and of the battle of Philippi at which both sides were Romans – *paribus telis*; and its final passage is a desperate prayer to heaven that Octavian Caesar should be permitted to restore peace and order to a 'ruined generation'. Here is the passage, a passage that is vital for a proper understanding of the relief and exhilaration which greeted the fulfilment of the prayer, and which prevailed during the time when Virgil was writing the *Aeneid*.

> *di patrii, Indigetes, et Romule Vestaque mater,*
> *quae Tuscum Tiberim et Romana Palatia servas,*
> *hunc saltem everso iuvenem succurrere saeclo*
> *ne prohibete. satis iam pridem sanguine nostro*
> *Laomedonteae luimus periuria Troiae;*
> *iam pridem nobis caeli te regia, Caesar,*
> *invidet atque hominum queritur curare triumphos,*
> *quippe ubi fas versum atque nefas; tot bella per orbem,*
> *tam multae scelerum facies, non ullus aratro*
> *dignus honos, squalent abductis arva colonis,*
> *et curvae rigidum falces conflantur in ensem.*
> *hinc movet Euphrates, illinc Germania bellum;*
> *vicinae ruptis inter se legibus urbes*
> *arma ferunt; saevit toto Mars impius orbe;*
> *ut cum carceribus sese effudere quadrigae,*
> *addunt in spatia, et frustra retinacula tendens*
> *fertur equis auriga neque audit currus habenas.*

(*Geo.* 1. 498–514)

Gods of our fatherland, Indigetes, Romulus and mother Vesta, who guard the Tuscan Tiber and the Roman Palatia, at least do not forbid this young man to save our ruined generation. Long enough now have we atoned with our blood for the perjury of Laomedon's Troy; long enough, Caesar, has the kingdom of heaven begrudged you to us, complaining that you concern yourself with men's triumphs. For indeed here right and wrong are confounded – so many wars in the world, so many shapes of sin, no proper respect for the plough, the fields gone to ruin with the farmers driven out, the curving sickles converted into iron swords. Here Euphrates threatens war, there Germany; neighbouring cities break their agreements and fight each other;

Mars, the god of civil war, rages all through the land. It is as when chariots speed from the starting-posts, going faster and faster through the laps, and the charioteer vainly clutching the leather thongs is swept on by the horses and the chariot does not obey the reins.

Equally powerful pessimism and indeed guilt is expressed in the same period by Horace: here is *Epode* 7, addressed to the Roman people:

> *quo, quo scelesti ruitis? aut cur dexteris*
> *   aptantur enses conditi?*
> *parumne campis atque Neptuno super*
> *   fusum est Latini sanguinis?*
> *non ut superbas invidae Carthaginis*
> *   Romanus arces ureret,*
> *intactus aut Britannus ut descenderet*
> *   Sacra catenatus Via,*
> *sed ut secundum vota Parthorum sua*
> *   urbs haec periret dextera.*
> *neque hic lupis mos nec fuit leonibus,*
> *   nunquam nisi in dispar feris.*
> *furorne caecus an rapit vis acrior*
> *   an culpa? responsum date!*
> *tacent et ora pallor albus inficit,*
> *   mentesque perculsae stupent.*
> *sic est: acerba fata Romanos agunt*
> *   scelusque fraternae necis,*
> *ut immerentis fluxit in terram Remi*
> *   sacer nepotibus cruor.*

Where, where are you rushing to, men stained with crime? Or why are swords once sheathed now grasped in your hands? Has not enough Latin blood been shed on land and sea? – not so that the Romans might burn the lofty citadels of envious Carthage, or that the Britons, unattacked yet might pass in chains down the Sacred Way, but so that, as the Parthians dearly wish, this city might perish by its own right hand. This has not been the way of wolves or lions who never attack their own kind. Is it mad frenzy or some fiercer power that drives you on – or guilt? Give answer! They give none, and a white pallor overspreads their faces, and their thoughts are shaken and dazed. Thus it is: bitter fate pursues the Roman people, and the crime of a brother's murder, ever since the blood of innocent Remus stained the ground, a curse upon generations to come.

Horace here, in one of the most moving and passionate poems in Latin literature, expresses by means of the legend of Romulus killing his twin Remus the horror of family feuds and internal violence. It is a guilt-feeling which he reiterates elsewhere, for example, *Epode* 16. 9: 'we, a generation of accursed descent, shall ourselves destroy Rome'.

The two quoted passages written by the two leading poets of the time during the last ten years of the long period of civil wars give a most vivid picture of horror and guilt against which to set the relief and new hopes following the final defeat by Octavian of Antony and Cleopatra at the Battle of Actium in 31 BC. We see preliminary glimpses of optimism at the beginning of *Georgics* 3 and the end of *Georgics* 4, and the new regime is celebrated in the *Aeneid* both directly (at the end of *Aeneid* 8 where the battle and Octavian's subsequent triumph in Rome are depicted) and indirectly in many ways, as we shall see. It is celebrated also by Horace, for example in *Epode* 9 and *Odes* 1. 37, and later in *Odes* 4. 15.

One of the main claims of Octavian (now to be called Augustus) was that he was 'restoring the republic' both politically (by divesting himself of certain powers) and morally, by enabling the Romans once more to be true to themselves by returning to the old virtues, the customs of their ancestors (*mos maiorum*). This was the moral message of Livy's history, the early part of which was being written at about this time; the Romans of old are depicted idealistically as people of simple virtues, brave, pious, just, disciplined, resolute, unyielding. Livy is writing in order to recall the Romans to these romanticized glories of their past; this is also one of the major aspects of the *Aeneid*. Horace too proclaims this moral aim both in the gentle philosophizing of his satires and epistles and in a number of his *Odes*, especially the first six *Odes* of Book 3, often known as the Roman *Odes*. The second of these, extolling bravery in warfare, recalls Livy's pictures of Roman warriors of old; the third (like the second) has a strongly Stoic flavour and a speech from Juno (proclaiming that she will give up her hostility against the Roman descendants of Troy provided that they give up their Trojan characteristics) which bears a remarkable resemblance to the *Aeneid* (12. 819 ff.). The fourth is particularly interesting in that it shifts in the middle from an autobiography of Horace as a child of the Muses to include Augustus as a lover of the Muses too and then by implication to involve him in Horace's moral advice, portrayed in the myth of the defeat of the giants and Titans and summarized in the memorable maxim:

> *vis consili expers mole ruit sua;*
> *vim temperatam di quoque provehunt*
> *in maius . . .*   (3. 4. 65–7)

Force without wisdom is destroyed by its own impetus; but force
which is properly controlled is supported by heaven too . . .

The fifth of these *Odes* tells the story of Regulus, an early Roman
general who placed bravery and patriotism above his own life and
family; and the sixth is a most remarkable attack on current
immorality in contrast with the stern discipline of the past.

This then was the social and political climate within which two
of Rome's greatest writers, Horace and Virgil, expressed their disgust
and guilt at the sins of the past and their hopes and confidence that
under the new regime the Romans would return to their old
traditions and move forward to a new world of excitement and
achievement.

Sometimes the imagery in which gratitude to the new emperor is
expressed by the poets strikes the modern reader as excessive: the
future deification of Augustus is referred to several times by Horace
(*Odes* 3. 3 *init.*, 3. 5. *init.*, etc.) and by Virgil (*Geo. 1. 24 ff., Aen.*
1. 289 ff., etc.). Suffice it to say here that it must be borne in mind
that the Roman attitude towards deification was entirely different
from ours: their mythology was full of great heroes who had become
gods (Hercules, Bacchus, Castor and Pollux).

Were these expressions of support for Augustus genuine? Of
course they were: the evidence, as we have seen, is overwhelming.
The *Aeneid* fits into its time: it was an epoch when optimism was
in the air, perhaps not unlike the period of Elizabeth I in England.
But this is not to say that the optimism was unreasoning, and we
shall see that a primary aspect of the greatness of the *Aeneid* is that
it faces the problems at the same time as it expresses the hopes of
Rome reborn.

We have now looked at the literary scene as it was affected by the
social and political situation in Rome. Next we should consider
Virgil's environment from the purely literary angle.

The period of Virgil's youth was marked by a new movement in
Roman literary circles – a rebellion against the old traditions of long
narrative poems in favour of the shorter and more personal lyric or
elegiac poem, or the brief and emotional epyllion. This movement,
of which Catullus was one of the chief members, gained for its
followers the title of *novi poetae* and became highly influential,
though disliked intensely by traditionalists like Cicero. The *novi
poetae* based their work on the Greek Alexandrian (or Hellenistic)
poets such as Callimachus and Philetas and Theocritus and aimed
at personal expression of intensely felt emotion, very often the
emotion of love. They sought an immediacy of impact concerned
with individual emotions; they were not interested in large national

or social issues but in the more intimate, personal world of the poet's own feelings. This they wished to express briefly, elegantly, descriptively, above all intensely. Virgil was very much under their influence in his earliest poetry, and the *Eclogues* owe much to Theocritus in particular but also in a wider sense to the *novi poetae* in general. The debt is much less in the *Georgics*, except for the second half of the fourth book, and in the *Aeneid* this aspect appears only quite rarely, but when it does appear it has a tremendous impact. This is discussed further in Chapter 3.

Meanwhile important poetic contemporaries and friends of Virgil strongly proclaimed themselves as followers of the *novi poetae*, and refused the epic mode which Virgil had undertaken. All three of the outstanding elegists, Gallus, Propertius, Tibullus (and later Ovid) were to a large extent followers of Callimachus and his school. We unhappily possess practically none of Gallus' poetry, but both Propertius and Tibullus are explicit in their rejection of national poetry in favour of the emotion of the individual, as well as in their insistence on smoothness of expression. For example, Tibullus (1. 1. 53 ff.):

> te bellare decet terra, Messalla, marique
>> ut domus hostiles praeferat exuvias:
> me retinent vinctum formosae vincla puellae,
>> et sedeo duras ianitor ante fores.
> non ego laudari curo, mea Delia; tecum
>> dum modo sim, quaeso segnis inersque vocer.

It is right for you, Messalla, to wage war on land and sea, so that your house may display spoils taken from the enemy: but for me, the bonds of a beautiful girl hold me in their grip, and I sit keeping watch at her unkind doors. I do not care for glory, my Delia: provided only that I am with you I ask to be called lazy and inactive.

Near the end of the same poem he says:

> vos, signa tubaeque
> ite procul, cupidis vulnera ferte viris . . . (1. 1. 75–6)

Depart far off from me, you banners and trumpets: take your wounds to men of greedy ambition.

The same attitude is frequent in Propertius: for example, *non ego sum laudi, non natus idoneus armis: hanc me militiam fata subire volunt* ('I was not born a man fit for glory or warfare: these are the battles' – i.e. the battles of love – 'which the fates wish me to engage in', 1. 6. 29–30). He makes his Alexandrian literary ancestry clear very often, for example:

> Ennius hirsuta cingat sua dicta corona:
>   mi folia ex hedera porrige Bacche tua,
> ut nostris tumefacta superbiat Umbria libris,
>   Umbria Romani patria Callimachi.   (4. 1. 61 ff.)

Let Ennius crown his poetry with an untrimmed garland; but Bacchus, give me leaves from your ivy, so that Umbria may boast and be proud over my writing, Umbria the home of the Roman Callimachus.

This last quotation indicates precisely, as other passages in Propertius do, that he belongs to the Alexandrian school in the spirit of his writings and also in style. The metaphorical contrast between the 'untrimmed' or 'shaggy' nature of Ennius' rough and robust poetry and the shining 'ivy' of Callimachus shows very well the stylistic aims of the *novi poetae*.

The achievement of Virgil in the *Aeneid* was to combine the robustness of traditional epic with the soft sensitivity and smooth flow of the *novi poetae*, and to allow the contrast between the two to set up tensions of many kinds. He had in his youth been fascinated by the type of poetry which the Alexandrians wrote, and he retained enough admiration for it to incorporate it from time to time in the grandeur of the full-scale national epic. In the *Aeneid* the heightened tone of war and empire blends with the lyrical tone of the Alexandrian school. The world of humanity in the *Aeneid* is viewed from both sides, comprising both the massive scale of events and movements which make history and the tiny world of the individual.

CHAPTER 3

The Literary Sources of the Aeneid

Before we come to a literary analysis of the qualities and purposes of the *Aeneid* itself it is vital to consider in some detail the literary sources which Virgil employed, especially his use of Homer as a poetic model and also as a counterweight for his own exploration of human character and behaviour. We have already looked at the historical and social conditions which gave birth to the *Aeneid*; but the poem was the child not only of Augustan peace after civil strife, but also (importantly and essentially) the child of the literature of the past as it had presented its visions of the human condition.

The writers of the ancient world were, with very few exceptions, greatly influenced by literary tradition, particularly in selecting their genres and in following the rules of that genre. Their claims to originality would depend upon the way in which they treated the genre, and perhaps adapted it, but – as Horace explains at length in *Ars Poetica* (73 ff.) – each particular type of poetry had traditional requirements of metre, style, subject-matter and so on.

It was natural therefore that by far the most important model for Virgil was the epic poetry of Homer: *res gestae regumque ducumque et tristia bella quo scribi possent numero monstravit Homerus* ('Homer has shown in what metre the deeds of kings and generals and sad warfare can be written', Horace, *Ars Poet.* 73–4). Horace's reference to metre may fairly be extended to many other aspects of Homer's poetry. The aspiring Roman epic poet would therefore wish to try to rival the Greek master by using a similar form of poetry adapted to the Latin language and the requirements of a Roman theme. In famous phrases in *Ars Poetica* Horace urges the Roman poet to handle Greek models night and day: *vos exemplaria Graeca nocturna versate manu versate diurna* (268–9). The word *exemplaria* here sums up the point: as in history, politics, philosophy, law, ethical behaviour, so in literature the Romans sought *exempla*, patterns to which they could cut their material and then make it into something new, based on the old. This is what Horace claimed to do, and did do, in his *Odes*; this is what Virgil had already done in his *Eclogues* and his *Georgics*. Imitation is not the best word to describe this traditionalism in Roman literature; the Latin word *aemulatio* (rivalry in a similar area) would be a better one.

(i) HOMER

Everything in the literary tradition, then, pointed towards a Homeric form for the *Aeneid*, but there was an additional powerful reason for Virgil to wish to be the Roman Homer. This was his profound love for the *Iliad* and *Odyssey*, in which he was clearly steeped (like so many other Romans of his time), coupled with the fact that the subject which he chose for his epic was itself Homeric. Aeneas is an important figure in the *Iliad*, and his journey westward towards Italy occurred at about the same time as Odysseus' journey home to Ithaca. Thus Aeneas belonged to the Homeric world, but unlike the other heroes of the *Iliad* and *Odyssey* he had to move out of it, to leave it behind and begin the long process which would eventually lead to Augustan Rome.

The debt which Virgil owed to Homer was very great indeed, but, as we shall see, almost always Homer is a model or a starting-point from which Virgil can adapt material suitable for his own entirely different poetic aims. First we should consider the extent and nature of this debt, before discussing in later chapters the vital aspects of Virgil's poem which have no precedent in Homer, and give the *Aeneid* in the end a totally different impact from its Homeric models. Chief among these, as will be fully shown later, are the importance for mankind of the march of fate and Rome's destiny, the different attitude towards war, and the emotional intensity of Dido's tragic love-story.

The ancient critics emphasized the similarity between the *Aeneid* and Homer's poems: the Suetonius–Donatus life (*Vita Vergilii*, 21) speaks of the *Aeneid* as *quasi amborum Homeri carminum instar* ('a kind of equivalent of both Homer's poems') and Macrobius (*Saturnalia*, 5. 2. 13) says *quid quod et omne opus Vergilianum velut de quodam Homerici operis speculo formatum est* ('what about the fact that the whole of Virgil's poem is a kind of mirrored reflexion of Homer?'). The fifth book of Macrobius' *Saturnalia* is filled with parallel passages of Homer and Virgil, intended primarily to show the skill with which Virgil could take passages which he needed from his model (as if each new example of 'imitation' was a further indication of Virgil's quality); but Macrobius does sometimes comment on the way Virgil has adapted the material (using phrases like *densius excoluisse* – 'developed it more richly'). Quintilian (10. 1. 85–6) says that just as Homer is the model and source for Greek education, so Virgil is for Roman: *omnium eius generis poetarum Graecorum nostrorumque haud dubie proximus* ('being of all the poets of that genre, Greek and Latin, undoubtedly second'); and he then quotes Domitius Afer as saying 'Virgil is second, but nearer first than third'. Quintilian then contrasts the 'divine and immortal inspiration' of Homer with Virgil's greater 'care and diligence', and ends by saying that perhaps the Roman poet compensates for Homer's superiority in brilliance by his own uniform excellence (*aequalitas*).

The innumerable parallel passages between Homer and Virgil have long been the subject of scholarly investigation, and the massive work of G. N. Knauer, *Die Aeneis und Homer*, with its huge indexes (Homer to Virgil and Virgil to Homer) containing literally hundreds of Homeric parallels in each separate book of the *Aeneid* gives a fair picture of Virgil's debt. Very many of these, of course, are short verbal echoes or translations (like 'his armour clanged about him', or 'three times and four times blessed', or 'when they had satisfied their hunger'). Some of these are given added or new significance by the Virgilian context; but it is of the larger aspects of Virgilian imitation that I wish now to speak.Some of these larger aspects will be discussed at greater length elsewhere in the book (because so much that is essentially Virgilian springs from and is developed out of Homeric material), but it will be helpful to list the chief ones here, indicating briefly both the similarities and the differences.

First there is the metre, the heroic hexameter, accepted by all epic writers in Greece and in Rome (after Ennius) as the appropriate one because it was Homer's choice. But the movement of Virgil's hexameter is entirely different from that of Homer, partly because the Latin language is slower moving and more sonorous than the dancing dactyls of Greek, but partly also because Virgil's more reflective method of narrative slows his metre. Similarly with style: like Homer's, Virgil's is elevated and conventional, far removed from ordinary speech. But in Homeric recited epic the narrative must move fast and the listener's concentration be helped by stock epithets and repetitions: there is no such requirement in written or 'literary' epic, and Virgil's style is much denser, much less precisely presented, enriched with images and implications flitting around the penumbra, as opposed to what Auerbach called the 'perpetual foreground' of Homer.

A particular feature of style which Virgil took from Homer (as did all other Latin epic writers) is the extended or 'Homeric' simile, a comparison several lines long which does not necessarily confine itself to the actual point or points of comparison, but may develop the new picture for its own sake. In Homer these similes are powerful and vivid aids to visualizing the narrative, and tend to occur particularly at moments of high excitement (the more intense *Iliad* has some two hundred similes altogether, compared with forty or so in the *Odyssey*). In Virgil the similes may indeed be of this kind, but often they also contain subtle links with the narrative and the main themes of the poem: for example the simile (4. 69 ff.) comparing the love-smitten Dido with a wounded deer looks backwards to Aeneas as the hunter unaware that he has wounded the deer, and forwards to the dire consequences when the shaft is called 'death-bringing'.

A vitally important technique in the method of the *Aeneid* which Virgil took from Homer was the two-tier narrative, partly concerned with the mortal scene on earth and partly with the doings of the gods and goddesses in Olympus. This both varies the narrative by a total change of scene and activity, and dignifies it by raising it to a more than human level. To adopt this presented Virgil with considerable difficulties (because Homer's audience probably believed literally in these divinities whereas Virgil's did not), but he overcame them to a large extent not only by treating his gods and goddesses pictorially but by making them symbolize forces which humans encounter in life. Virgil's Olympus is far less literally real than Homer's (though not less pictorially visualized) but it very successfully serves other purposes.

Many other features of epic method, or 'machinery', were employed by Virgil as being proper to epic because Homer had used them – flashback technique in narrative, description of armour, catalogue of forces, description of athletic games, encounters with monsters, conversations with ghosts of the underworld: these will best be considered at this point by means of a brief book by book analysis of the *Aeneid* showing how Virgil has incorporated these features and by summarizing in what ways he has altered the Homeric model to suit his own poetic purposes. Many of these similarities and contrasts form major themes in the *Aeneid*, and will be considered at greater length later.

Aeneid 1 shows an astonishing similarity of episode and structure with *Odyssey* 5–8. In both authors our first introduction to the hero (in Homer, of course, Odysseus himself does not appear until Book 5) shows him at the mercy of an angry divinity (Juno, Poseidon); both heroes are shipwrecked and reach shore in bad shape: Aeneas is met and hidden in a cloud by a goddess in disguise (Venus) as Odysseus is by Athena. Both come to a glorious city (Dido's Carthage, Alcinous' Scheria) at which they marvel. Both are most hospitably received by the ruler of the country and entertained at a great feast, including a performance by a minstrel: both are asked to tell the story of their adventures, and Aeneas does so in the flash-back of *Aeneid* 2 and 3 as Odysseus does in the flashback of *Odyssey* 9–12. The only differences in Virgil's imitation of narrative structure are in the passages concerned with the gods: the proem about Juno, the great patriotic speech of Jupiter, and the intervention of Venus to make Dido fall in love with Aeneas.

It is an extraordinary similarity, and it challenges us to consider whether the proto-Roman hero of our poem is to be a second Odysseus, or whether he has to show different qualities from Homer's hero. The differences are in fact profound, and will be discussed in the section on Aeneas' character. These differences emerge all the more clearly because of the deliberately sought similarity of episodes.

Aeneid 2, the story of the sack of Troy, is Homeric in the form of some of its battle descriptions, but as so often in Virgil the pathos and futility of slaughter are much more intensely expressed than in Homer (as for instance the murder of old King Priam), and the horror of destruction is all the greater because the Virgilian narrative is given from the point of view of the vanquished Trojans, not – as in the *Iliad* – from the point of view of the victorious Greeks (seen in the prowess and victory over Hector of Achilles). As in Book 1 Virgil uses divine intervention in the Homeric manner (Venus appears to her son to tell him to save his family). The most interesting point of similarity with Homer in *Aeneid* 2 is in the picture we get of Aeneas as a true Homeric hero (anxious to die fighting, to sell his life dearly when all is lost, and not yet at all ready to abandon the Homeric ethos and obey his mission). He ignores the warning he receives in the dream of Hector (2. 289 ff.) that he must leave; later he is so battle-mad as to consider killing Helen until he is restrained by Venus; finally when he loses Creusa he dashes madly back among the Greeks looking for her, careless of the personal safety upon which his as yet imperfectly accepted mission depends. There is further elaboration in a later chapter of this Homeric aspect of Aeneas' character before he leaves Troy.

The third book of the *Aeneid* is a curious, and in some ways unsuccessful, blend of the Odyssean world of strange adventures with supernatural beings and the Augustan world of the well-known Mediterranean. The geography of Aeneas' seven-year voyage from Troy to the Tiber is easily charted, whereas the journey of Odysseus is essentially vague, and often set in a kind of mariner's fairyland. For example Virgil mentions the famous towns of southern Italy (3. 551 ff.) as Aeneas nears Sicily, and also the great ports of Sicily as he sails round the south coast (3. 699 ff.). In particular Virgil makes a special point of a stop at Actium (a variation on the usual legend), where the Trojans hold games (3. 280), thus bringing us immediately in thought to contemporary events, Augustus' victory at Actium and his proclamation of celebratory Actian games. But in among these very real Mediterranean places Virgil inserts supernatural episodes of an Odyssean type. On the Strophades Islands (3. 209 ff.) the Trojans are attacked by the Harpies, fierce birds with the faces of women, and actually fight against them. This is not itself an Odyssean episode (the main source is probably Apollonius Rhodius, 2. 178 ff.) but its spirit is wholly Odyssean. And the last long episode in Book 3 (588–691) is a very close imitation of Odysseus' encounter (*Od*. 9. 106 ff.) with Polyphemus the Cyclops. The closeness is underlined by the fact that Achaemenides had been left behind (presumably just a few months earlier) by Odysseus, and he tells the story of how Odysseus got away by blinding the Cyclops. Virgil is of course careful not to bring Aeneas into direct contact with Polyphemus, but it still seems an incongruous episode in the story of Rome's foundation. There are some indications that Virgil was perhaps planning to remove the whole episode, but what we may learn from it is that while Virgil was aiming to adapt Homer to the Roman requirements of his theme he also was sufficiently enchanted with the Greek poet to wish to rework one of the most famous episodes of the *Odyssey*, even though it was not wholly suitable.

Aeneid 4 may be dealt with briefly here, because it is by far the least Homeric part of the whole work, dealing as it does with the intimate portrayal of emotional love in a way quite alien from Homeric epic. This is discussed in the section on Dido.

Most of Book 5 is an interlude describing the anniversary funeral games for Anchises, based upon the description of funeral games for Patroclus in *Iliad* 23. This plays a crucial part in diminishing the emotional intensity between the tragedy of Book 4 and the mysterious majesty of Book 6, and Virgil has altered the normal version of the legend (adding this second visit to Sicily) in order to place his games where he wanted them in the structure of his poem. In addition to the Homeric precedent Virgil had a further reason for including a description of games, namely the keen interest Augustus was taking in the revival in Rome of the Greek type of athletic games, and especially in the great Actian games just inaugurated and planned to occur every four years like the Olympic games. But there were problems to be overcome in imitating *Iliad* 23. There was a gusto and an immediacy about Greek games which Homer captured, and which no Roman was likely to recapture in the same way. Virgil therefore has substituted for the breathless succession of the eight events in Homer a carefully structured pattern of only four contests – a long description of the boat race, a short one of the foot race, a long and almost mythological description of the boxing match, and a short archery contest, and he has rounded it all with an equestrian cavalcade, the *lusus Troiae*. Additionally, he has made many of his favourite aetiological links with his own times: the elaborate religious ceremonies before the games recall the Roman *Parentalia*, the names of sea captains are connected with famous Roman *gentes*, the portent of the arrow bursting into flames connects Acestes with Segesta (some would say that it refers to the comet indicating Julius Caesar's deification), and finally the *lusus Troiae* has explicit reference to its subsequent performance in Roman times.

The sixth book provides an outstanding example of the use of a Homeric model to produce something entirely different. It is based on Homer's book of the ghosts in *Odyssey* 11, but in Homer the ghosts come up to Odysseus, whereas in Virgil Aeneas goes down to the underworld, thus enabling Virgil to take advantage of the post-Homeric descriptions of descents to the underworld (catabaseis) with all the pictorial and religious possibilities which this offered. Virgil uses a number of details, striking ones, from Homer: for example the first ghost which Aeneas meets is his helmsman Palinurus, very recently dead, just as in Homer the first ghost is the recently dead helmsman Elpenor. The great sinners in Tartarus are partly taken from Homer's list, and one of the most memorable passages of all in *Aeneid* 6 is when the angry ghost of Dido turns away from Aeneas' pleas without a word of answer, as Ajax turns from Odysseus' pleas in *Odyssey* 11. 563 ff.; Longinus comments on this Homeric silence as 'more sublime than any words could be'.

But of course in essence *Aeneid* 6 is totally different from *Odyssey* 11. There is no equivalent, naturally, in the *Odyssey* for Virgil's patriotic pageant of Roman heroes waiting to be born with which *Aeneid* 6 ends, nor is there the remotest resemblance in the religious message. Homer's afterlife was one of gloom and hopelessness save for the children of divinities: Virgil's is such that this life is seen merely as a preparation for a richer life hereafter in which virtue will have its reward (as it rarely seems to in the mortal narrative of the *Aeneid*).

Aeneid 7 once more illustrates the use of a Homeric epic technique for a changed purpose. The book ends with a long catalogue of forces mustered for battle, recalling the catalogue of Greek ships at the end of *Iliad* 2. But Virgil's list, unlike Homer's, is of the enemy forces, of the Italians who rally to withstand the Trojan invasion, and it plays a vital part in the development of one of the great themes of the *Aeneid*, namely the paradox of Italian dominance over the victorious Trojans in their future offspring, the Roman people. The Italians are portrayed in the catalogue with the greatest sympathy as they line up against Aeneas and his men: the contingents from the little towns and districts so familiar to the Italians of Virgil's day are shown as brave and simple people, destined to be losers in the battle but worthy ancestors of the Romans.

At the end of *Aeneid* 8 Virgil describes the pictures on the new shield which Vulcan at Venus' request made for Aeneas. In *Iliad* 18 Homer describes the new shield which Hephaestus made for Achilles. The narrative motivation in Homer is much more direct than in Virgil. Achilles has lost the shield which he had lent to Patroclus and it is natural that the new shield should be described, with all its vivid depiction of scenes of various aspects of Greek life. Aeneas has not lost his shield, but Virgil wants an opportunity of illustrating once more (as he has at the end of Book 6) scenes from the future destiny of Rome whose fulfilment rests on Aeneas' shoulders. This is the part of the poem immediately preceding the outbreak of full-scale fighting, and it is here that Virgil wishes to reiterate why the battles must be fought and what depends on them, and it is by means of this Homeric device that he is enabled to do so.

In the battle scenes which dominate Books 9–12 Virgil uses the Homeric technique of devoting long, continuous sections to the deeds of prowess (*aristeia*) of individuals – of Turnus (especially in the second half of 9 and in 10 and 12), of Camilla in 11, of Aeneas in 10 and 12. But his method of describing warfare, Homeric in many external features, leaves on the reader a totally different impression. In Homer battle scenes, though often tragic, are an accepted part of the heroic environment of the time: in Virgil there is a strong feeling of the futility and pathos of an activity which he knew well enough had played a great part in Rome's rise to power but which he could not feel was wholly acceptable and glorious. One might perhaps say that he tried to make the battle scenes glorious, but so often found his focus shifting to the victim rather than the victor.

In the last three books of the *Aeneid* Virgil's plot is clearly intended to echo Homer's in the *Iliad*. Just as Achilles' close friend Patroclus is killed by Hector and therefore Achilles sets out for vengeance, so Aeneas' protégé Pallas is killed by Turnus and Aeneas determines on vengeance. Throughout the last part of Book 12 Virgil again and again recalls the episodes and phraseology of *Iliad* 22 (see the section on Turnus) and makes the reader feel that the well-known Homeric story is being re-enacted in reverse, with the Trojan this time destined to win and the new Achilles-figure, Turnus, in the loser's situation. We are led to expect that at the end when Turnus is brought low and begs for mercy Aeneas (a less warlike character than Achilles) will spare him, as Achilles did not spare

Hector. It is a grim shock when Aeneas acts towards his suppliant exactly as Achilles did.

I have written at length about Virgil's use of Homer, because this is a case not just of following in the steps of the master but rather of adapting Homeric conventions to suit the development of his theme and of using the heroic world as depicted by Homer as a point of comparison with the proto-Roman world which Aeneas is destined to found. Homeric ideals and standards of conduct are used as a counterpoise against which to weigh Roman ideals and standards.

(ii) POST-HOMERIC GREEK LITERATURE

Tragedy

No other author, Greek or Latin, not even Ennius, exercised anything like the same influence on Virgil as Homer did. Nevertheless he drew inspiration from many others in greater or lesser degree, and in some ways the *Aeneid* might be said to be a literary synthesis of the aspects of human existence as Virgil found them expressed by the long line of great Classical authors who had preceded him.

Virgil was evidently quite familiar at first hand with the Greek tragedians (and presumably also with their Latin followers). This debt is to be seen in some verbal parallels (*Aen.* 12. 435–6, *disce puer virtutem ex me verumque laborem, fortunam ex aliis* – 'Learn, my son, valour from me and real toil, but good luck from someone else'; Sophocles, *Ajax*, 550–1, 'My son, may you be luckier than your father, but otherwise the same'); but much more important is the correspondence of major episodes in the *Aeneid* with the spirit of Greek tragedy. The story of Turnus is that of a virtuous hero brought to total disaster by a flaw in his character (violence and lack of respect for the divine will); the downfall of Troy in Book 2, and especially the tragic reversal (the peripeteia) of Priam's prosperity, is reminiscent of the powerful pathos of Euripides, especially in the *Troades* or the *Hecuba*. But most of all the story of Dido is treated as a Greek tragedy, with a great and glorious queen brought to utter ruin by infatuation; there are details which correspond with the structure of Greek tragedy (Mercury and Anna representing messengers, occasional choral reflections from Virgil himself, the quiet ending after the disaster); and the tragic nature of the whole grim story is specially signalled by Virgil in a memorable double simile describing Dido's nightmares:

Eumenidum veluti demens videt agmina Pentheus
et solem geminum et duplices se ostendere Thebas,
aut Agamemnonius scaenis agitatus Orestes,
armatam facibus matrem et serpentibus atris
cum fugit ultricesque sedent in limine Dirae.   (4.469–73)

Like Pentheus when maddened he sees the bands of Furies, and
two suns and two cities of Thebes appearing; or like Orestes, son
of Agamemnon, hounded on the stage as he flies from his mother
armed with torches and black snakes, and the avenging Furies
wait on the threshold.

This simile is an explicit reference first to the *Bacchae* of Euripides
and then to the *Oresteia* of Aeschylus; and it is expressly to be noted
that the second comparison is not merely to the well-known story
but to a theatrical performance of it (*scaenis agitatus*).

The Alexandrians

In Virgil's time the post-Classical poets of the Alexandrian period
enjoyed great popularity with many (though not all) of the leading
figures in Latin literature, and Virgil had already shown his
familiarity with them in taking Theocritus as his model in the
Eclogues and using didactic poets such as Aratus and Nicander in
the *Georgics*. It is evident too that he was well acquainted with
Callimachus, but it was Callimachus' literary rival, Apollonius of
Rhodes, who exercised the main influence on the *Aeneid*.
Apollonius had gone against the main stream of thought of his
contemporaries by writing an epic poem (regarded as an archaic form
of literary expression by the Callimachean school); but he
represented the interests of his times by introducing into his
Argonautica a love-story, not only describing love's manifestations
but treating it as lyric and elegiac writers treated love, emotionally
and intimately, with the revelation of the innermost thoughts of the
lover. This demanded from the reader empathy as well as sympathy,
that is to say personal identification with the emotions and
dilemmas of the lover.

The third book of Apollonius' poem is taken up entirely with the
story of Medea's love for Jason, and this gave Virgil a precedent, a
wholly non-Homeric one, for the intimate and romantic description
of love in the genre of epic poetry. There are some notable points of
similarity – goddesses scheming to ensnare the heroine in the net
of love; a long passage descriptive of the peace of night which the
tortured lover cannot enjoy (*Arg.* 3. 744 ff., *Aen.* 4. 522 ff.); Dido's
recourse to magic, the special art of Medea – and Servius remarks

at the beginning of his commentary on *Aeneid* 4 that the whole of the book is taken from Apollonius. But there is very little similarity in tone: Dido is a far more regal and mature character than the young princess Medea, and Virgil has added the element in the love-story which makes it truly tragic for Dido, namely the conflict in Aeneas between love and duty.

(iii) LATIN LITERATURE

It is a sad quirk of fate that the poet whom the Romans regarded as the father of their literature should survive for us only in fragments. About the beginning of the second century BC, Quintus Ennius composed his *Annals*, an epic poem in chronicle form about the history of Rome from its legendary beginnings to his own time. We possess small fragments of a somewhat earlier Roman epic, the *Punica* of Naevius, and this had some influence on Virgil, perhaps including the visit to Carthage in the Aeneas legend; but it was Ennius whom the Roman literary public knew and venerated, and his influence on Virgil was incalculable. There are countless echoes, indeed sometimes virtual quotations from him in the *Aeneid*; for example, the line describing Fabius Maximus which closes the pageant of Roman heroes in *Aeneid* 6, *unus qui nobis cunctando restituis rem* (6. 846), is a quotation of Ennius' line about the same Fabius, *unus homo nobis cunctando restituit rem*. A comment by Seneca is preserved in Aulus Gellius (12. 2) to the effect that Virgil used Ennian metrical effects 'in order that the people who knew Ennius so well should recognize an archaic touch in a modern poem'. It was not only in verbal echoes (of which we should doubtless recognize even more than we can now if Ennius's poem had been preserved intact) that Virgil looked back to his archaic predecessor: there are fragments surviving which show how Ennius could express memorably the traditions and ideals of early Rome, the *mos maiorum* so nostalgically praised and sought after in the Augustan age. The Ennian line *moribus antiquis res stat Romana virisque* ('the Roman state stands firm on its ancient traditions and its men'), with its simple effectiveness, would strike a patriotic chord in the hearts of many of Virgil's contemporaries.

But by far the greatest debt which Virgil, like all other Roman epic poets, owed to Ennius was the introduction into Latin of the Greek quantitative hexameter, the metre of Homer. Prior to Ennius Latin poets (for example Livius Andronicus and Naevius) had used the Saturnian metre, based on stress (or word-accent) as our own poetry is; this rhythm corresponded with the way in which Latin was in fact spoken. But Ennius made the extraordinarily bold experiment of basing his verse (like that of the Greek poets) on the quantity of vowels (or, more strictly speaking, of syllables). This meant that many of the Latin words would have a metrical rhythm different from the way in which they were pronounced. For example *ámant* would be pronounced in speech as a trochee, but have a metrical value, *āmānt*, as an iambus. This had the effect of giving Latin verse two rhythms going at the same time, the one accentual and the other quantitative; and it meant that the two rhythms could be made to coincide or to conflict, and to alternate as the poets wished. In English imitations of the Latin hexameter the metrical rhythm has generally been based on accent, not quantity, giving a monotonous effect, as in Longfellow:

Once in an ancient city, whose name I no longer remember,
Raised aloft on a column a brazen statue of Justice
Stood in the public square, upholding the scales in its left hand,
And in its right a sword, as an emblem that Justice presided
Over the laws of the land, and the hearts and the hands of the
　　people.
　　　　　　　　　　　　　　　　　　　　　(*Evangeline*, 1. 3.)

There have been experiments in English to use a quantitative instead of an accentual base, but they have lacked the success which Ennius achieved; for example Bridges:

They wer' amid the shadows, by night, in loneliness obscure
Walking forth i' the void and vasty dominion of Hades;
As by an uncertain moonray secretly illumined
One goeth in the forest, when heav'n is gloomily clouded
And black night hath robb'd the colours and beauty from all things.
　　　　　　　　　　　　　　　　　　　　　(*Ibant obscuri*, 1. 1–5)

Observe here how the second line sounds much less strange to the ear as a hexameter than the others: this is because Bridges has caused the quantities of the syllables to coincide with the word-accent expected by the English reader. But in the lines where there is not total coincidence the effect seems very strange and unacceptable.

The successful introduction by Ennius of this new Latin poetic scheme based on quantity meant, as I have said, that there became available a variety of rhythms in which the accentual pronunciation of the words could accord with or struggle against the metre. It is only quite recently that detailed study of this feature has been made by students of Latin poetry; it was pioneered in modern times by

W. F. Jackson Knight, who used the terms homodyne and heterodyne to indicate coincidence and conflict. It has become increasingly evident that it was in Virgil's poetry more than in any other author's that the rhythmic possibilities of reflecting by this means the sense and mood of a passage were fully appreciated. Ennius was the pioneer who made possible, though he himself rarely achieved, the infinite beauties of the 'stateliest measure ever moulded by the lips of man'.

There seems to have been a gap (of well over a century) in important Latin hexameter verse between Ennius and the authors belonging to the generation before Virgil. But the works of his immediate predecessors were of great importance in adapting and polishing the rugged measures of Ennius. Cicero wrote some translations and some original works in tolerably good hexameters (for all the ridicule which they attracted from subsequent critics); Lucretius, though (as he confessed) he found the metre difficult for his philosophic and scientific poem *De Rerum Natura*, produced descriptive passages of a power and breath-taking beauty very different from Virgil, but not inferior; Catullus brought to the hexameter an elegance and a smoothness suitable for his little epic (epyllion), Poem 64, which Virgil could use where he wished as a variation on his normal stronger style.

The debt of Virgil to Lucretius was great, but will not be discussed at length here because the chief debt was in the *Georgics* rather than the *Aeneid*. Lucretius was the first of the Romans to write a successful didactic poem, and many passages in the *Georgics* show Virgil's admiration for him. In the *Aeneid* there are verbal echoes, and Virgil pays a compliment to Lucretius in the minstrel's song (*Aen.* 1. 742 ff.) and in *Aeneid* 6. 724 ff, where his near-Stoic description of the future life uses Lucretian phrases and archaisms (*principio, modis . . . miris, aurai*) although the subject-matter is the exact opposite of Lucretius' Epicurean denial of a future life.

The number of echoes of Catullus in the *Aeneid* is small compared with Homer and Ennius, but the echoes occur in passages of the highest importance, particularly in those which express sadness and pathos. Tennyson called Catullus 'tenderest of Roman poets 1900 years ago', and it was in this that Virgil had much in common with the most intensely emotional poet of all Roman literature. In particular the pathos of Dido's desertion by Aeneas is deepened and enriched by marked reminiscences of Catullus' account of the desertion of Ariadne by Theseus (Poem 64). Compare, for example, Dido's plea to Aeneas (4. 316), *per conubia nostra, per inceptos hymenaeos*, with Ariadne's words in Catullus, 64. 141, *sed conubia laeta, sed optatos hymenaeos; Aen.* 4, 365 ff. with Catullus,

64. 154; *Aen.* 4. 657–8, *felix heu nimium felix si litora tantum numquam Dardaniae tetigissent nostra carinae*, with Catullus, 64. 171–2, *Iuppiter omnipotens utinam ne tempore primo Gnosia Cecropiae tetigissent litora puppes*. These are not merely verbal reminiscences; they serve to identify Dido's plight with that of Ariadne, and they link Virgil with the most characteristic and all-pervasive theme of Catullus' poetry generally, the theme of desertion by friend or lover. One further and quite astonishing link with Catullus occurs in Dido's plea in *Aeneid* 4. 328–9, *si quis mihi parvulus aula luderet Aeneas* . . . . This recalls Catullus, 61. 209 ff., *Torquatus volo parvulus* . . ., and totally violates the expectation of epic diction by using the diminutive ('darling little child of Aeneas') so characteristic of the lyric and elegiac poetry of Catullus, but utterly unexpected in epic. Nowhere else in the *Aeneid* does Virgil use a diminutive adjective.

Reminiscences of Catullus occur elsewhere in passages of intense pathos: for example, the flower similes at the death of Euryalus (9. 435 ff.) and at the funeral of Pallas (11. 68 ff.) recall Catullus, 11. 21 ff. and 62. 42 ff.; the account of Pallas' funeral has some typically Catullan rhythms (especially Poems 66–8), and Aeneas' last words at the funeral are *salve aeternum mihi, maxime Palla, aeternumque vale*, which recalls one of the most famous of all Catullus' poems, that composed at the tomb of his brother which ends *atque in perpetuum frater ave atque vale* (101.10).

J. W. Mackail, in a memorable epigram, has said: 'It is not what a poet makes his poems out of, but what he makes them into, that matters' (*Lectures on Poetry*, p. 58). In the case of Virgil the literary source-material he uses is precisely that which expresses the different polarities between which his poem operates. In Greek literature, Homer gave him a heroic concept of individual leadership and personality against which he could measure a Roman concept of leadership, and Greek tragedy gave him a pattern for depicting grandeur in defeat. In Latin literature, Ennius had presented the robust and vigorous aspect of great events and great men in Roman history, while Catullus saw the world in terms not of history but of people and personal relationships and the all-enveloping sadness of loss, whether by desertion or death. It was Virgil's remarkable achievement that as he wrote of the Roman march towards empire and of the long processes of history he could successfully implant into the grandiloquent setting of epic something of the soft sensitivity of lyric and elegy.

CHAPTER 4

The Composition of the Aeneid

(i) CHOICE OF SUBJECT

We have some evidence about Virgil's ideas as he began to consider writing an epic poem, his ultimate literary ambition. There is a statement in the Donatus life (*Vita Vergilii*, 19) that he made a start on a Roman subject, but finding the material uncongenial (*offensus materia*) turned instead to the *Eclogues*. This is echoed and somewhat amplified by Servius, who says that Virgil began an epic poem on the Alban kings, but abandoned it because of the harshness of the names. Virgil himself gives some indication of his plans at the beginning of *Georgics* 3, where he says that he will not sing of the trite themes of mythological epic such as the stories of Eurystheus or Hylas or Pelops, but instead will aim at literary fame such as that achieved by Ennius (he uses a well-known Ennian phrase in line 9, *victorque virum volitare per ora*) by building a temple of song in the midst of which will be Caesar: *in medio mihi Caesar erit templumque tenebit* (3. 16). In a long allegorical description of this temple of song he speaks of how he will depict the innumerable battles and triumphs of Augustus Caesar. This he tells us is his plan, and when he has finished his *Georgics* he will gather his powers to embark on this new subject.

The subject which he actually chose, the legend of the Trojan prince Aeneas and his mission to found a city in Latium from which ultimately Rome would spring presented him with a number of crucial advantages compared with the direct panegyric of the Emperor's achievements which he had sketched out in the *Georgics*. First and foremost it was indeed a Roman theme, but a legendary rather than a historical one. His expressed desire to sing the praises of Caesar could thus be achieved, but in subtle and indirect ways, far more acceptable than the straightforward account of contemporary events which the *Georgics* passage seems to suggest. Because it was so remote in time, it made it possible for him to use the traditional Olympian gods as an indication of the divine favour under which Rome had achieved her greatness and by means of supernatural prophecies to link his ancient material with the later Roman world.

Secondly the Aeneas legend was well known in Virgil's day, but very fluid in its details and remote enough for poetic adaptation (compare our King Arthur legend before Malory). Thus Virgil could vary the details for his own special purposes: for example the second visit to Sicily which gives opportunity for the ceremonies of Book 5 was not in the normal version of the legend; other details of the journey were altered, such as the place of Anchises' death, the burning of the ships, the stage at Actium; the details of the relationship in the second half of the poem between the Italian leaders, Latinus, Mezentius, Evander and Turnus, could all be altered, and were, to suit the intention of Virgil's narrative; and most importantly the story of Dido could be given far greater prominence than was normal in the Aeneas legend; indeed there is some doubt whether it figured at all in the story.

Thirdly the dramatic date of Virgil's poem is the same as that of Homer's *Odyssey*; Aeneas was travelling west in search of Italy at the same time as Odysseus was returning to Ithaca, and Aeneas indeed had been an important Trojan warrior in the *Iliad* (though not so strongly delineated as to restrict Virgil's intention to make him into a prototype of a Roman leader). This means, as we have seen in detail in Chapter 3, that Virgil could use the Homeric poems not only for episodes and for epic machinery, such as the double action in Olympus and on earth and the use of long similes, catalogues, funeral games and so on, but also as a touchstone for the examination of Roman values. In what ways, if any, should Aeneas the ex-Trojan warrior but now proto-Roman ruler differ from the Homeric warriors? (This aspect will be discussed in the section on the character of Aeneas.)

We may say then, in summarizing the reasons why Virgil chose the Aeneas legend, that it could embody his two main poetic aims: to write about the past, present and future greatness of Rome without being confined to recent historical events; and to produce a work which would bear direct comparison with Homer. This is the essence of what Servius says very succinctly and perhaps too baldly: *intentio Vergilii haec est: Homerum imitari et Augustum laudare a parentibus* ('Virgil's intention is this – to imitate Homer and to praise Augustus through his ancestors') (Thilo and Hagen (eds), p. 4, l. 10). The Donatus life says the same, speaking of the *Aeneid* as *quasi amborum Homeri carminum instar . . . et in quo, quod maxime studebat, Romanae simul urbis et Augusti origo contineretur* ('a kind of equivalent of both Homer's poems . . . in which – and this was his special aim – there should be contained the origins of the city of Rome and of Augustus', *Vita Vergilii*, 21). We might paraphrase these two ancient authorities by saying that

Virgil's intention was to use and rework the tradition of Homeric epic not only for dramatic and literary effect but also in order to present and examine the Roman way of life, its past achievements (and failures) and its hopes for the future.

(ii) METHOD OF COMPOSITION

We are given some precise information by the ancient authorities concerning Virgil's method in composing the *Aeneid,* and the conditions under which the unrevised poem was published after his death. We read in the Donatus life: 'He first drafted the *Aeneid* in prose, and divided it into twelve books, and began to compose it piece by piece [*particulatim*], taking it up just where he felt like it, not at all in any order. And so that nothing should interrupt his impetus, he left some places unfinished and others he filled up as it were with stop-gaps, which jestingly he used to say were put up as props to hold up the work until the solid columns came' (*Vita Vergilii,* 23–4). This is reinforced by more information from Donatus (31 ff.) that very early on, as soon as Virgil had made a start on the poem, 'Augustus wrote to him in jestingly threatening letters asking that he should be sent either the first draft of the poem, or some section of it', but it was only much later, 'when the material was at last ready, that he read to him three of the books, the second, fourth and sixth'. He also 'gave recitations to larger audiences, but not often and generally passages about which he was not happy, in order to test the audiences' opinions'.

Both Servius and Donatus give full information about the posthumous publication of the poem, at Augustus' instructions, in contravention of Virgil's wish that it should be burned. Servius says that Varius and Tucca were instructed by Augustus to revise it 'in such a way as to remove what was redundant (*superflua*), but not to add anything – hence we find incomplete lines' (Hardie, *Vitae Virgilianae,* 'Vita Servii', 30). Donatus says that instructions from Virgil to Varius and Tucca, when his request to have the poem burned was refused, were that 'they should not publish anything which he would not have published', and consequently it was published 'with only a few corrections and the incomplete lines were left as they stood' (Hardie, *Vitae Virgilianae,* 'Vita Donati', 41).

These pieces of ancient evidence give a wholly convincing account of the *Aeneid* as we now have it. It does contain some fifty or so incomplete lines, generally called 'half-lines', and although some scholars have tried to show that such half-lines were a deliberate poetic technique, they have not been successful. It does contain stop-gaps (*tibicines*) which fall short of Virgil's usual standard of excellence. It does also have minor inconsistencies in chronology and attribution of prophecies. But in no sense is it an unfinished poem.

(iii) STRUCTURE

Even more than in his earlier works, the *Eclogues* and the *Georgics*, Virgil took great pains with the structure of the *Aeneid*. An epic poem, indeed, perhaps more than any other genre requires that it should be built to a plan on a large scale; the architecture must be organized for symmetry and contrast in all sorts of ways, by subject-matter, by thematic linkage, by emotional tone. This is not to say that structure is the main consideration: it should be subordinate to the total poetic intention of the poem in human terms, but it must not only assist this poetic intention but provide aesthetic satisfaction in its own right.

Much has been written in recent times about this aspect of the *Aeneid*, especially by Otis and Duckworth: the latter has gone to extreme lengths to analyse the sections of the poem mathematically, basing this analysis on an alleged fondness of Virgil for the golden section (a proportion of 1:0.618). However indisputable the part which this proportion plays in visual art, it is unconvincingly complicated and unrecognizable in poetry.

But there is much that can and should be said about the symmetries and contrasts of the *Aeneid*. First and most obviously it falls into two halves: Books 1–6 (Aeneas' journey to Italy) corresponding with Homer's *Odyssey* and Books 7–12 (the events and battles in Italy) with the *Iliad*. This bipartite division is emphasized by Virgil by means of the new invocation in Book 7 ('I now undertake a greater task', 7. 45), and by the correspondence of some of the major events in Book 7 with those in Book 1. In both cases the Trojans are on the point of success at the beginning of the book when an intervention by Juno brings disaster. The angry speeches of Juno (1. 37 ff. and 7. 293 ff.) are very similar, the second one being an even more angry elaboration of the first. This not only produces what the Romans would immediately have recognized and saluted as an indication that the *Aeneid* vied with Homer, but also sets up a comparison of Aeneas with Odysseus in the first half of the poem and in the second half with Achilles. The similarities and differences between Aeneas and the two Homeric heroes was one of the main themes Virgil wished to explore, and more will be said on this later. Thus this very simple structural device serves the wide poetic intention.

Secondly the *Aeneid* divides very naturally into three sections of four books each – the first four concerned with the tragic story of Aeneas and Dido, the last four with the tragic defeat and death of Turnus at Aeneas' hands, and the middle four forming a great central block containing within it long and crucial passages about the destiny of Rome, such as the pageant of Roman heroes at the end of Book 6, the catalogue of Italian ancestors of the Romans at the end of Book 7, the account in Book 8 of Evander's settlement on the seven hills where later Rome was to be built, and the pictures of Roman heroes on the shield of Aeneas at the end of Book 8. Additionally it contains many episodes concerned with religious belief, especially the descent into the underworld and the description of the blessed in Elysium in Book 6, the ceremonies conducted at the tomb of Aeneas' father, Anchises, in Book 5 (*Parentalia*), Faunus and the oracle in Book 7 (*Faunilia*), the worship of Hercules in Book 8 (celebrated with great pomp at the Ara Maxima in Virgil's time). By flanking this central portion with the tragedies of Dido and Turnus, the two great enemies – of a very different kind – of the Roman mission, Virgil has enriched the pathos of the fate of each of them. Each has qualities of greatness, but each comes to disaster and death in order that the foundation of Rome may not be frustrated.

Another very marked feature of the structure is the alternation of intensity between adjacent books. The first book, after presenting to us in an introductory way most of the important themes of the whole poem, then moves on to a peaceful and happy concluding section about the welcome of Aeneas and the banquet which Dido gives the Trojans. The second book, in total contrast, is intense, tragic, horrific, as Aeneas tells the story of the bloodshed and horror of Troy's last night. The third book, linked with the second as part of Aeneas' story to Dido, is far less intense than the second; it tells the weary story of seven long years of wandering and makes much less emotional demand on the reader. It plays its part in the thematic development of the poem, but its poetic level of intent is much lower than that of the two books which flank it and are perhaps the two most moving in the whole poem.

Following the intensity of the fourth book, Virgil uses the same method of relaxing the tension and the demands made on the reader, and Book 5 for the most part is the least emotional of all, concerned as it largely is with the anniversary games at Anchises' tomb. But towards the end the tension mounts as the women burn the ships, and later as the faithful helmsman Palinurus is drowned. The tension is now high enough for a natural transition to the mystery and majesty of Book 6, the book of the underworld.

A similar alternation can be seen in the second half of the poem. Book 7 sets the horrific scene for violence by the agency of Juno and Allecto, while Book 8 is gentle and serene. Book 9 is a battle interlude leading up to the decisive and tragic events of Book 10, with the death of Pallas; Book 11 is another battle interlude before the denouement of the events of Book 10 in the final scenes of Book 12.

Within the individual books careful organization of structure can be seen. Virgil's favourite method is to use three sections (for example, in Book 2, the wooden horse, the destruction of Troy, Aeneas' personal fortunes; in Book 3, three groups of three landfalls; in Book 6, the preparations for the descent, the descent itself, the meeting in Elysium; in Book 7, joyful arrival, intervention, catalogue of forces). But sometimes he prefers two sections (for example, in Book 1, introduction of themes, the story of Dido; in Book 4, Dido's pathetic love, her furious desire for vengeance), and sometimes he will interweave two themes throughout the book (in Book 8, meeting with Evander, making of Aeneas' shield). Much more could be said about structural symmetry and contrast, and the work of Conway, followed by that of Pöschl, Otis, Duckworth and many others, has emphasized the importance of this aspect of the *Aeneid*; but in the end we have to remember that in architecture (a word often used by the critics in discussing the *Aeneid*) the structure is an end in itself, while in poetry it is a means to an end. So we turn now to the themes which Virgil explored in his poem.

CHAPTER 5

The Main Themes
of the Aeneid

(i) THE OPENING SCENES OF THE POEM –
A FORETASTE

A remarkable aspect of the organization of the *Aeneid* is that practically all of the main themes of the poem are given expression in the opening scenes of Book 1. The first seven lines indicate clearly that the *Aeneid* is to be an adaptation of the Homeric epics to a Roman setting. The poem begins: *arma virumque cano, Troiae qui primus ab oris* ('I sing of battles and the man who first from the shores of Troy . . .'); *arma* recalls the most famous battle poem of antiquity, Homer's *Iliad*, and *virum* the subject of Homer's *Odyssey*, of which the first word is *andra* ('the man'), and which is centred round one individual hero; the word *Troiae* confirms the Homeric subject-matter. But in the second line we have an indication of the difference in this new poem: Aeneas is *fato profugus* ('an exile because of fate'), and the historical dimension of Virgil's poem (absent from Homer) as a process of events divinely ordained by the powers above immediately becomes apparent. The next line presents what is to be the ever-present theme of human suffering (*multum ille et terris iactatus et alto*; 'much made to suffer on land and sea'); and the next introduces the goddess Juno who is to be the cause of this suffering. Finally the opening paragraph is rounded off with a definition of the mission of Aeneas – 'to found a city, and bring his gods to Latium, whence would spring the Latin race, and the fathers of Alba Longa and the walls of lofty Rome'.

Now follows the invocation to the Muse. Virgil does not, as Homer does, ask to be inspired to tell the events of his narrative, but to be given the reasons behind it (*Musa, mihi causas memora*), i.e. the reasons for Juno's persecution of Aeneas and the suffering she caused to a man outstanding for his *pietas*, his devotion to his divine duty (*insignem pietate virum*). This is the great unanswered question of the *Aeneid*: *tantaene animis caelestibus irae*? ('can there be such wrath in the minds of gods?'). Unlike Milton, Virgil in the end cannot 'justify the ways of God to men'.

It seems that after the invocation we are ready to begin the

narrative, but first Virgil pauses to elaborate on one of the themes
mentioned twice already, namely the hostility of Juno. This is
attributed mainly to her support for the Carthaginians, the people
which she aimed to make rulers of the world; but she has heard that
a race descended from the Trojans will overturn Carthage.

She has other reasons too for hostility to the Trojans – the
damage they have inflicted upon her beloved Greeks, the judgement
of Paris, Jupiter's fondness for Ganymede; but it is the historical one
which is of most importance and therefore given most prominence,
and it serves as a background to the conflict (described in Book 4)
between Aeneas' Roman mission and his love for Dido, Queen of
Carthage. It was due largely to Juno that 'it was so great a task to
found the Roman race' (*tantae molis erat Romanam condere
gentem*, 1. 33), the line with which Virgil concludes his pre-
narrative introduction.

The modern reader would be justified in seeing Juno not only as
playing the anthropomorphic part of a formidable and angry goddess
in Olympus, but also as symbolizing in personified form the
apparently undeserved blows of ill-fortune which beset the human
race. Certainly the first narrative action following an angry soliloquy
from Juno is the arousing of a great storm to batter the Trojan ships
just on the point of their departure from Sicily. A storm is one of the
most obvious manifestations of ill-fortune, and Virgil lingers long on
his description, a magnificent and terrifying mixture of supernatural
forces (Aeolus, Juno, Neptune) intermixed with naturalistic pictures
of huge waves, sandbanks, whirlpools. We see, at this very early
stage, that in writing a poem about the grave issues of empire and
war, triumph and suffering, Virgil is also a lover of language and
sound: he follows the rhetorical fireworks of Juno's speech with a
marvellously evocative picture of the mountain of the winds ruled
by Aeolus, and of the terrors of the storm, calmed at last as King
Neptune rides serenely over the waves in his chariot.

During the storm we meet the hero of the poem for the first time,
and we immediately learn what kind of a man it is to whom the task
of inaugurating the foundation of Rome has been entrusted. He is no
superhuman figure of qualities far beyond those of ordinary mortals;
on the contrary he is very much an ordinary mortal, frightened and
downcast at this sudden blow of fortune:

> *extemplo Aeneae solvuntur frigore membra;*
> *ingemit et duplices tendens ad sidera palmas*
> *talia voce refert: 'o terque quaterque beati,*
> *quis ante ora patrum Troiae sub moenibus altis*
> *contigit oppetere . . .'*   (1. 92–6)

Immediately Aeneas' limbs were paralysed with panic fear; he groaned and holding out his two hands to the stars thus he spoke: 'O three times and four times blessed, those whose lot it was to fall dead before their parents' eyes beneath the lofty walls of Troy . . .'

These lines are closely based on Odysseus' words in Homer (*Od*. 5. 306 ff.), and they prepare us for the comparison of Aeneas with Odysseus which is so marked a feature of *Aeneid* 1 (see the section on Aeneas' character).

The first full-scale simile in the poem occurs to illustrate the calming of the storm by Neptune (1. 148–54). It commands attention partly because it is the first, and partly because it is inverted. Instead of the usual comparison of human activity with some other aspect of nature, Virgil here compares the calming of the storm with the human activity of a statesman calming an unruly mob. This simile foreshadows a theme with which the *Aeneid* is constantly preoccupied: the nature and importance of *pietas* in humans, and the chief failing of humans, i.e. *furor*, wild irrational passion. The tragedies and disasters in the poem are very largely, indeed, due to this violent and unreasoning element in human behaviour. Here is the simile, in which both of these key value-words occur:

> ac veluti magno in populo cum saepe coorta est
> seditio saevitque animis ignobile vulgus;
> iamque faces et saxa volant, furor arma ministrat;
> tum, pietate gravem ac meritis si forte virum quem
> conspexere, silent arrectisque auribus astant;
> ille regit dictis animos et pectora mulcet:
> sic cunctus pelagi cecidit fragor . . .   (1. 148–54)

And just as often happens in a great nation when rioting breaks out and the common mob become wild with passion, and now firebrands and stones fly about, madness supplies weapons: then if it happens that they see some man respected for his selflessness and service, they fall silent and stand listening intently; he controls their passions with his words and calms their hearts. So it was that all the rage of the sea subsided . . .

After the storm the scene shifts to Olympus, where Venus complains to Jupiter of the sufferings of her son, who is dutifully attempting to carry out his divinely imposed mission: she ends with the indignant question, *hic pietatis honos?* ('Is this the reward for devotion to duty?', 1. 253). Here again is an expression of the bewilderment at the ways of providence which Virgil had expressed in his invocation, and which the poem constantly confronts, and constantly fails to solve.

Jupiter's reply is a serene and optimistic forecast of the destiny and greatness of the Roman race of whose first foundation Aeneas is the chosen agent: it is analysed fully in the next section. And at the end of his speech (1. 297 ff.) he sends Mercury down to apprise Dido of the arrival of the Trojans and to cause her to welcome them hospitably. So begins the story of Dido which dominates the first third of the poem.

Thus in the opening part of *Aeneid* 1 Virgil has shown in what ways he intends to use Homeric episodes and epic techniques, how he proposes to add non-Homeric elements to suit his Roman subject, how his special descriptive skill will add beauty and lustre to the narrative. Above all he has set in motion many of the main trains of thought which he is to explore throughout the poem.

(ii) THE OPTIMISTIC VISION – ROME'S GREATNESS. PAST, PRESENT AND FUTURE

There can be no doubt that a major intention of the *Aeneid* was to glorify Virgil's own country; the fact that very strong qualifications to this optimistic view arise in the course of the poem, which will be discussed in the next section, does not alter the primary fact. Virgil was in love with the past of his country and with his idealized vision of the future, and this love finds expression in many ways in the *Aeneid*. If we ask ourselves, 'Is this a patriotic poem?', the answer is 'Yes'. If we ask ourselves, 'Is it a piece of Augustan propaganda?', the answer must be much more qualified.

It was essential that Virgil should find effective ways of associating the far-off events of the Aeneas legend with material relevant to his own time, and one of the outstanding features of the *Aeneid* is the linking of the distant past with the nearer past, with the present, and with the future hopes which the present inspired. This section will be concerned with the prophecies and supernatural revelations of the future, and with the various kinds of aetiological references which bring Augustan Rome into the Trojan time-scale.

There are four major passages in the *Aeneid* (and many shorter ones) which refer to events far ahead of the story of Aeneas. With consummate literary skill Virgil has used quite different poetic techniques for all four of them. They are (i) the prophecy of Jupiter in Olympus to his daughter Venus (1. 257–96); (ii) the pageant of heroes of Roman history awaiting birth in the underworld (6. 756–886); (iii) the pictures of scenes from Roman history on the shield of Aeneas (8. 626–728); (iv) the reconciliation between Jupiter and Juno, with the promise of major Italian participation in the Trojan–Italian alliance from which the Roman race is destined to spring (12. 791–842). All of these passages contain in different degrees both an indication of the nature of Rome's greatness and its beneficial contribution to the world's civilization and some suggestion of the cost involved in achieving this both to Rome herself and to others.

The Prophecy of Jupiter to his Daughter Venus (1. 257–96)
This passage occurs very early in the narrative of the poem, just after we have heard of the latest disaster to Aeneas in his quest, the storm which drove him southwards from Sicily after seven years of wandering to find his western land, destroyed one of his ships, and scattered the rest in poor shape to the coast of north Africa. During the storm we have seen him in despair, we have doubted his ability to carry through his mission to found Rome; now we have a serene and optimistic statement from the king of heaven that Aeneas will be successful. It is important to notice that Aeneas himself, though sadly in need of encouragement, does not of course hear this speech in heaven. We the readers hear it, and through the tragedies and disaster of the subsequent books it brightens the darkness and shines as an ideal which must be pursued in spite of the suffering involved. Jupiter's speech acknowledges the suffering involved, especially in the wars that will have to be fought, but its emphasis is wholly on the achievement. Aeneas will crush the fierce opposition and establish for his people city walls and a way of life – *moresque viris et moenia ponet*. Here is an important foreshadowing of a major theme of the poem: Aeneas is to be the founder not only of a city but also of a way of life, a new non-Trojan, non-Homeric way of life. Jupiter then goes on to give an account of the preliminaries to the foundation of Rome itself (Lavinium for a short period, then Alba Longa for three hundred years, and finally Rome). Of Rome Jupiter says:

> *his ego nec metas rerum nec tempora pono:*
> *imperium sine fine dedi.*   (1. 278–9)

To these I set no bounds in space or time; I have given them rule without end.

He continues by promising that Juno will cease her opposition, and with him cherish the Romans: *'rerum dominos gentemque togatam'* ('lords of the world, and a people wearing the toga'). This expresses for the first time the two-fold concept of the Roman mission which dominates the *Aeneid*: first military conquest, and then peace and a civilized way of life for the conquered.

Jupiter mentions only two periods of Roman history: the conquest of Greece, with reference to the names so hateful to Aeneas – Agamemnon, Achilles, Diomedes; and the period of Augustus, who will conquer the East and one day be deified (it is thought by some that the reference here is to Julius Caesar, but the evidence the other way is overwhelming). Then he says there will come a time of universal peace and gentleness:

> *Aspera tum positis mitescent saecula bellis*:

> Then wars will be laid aside and the fierce generations grow gentle.

This is the fair vision of Augustus' golden age, and Jupiter ends by saying that traditional values will be restored, the Gates of War closed, and mad frenzy (*Furor impius*), which has caused so much suffering in human history – and did especially in the civil wars which preceded the reign of Augustus – will be for ever tamed.

This idealistic and optimistic prophecy, which may have seemed in Virgil's time likely to come true, certainly represents the gentle Virgil's hopes. That it did not come true, certainly not in its entirety, we all know; but this was the hope (albeit an increasingly uncertain one as the poem progressed) in which the *Aeneid* was written.

The Pageant of Roman Heroes (6. 756–886)

This is the longest of the patriotic passages in the *Aeneid*; in it the ghosts of future Roman heroes waiting to be born are described by Anchises in the underworld to Aeneas. Like Jupiter's prophecy and like the description of Aeneas' shield it contains direct reference to Augustus. It falls distinctly into two parts, with a pendant added about Marcellus. The parts are divided by Anchises' question to Aeneas (6. 806–7), immediately after the description of the ghost of Augustus, when he asks 'Do we still hesitate to enlarge our prowess by deeds, or does fear prevent us from settling in Italy?'

The first half begins quietly with description of some of the kings of Alba Longa before swelling to a crescendo for Romulus, son of Mars and Ilia, founder of Rome, the city which will 'make its bounds equal to earth's extent, and its courage high as the heavens, happy in its offspring of heroes'. The trumpet notes now sound even louder as we come to Augustus, out of chronological order so that he, as the 'second founder' of Rome, may come next to Romulus. This is the fullest description of Augustus in the poem, and we should look at it in detail:

> *hic vir, hic est, tibi quem promitti saepius audis,*
> *Augustus Caesar, divi genus, aurea condet*
> *saecula qui rursus Latio regnata per arva*
> *Saturno quondam, super et Garamantas et Indos*
> *proferet imperium; iacet extra sidera tellus,*
> *extra anni solisque vias, ubi caelifer Atlas*
> *axem umero torquet stellis ardentibus aptum.*
> *Huius in adventum iam nunc et Caspia regna*
> *responsis horrent divum et Maeotia tellus,*
> *et septemgemini turbant trepida ostia Nili.*
> *nec vero Alcides tantum telluris obivit,*
> *fixerit aeripedem cervam licet, aut Erymanthi*
> *pacarit nemora et Lernam tremefecerit arcu;*
> *nec qui pampineis victor iuga flectit habenis*
> *Liber, agens celso Nysae de vertice tigres.*   (6.791–805)

This is the man, yes this is he whom you often hear promised to you, Augustus Caesar of divine descent, who will once again set up a Golden Age in Latium, in the territory once ruled over by Saturnus, and will extend his empire beyond the Garamantes and Indians; his territory lies beyond the stars, beyond the paths of the year and the sun, where heaven-bearing Atlas turns on his shoulder the vault of heaven studded with its shining stars. In anticipation of his coming even now the Caspian regions shudder at the oracular responses they receive, and the Maeotian land, and the trembling mouths of the seven-deltaed Nile are in turmoil. Indeed neither Hercules covered so much of earth, though he transfixed the bronze-footed stag and made Lerna tremble with his bow, nor Bacchus, he who triumphantly guides his yoked team with reins of vine-leaves as he drives his tigers down from the lofty height of Mount Nysa'.

The passage begins with the promise of a new Golden Age for Rome. Virgil refers to the mythical golden age under Saturn when Nature produced freely everything needful for men before Jupiter, the new king of the gods, decided that it was good for men to win their livelihood by hard work. This is the theme of the *Georgics* and is specifically described in *Georgics* 1. 121 ff. Here of course Virgil uses the phrase 'golden age' in a different sense, not mythically but practically, an age of peace and happiness. The majority of the passage is concerned with military supremacy, with special importance attaching to the panic of the River Nile at Augustus' coming (6. 800), a reference to Augustus' victory over Antony and Cleopatra at Actium in 31 BC, the subject of the central scenes on Aeneas' shield. The comparison of Augustus at the end with Hercules and Bacchus has special significance. The actual point of comparison is the large area of the world covered by the three; but a secondary point, perhaps a more important one, is that Augustus, like the other two, will be a great civilizer. Hercules freed the world from monstrous creatures (compare the story in *Aeneid* 8. 185 ff. about how he rid Evander's people of the monster Cacus), and Bacchus symbolized the conquest by man of wild nature (as shown in the image of the tigers drawing his chariot). A third point, which Virgil does not here make explicit as he did in Jupiter's prophecy (1. 289–90), is that both Hercules and Bacchus were mortals who had become deified because of their services to mankind; the implication is here that Augustus will receive the same reward.

The second half of the pageant is much more crowded with characters than the first half; and very significantly it contains, unlike the first half, passages of sorrow and unhappiness, intermingled with the triumphs – the history of Rome's progress towards her new Golden Age has not been without much suffering and disaster. It begins quietly with the kings of Rome who succeeded Romulus, placing emphasis on the peaceful and religious achievements of the second king, Numa. He is conspicuous with the olive branch of peace, he carries the sacred emblems, he will found the city upon the rule of law. The whole Roman mission is symbolized by its two first kings, Romulus the conqueror, Numa the man of peace and civilization.

The first note of disquiet is struck with the mention of Brutus, the founder and hero of republican Rome, who was renowned for having got rid of the dictatorial tyranny of kingship, as seen especially under Tarquin the Proud. Most surprisingly the epithet 'proud' is transferred from Tarquin to the 'proud spirit of the avenging Brutus', and the story of how Brutus subsequently as consul put his sons to death for plotting rebellion is presented not as a great example of Roman devotion to duty regardless of personal feelings but as a sad event in which Brutus' 'love of his country and immense desire for glory' motivated him. The last phrase is a disquieting one.

There follows a rapid mention of the great families of the Decii and Drusi, and of Torquatus and Camillus, before another note of pathos is struck with the mention of Julius Caesar and Pompey fighting a civil war:

ne, pueri, ne tanta animis adsuescite bella
neu patriae validas in viscera vertite viris;

(6. 832–3)

Do not, my children, make such warfare normal and acceptable in your thoughts, and do not turn your mighty strength against your country's heart.

And Anchises appeals to Julius Caesar especially, as being of his own blood, to refrain.

The tone changes again from sorrow to triumph as the pageant ends with a crowd scene of Roman victors, the conquerors of Greece, the Gracchi, the Scipios, Regulus and others, and it concludes with Quintus Fabius Maximus Cunctator, the Roman leader who won no victories but, by defensively avoiding further pitched battles with Hannibal, finally ensured the survival of Rome in her darkest hour of all. His achievement is summarized in a quotation from Ennius, Virgil's great predecessor in Roman patriotic epic, describing Fabius as 'the one man who by delaying tactics saved the situation'.

Now follow (6. 847–53) the most famous lines in the poem, expressing more precisely than anywhere else in the epic the nature of Rome's mission for the world as Virgil saw it. The lines begin with concessions to the Greeks as being superior in sculpture, oratory and astronomy, and continue:

tu regere imperio populos Romane memento –
hae tibi erunt artes – pacique imponere morem,
parcere subiectis et debellare superbos.

Roman, you must remember to rule the peoples with your government – these shall be your arts – to build civilization upon a foundation of peace, to spare the conquered and destroy proud aggressors.

'To rule the peoples with your government' – this is the Roman imperial concept which they considered to be their divine mission. This idea that empire was the destiny which the gods had laid upon the Romans is dominant throughout the *Aeneid*, and seems to have been widely believed in Virgil's time – for example Horace says (*Odes* 3. 6. 5.): *Dis te minorem quod geris imperas* ('Because you are servants of the gods, you rule on earth').

'These shall be your arts'. The Romans were often conscious of an inferiority complex in comparison with the artistic achievements of the Greeks, and here Virgil pinpoints what they achieve instead: no Parthenon, but peace and stability for the world.

'To build civilization upon a foundation of peace'.This is the translation of the phrase with the reading *pacique*; most texts until recently accepted the reading *pacisque*, which would give the meaning 'to impose the habit of peace', a much weaker phrase. There is no doubt that *pacique* is correct, being the reading of all the MSS: it is extraordinary that *pacisque* should have been printed by so many editors until now; it seems to have been based on a misreading of the commentator Servius. So with the correct reading we have a brilliant description of the bright side of the Roman imperial concept: first, as a foundation, to establish peace through the world (by means, of course, of military conquest), and then to build on that foundation (*imponere*) the civilization of Rome. The word *morem* has the connotation of a 'moral', organized, settled way of life: it is more often used in the plural (*mores*) in this meaning, but Virgil has it again in exactly this sense in 8. 316, describing a primitive tribe *quis neque mos neque cultus erat*, 'who had neither civilization nor culture'.

Parcere subiectis: this was the great Roman claim, that having conquered they were generous to the conquered. In comparison with most other conquerors of the ancient world this was true – it was something which Julius Caesar especially prided himself on after his conquest of Gaul – but all students of Roman imperial history will easily think of plenty of exceptions, and what is particularly significant for students of Virgil is that at the end of the poem Turnus is *subiectus* to Aeneas and is not spared.

Debellare superbos: this again has special reference to Virgil's poem, in that Turnus is frequently called 'proud' ('arrogant' is another possible translation) and therefore must be brought low.

So much for the pageant and its summary: it would seem that this would mark the end of the book and the end of the first half of the poem on a note of triumph. But it was not Virgil's way to over-simplify the complexity of the human world as he saw it, and he adds – as a kind of pendant to the pageant – a passage referring to the tragic death of the young Marcellus, marked out to be Augustus' heir, at the age of 19. Anchises explains, as he laments Marcellus' fate, that Rome would have seemed too powerful to the gods if Marcellus had been hers to keep. And so the long pageant, mostly patriotically triumphant, ends on a note of bewildered tragedy. In Conway's memorable phrase, we have 'a sudden gust of tragedy, when the sky at last seemed clear'.

The Shield of Aeneas (8.626–731)

In this long 'ecphrasis', or descriptive passage, Virgil uses a pictorial method of presenting the history of Rome. It is very similar in its patriotic impact to the pageant of heroes at the end of Book 6, but its method is different, comprising a series of static pictures of individual events as compared with the moving procession of great heroes as Anchises described them to Aeneas. It falls into two sections, the first (8. 626–70) depicting various scenes around the edge of the shield, and the second (8. 675–728) focusing on Augustus' victory at the battle of Actium, described in three separate scenes. This is the most direct and longest reference to contemporary events in the poem and in it figure by name Augustus himself, Agrippa, and Antony and his Egyptian wife (Cleopatra).

A comparison with Homer's description (*Iliad* 18. 478 ff.) of the new shield made for Achilles sheds light, as we have seen, on Virgil's method of adapting an epic technique to his thematic requirement. In Homer the motivation for introducing a new shield into the narrative is direct, as Achilles has lost his, and the opportunity is taken to describe it, a splendid work of art with pictures of all sorts of aspects of Greek life, but with no special relevance to the immediate context in the poem. In Virgil there is no direct reason for Aeneas to have a new shield, but the opportunity at this particular point in the poem to present pictorially aspects of future Roman glory exactly suited his poetic requirement. This is the last moment in the *Aeneid* before the large-scale description of battles and bloodshed begins; the start of Book 9 describes Turnus' attack on the Trojan camp, and the whole of the book is taken up with deeds of slaughter, as indeed is very much of the rest of the poem. It is therefore essential that the reader should be reminded as strongly as possible of what is at stake in the battles which the Trojans have to fight, presented as they will be in all their full horror. Whether the slaughter was justified by the great outcome of the Trojan victory, the foundation of Lavinium, and the beginnings of Rome's mighty achievements, is something which the peace-loving Virgil seems often to leave uncertain; but if there was to be any justification at all for the violence and deaths of the last four books then the empire which had arisen as a result had to be put before the reader in all its glory.

The choice of the scenes depicted is governed by various factors. First and foremost the shield is a work of art and Virgil has depicted it as such, giving frequent indications of the location on the shield of the various scenes (*in summo, nec procul hinc, in medio*, etc.) and choosing scenes which lend themselves to pictorial representation (for example, the twins and the wolf, Horatius holding the bridge, the sacred geese saving the Capitol, the various aspects of the sea battle of Actium). Secondly the scenes chosen, as well as being well known in the legends and history of Rome, all give an illustration of qualities and ideals which the Romans regarded as vital parts of their national character. Let us consider them from this point of view.

The first of the six scenes around the edge of the shield depicts the she-wolf suckling the twins, perhaps the most famous emblem of Rome, represented on numerous monuments and coins. This symbolizes the toughness of the Roman race, the power of survival: the twins are 'fearless' (*impavidi*) in spite of the normal ferocity of wolves. Next comes a scene of the rape of the Sabine women, the resultant war and the subsequent peace and alliance between the two peoples. Here we see that as well as proving their martial valour the Romans thought of themselves as peace-makers – 'they made a treaty' (*iungebant foedera*), with all the appropriate sacrifical rites. We are reminded, as we had been in the pageant (6. 808 ff.), that the king who succeeded the martial Romulus was the Sabine Numa Pompilius, peace-loving and very deeply religious.

The third scene depicts the horrific story of how the third king of Rome, Tullus Hostilius, punished the Alban Mettus by binding him to two chariots and tearing him apart as they drove in opposite directions. Virgil here very explicitly shows the moral by entering the narrative with the comment 'Man of Alba, you should have kept your word' (*at tu dictis Albane maneres*). Here is an example of broken faith, *fides violata*, a particularly heinous crime to the Romans, frequently attributed to their worst enemies, as for example Hannibal.

There follows a picture portraying various aspects of the attempt to restore the expelled king Tarquin by means of a revolt against the newly established republic aided by Etruscans under Lars Porsenna. Two Roman ideals are illustrated here: firstly, 'the sons of Aeneas rushed to battle on behalf of freedom', (*Aeneadae in ferrum pro libertate ruebant*). The Romans always considered that the rule of kings was a denial of the liberty of the people: Julius Caesar knew well enough that he must not accept the offer of a 'kingly crown'. The word *libertas* occurs only twice elsewhere in the poem, once simply in the sense of permission, and on the other occasion in the same context of the expulsion of the kings. Titles such as *dictator*, and indeed later on the attribution of divinity to an absolute ruler did not carry for the Romans the same suggestion of the lost liberty of the citizens. And the second ideal, a very obvious one, illustrated by Horatius Cocles and Cloelia, is courage (*fortitudo*). Horatius was a frequent *exemplum* of *fortitudo*: in Valerius Maximus' collection of examples of the various Roman virtues Horatius gets first place under the heading of *fortitudo*.

The fifth scene is given the important position at the top of the shield (*in summo*) and it illustrates the emphasis which the Romans always put (as is obvious all through the *Aeneid*) on due religious belief and ceremonial. Manlius is shown defending Rome against the attack of the Gauls in 390 BC: he is in front of the temple, defending the Capitol and being warned of the enemy's advent by the cackling of the sacred geese (a story on which Livy (5. 47) comments that the gods saved the Romans because at a time of famine they had refrained from slaughtering the sacred geese). The scene is rounded off, after a brilliantly coloured picture of the Gauls in their shining armour, with a description of traditional religious ceremonies and artefacts: the dancing priests (the Salii), the Luperci, the sacred shield that fell from heaven, the matrons in religious procession through the streets (a special privilege given to them for having donated their golden ornaments to the state at the time of the Gallic crisis – Livy 5. 25. 9).

Last of the scenes around the edge, balancing the religious scenes at the top, is a picture, at the bottom, of the underworld. This is in two sections, the first the place of punishment in which languishes Catiline, the conspirator whose coup Cicero foiled; and the second the place of the blessed (*pii*: observe the word, the standing epithet of Aeneas, the adjective which more than any other summarizes Roman ideals). Here is Cato administering justice. This is quite evidently a reference to the younger Cato, the political adversary of Julius Caesar, killed in battle against him, and the example of an ideal Stoic rigidly holding to his principles against all pressures. It is very interesting here that Cato's Stoicism and inflexible righteousness, for which he was indeed considered a heroic Roman figure, eclipse the political aspect of his Republicanism and his hostility to Augustus' adoptive father, Julius Caesar. If evidence were necessary to show that Virgil is not a 'political' writer, it is available here, as well as in many other places.

So much for the scenes around the edge of the shield, their pictorial suitability and their illustrations of Roman ideals. If we compare them with the heroes in the pageant at the end of Book 6, we see that while they all have a counterpart in the pageant (except for Catiline and Cato in the underworld) they present a different aspect of the person or event involved. Romulus here is in his infancy, in Book 6 he had been in full regal splendour; the reconciliation of the Sabines and the use of the word Cures recall Numa (6. 808 ff.) but do not focus on him. Tullus is mentioned in Book 6 but not in connection with Mettus. The attempt to restore the Tarquins is made much of in Book 6, but in connection with Brutus and his sons, not with Porsenna, Horatius and Cloelia. The attack of the Gauls on the Capitol, treated fully here, is only hinted at in Book 6 by the mention of Torquatus and Camillus (6. 825). Finally Augustus is treated quite differently in Book 6, with more emphasis on his destiny as world-ruler and restorer of the golden age and only a glimpse at the battle of Actium in the mention of the Nile (6. 800). It is also noticeable that these scenes on the shield are presented in chronological order but do not extend (except for the underworld scene) beyond 390 BC, more than three hundred and fifty years earlier than Virgil's times. In this way greater attention is achieved for the central scene which is to follow, the description in the battle of Actium of contemporary events.

The centre-piece is isolated from the rest of the pictures by a border showing the waves of the sea with dolphins sporting around (8. 671–4). Then the subject of the centre-piece (*in medio*) is immediately revealed: 'brass-bound ships, the battle of Actium' (*classes aeratas, Actia bella*). The theme is presented in three separate parts.

The first is a picture of the opposing forces, beginning splendidly and majestically with Augustus standing on the leading ship:

> *hinc Augustus agens Italos in proelia Caesar*
> *cum patribus populoque penatibus et magnis dis,*
> *stans celsa in puppi, geminas cui tempora flammas*
> *laeta vomunt patriumque aperitur vertice sidus.*
>
> (8. 678–81)

Here is Augustus Caesar leading the Italians into battle, with the senators and the people, the household gods and the great gods, standing on the high stern; his serene brow gives forth twin flames, and his father's star is revealed on his head.

This is one of only two places in the poem where Augustus is given the title Augustus Caesar (the other being in the pageant of heroes in 6. 792), and one of only three where he is mentioned at all by name (the other being as Caesar in 1. 286). Here Virgil uses all his poetic powers to produce a densely packed picture of the victorious general of the forces of the western Mediterranean matched against the East: it is an ideological combat in Virgil's eyes between two contrasting ways of life. This is emphasized very strongly (and at first sight paradoxically in the context of the *Aeneid*, in which Aeneas fights against the Italians) by the word *Italos*: it is the peoples of Virgil's beloved Italy, the Italy of the *Eclogues* and of the *Georgics* as well as of the *Aeneid*, who stand together as a unity against the disparate eastern forces of Antony and Cleopatra. The line which follows (8. 679) has the strongest possible patriotic connotations: it links the senators and the people in unity, and it ends with the religious aspect of Rome's mission in a strange and memorable phrase, 'the household gods and the great gods', which is imitated from Ennius. Furthermore it is closely similar in rhythm and identical in its second half with a line already used in Book 3 (*cum sociis natoque penatibus et magnis dis*, 3. 12) which described the initial departure of Aeneas from Troy. Thus what Aeneas began many centuries before is now brought to its final conclusion by Augustus at Actium.

The pictorial impact of these four lines is very powerful indeed, to the point of exaggeration: the twin flames from Augustus' temples can be regarded as describing his helmet (like the new helmet of Aeneas, which gives forth flames, 8. 620), but this phrase also gives Augustus something of an aura of the supernatural, comparable with the flames around Iulus' head (2. 682 ff.) 'His father's star' is a reference to the comet which appeared shortly after Julius Caesar's death and was considered to have carried his soul to heaven: here again we may see it as a symbol on his helmet, but there is perhaps a suggestion that it shines from the man himself.

Next comes Agrippa, Augustus' right-hand man in government: he is given distinction by the naval crown won for his previous victories by sea, but there is here nothing like the dazzling radiance of the picture of Augustus.

Finally a picture of the opposition, portrayed as a motley crew of various eastern peoples: the word *barbaricus* is used, and the presence of Cleopatra is indicated by the paraphrase *Aegyptia coniunx*, and the parenthetical *nefas* ('the shame of it'). This part of the scene is rounded off with vivid pictures of the clash of battle, flames everywhere and the ships like mountains or floating islands, a suitably grandiloquent description for this most decisive of all Rome's battles.

The second part of the scene continues the ideological contrast between the two sides. Ridicule is directed at Cleopatra calling her troops to battle with the *sistrum*, an Eastern type of tambourine, and at the gods of Egypt:

> *omnigenumque deum monstra et latrator Anubis*
> *contra Neptunum et Venerem contraque Minervam*
> *tela tenent.*   (8. 698–700)

Monstrous shapes of gods of all kinds, and the yapping Anubis wield their weapons in opposition to Neptune and Venus and Minerva.

This trio of Roman gods is reinforced a few lines later by Apollo, Augustus's special patron deity, given the epithet of *Actius* and inspiring universal panic among the enemy. The section closes with Cleopatra in flight and a vivid and moving image of the River Nile sadly receiving the conquered into its embrace.

The last part of the Actium scene is set in Rome, as Augustus celebrates his triple triumph. Emphasis is put here on the religious thanksgiving of the Romans, and on the variety of the conquered peoples, stretching far away to the East and indicating the world-wide concept of the Roman Empire. The description (and the book) ends with Aeneas shouldering the shield:

> *Talia per clipeum Volcani, dona parentis,*
> *miratur rerumque ignarus imagine gaudet*
> *attollens umero famamque et fata nepotum.*   (8. 729–31)

He marvels at these scenes on the shield Vulcan made, the gift of his mother, and ignorant of the facts of history rejoices in the pictures of them, as he lifts up on to his shoulder the glory and destiny of his descendants.

This stirring conclusion brilliantly closes the episode as Aeneas literally shoulders the shield and metaphorically shoulders the responsibility for the whole future of Rome. He can of course know nothing except through visions and divine revelations of the consequences of his efforts to found his city, but dimly and darkly he continues his mission. All through the poem he has before him an *imago*, a vision yet unfulfilled, and this he pursues up to and often almost beyond his human powers.

The Final Reconciliation Scene in Heaven (12. 791–842)
The single combat between Aeneas and Turnus which is to decide the war is well under way when Virgil moves for the last time from the mortal scene to the activity of the divine powers in Olympus. Jupiter now directly intervenes in order that fate may be fulfilled. The main obstacle has always been Juno's opposition to the Trojans, both because of her love for Carthage (strongly stressed in the first few lines of the poem) and because she supports the Italian opponents of the Trojans. This latter is the aspect which is emphasized here in the strongest possible way, as we shall see.

Jupiter begins by insisting that Juno is well aware that the fates require that Aeneas should become the native deity (*indiges*) of the place, and that he can no longer tolerate her efforts to negate or postpone what is destined to happen. This should not be taken as an indication from Virgil that events are predestined: he is privileged, as author, as we are as readers, to look with hindsight on the events of history. Within the poem itself the whole of future history is dependent upon Aeneas' attempts to fulfil his mission.

Jupiter's speech ends with very powerful phrases describing the horrors which Juno's opposition has caused:

> *terris agitare vel undis*
> *Troianos potuisti, infandum accendere bellum,*
> *deformare domum et luctu miscere hymenaeos:*
> *ulterius temptare veto.* (12. 803–6)

You were able to hound the Trojans on land and sea, to instigate a hideous war, to harm the dynasty and wreck with sorrow the marriage: I forbid you to go any further.

'To instigate a hideous war'. Indeed the tone of the last four books of the poem has again and again indicated the horror of battle, especially of a battle which has been to all intents and purposes a civil war, between the two peoples who would unite to form the Roman race. This marriage (a marriage both literal, between Aeneas and Lavinia, and metaphorical, between the two peoples) has been caused by Juno to occasion grief and disaster (cf. her threats in 7. 308 ff.) Thus is symbolized the human folly which leads to such suffering.

Juno yields to Jupiter's commands, as she must: but she has some requests to make on behalf of the Latins, which she maintains are not ruled out by the dictates of fate. This is what she says:

> *cum iam conubiis pacem felicibus (esto)*
> *component, cum iam leges et foedera iungent,*
> *ne vetus indigenas nomen mutare Latinos*
> *neu Troas fieri iubeas Teucrosque vocari*
> *aut vocem mutare viros aut vertere vestem.*
> *sit Latium, sint Albani per saecula reges,*
> *sit Romana potens Itala virtute propago:*
> *occidit, occideritque sinas cum nomine Troia.* (12. 821–8)

When soon they make peace with happy wedlock – so be it then – when soon they make their agreements and treaties, do not order the native-born Latins to alter their name, or become

Trojans and be called Teucri, or to change their language or alter their dress. Let Latium exist, let there be Alban kings through the centuries, let the Roman stock be strong by means of Italian qualities. Troy has fallen – let it be fallen, name and all.

In the context of the *Aeneid* we would not for a moment expect these requests to be granted: Juno has all through the poem shown hostility and caused disaster for the Trojans, heroes of the poem, and that at her request they should virtually lose their identity after victory seems inconceivable. But in the context of history Juno's requests are not only destined to come true, but also they are highly desirable for the Romans (if not for the Trojans). The Romans of Virgil's time were of course people of Italian (not Trojan) qualities; we remember Augustus at Actium:

> *hinc Augustus agens Italos in proelia Caesar* . . .   (8. 678)

Troy in Virgil's time was associated with Italian distrust for the peoples of the eastern Mediterranean (compare Horace, *Odes* 3.3). In Virgil's poem they are the heroes who take the first steps towards the Roman Empire: but in the history of his own time they have no significance.

Jupiter assents serenely to Juno's requests and in sonorous and deliberate phrases grants her petition, yielding in the interests of Roman history to what she asks (notice the emphasis of the five consecutive monosyllables):

> *do quod vis et me victusque volensque remitto.* (12. 833)

I grant what you wish, and conquered and willingly I yield.

Not only this – Jupiter actually steps up her conditions in favour of the Italians, granting (as she asked) the retention of language and name, but expanding her word *vestem* ('way of dress') to *mores* ('way of life'). In his prophecy in Book 1 he had said that Aeneas would set up a city and a way of life for his people (*moresque viris et moenia ponet*, 1. 264); now he says it will be the Italian not the Trojan way of life that the Romans will inherit. He summarizes this virtual elimination of Trojan influence in the words:

> *commixti corpore tantum*
> *subsident Teucri* . . .   (12. 835–6)

The Trojan share in the union will be physical only, and they will be recessive partners.

And as a final touch he says:

morem ritusque sacrorum
adiciam faciamque omnis uno ore Latinos. (12. 836–7)

I will add the procedures and rituals of their religion, and I will make them all Latins, speaking one tongue.

Again the contrast with the beginning of the poem is very great: in line 6 of Book 1 we were told that Aeneas' task, for which he suffered so much, was to found his city and 'bring his gods' to Latium; and several times in the poem the *penates*, the household gods, which Aeneas was bringing with him from Troy, are stressed as a vital part of his mission.

Finally Jupiter says that the new race will be god-fearing as no other and that no other people will worship Juno more reverently. This had become historically true long before Virgil's time. Juno is satisfied and withdraws from events.

This very remarkable passage spans the two time-scales of the *Aeneid* and reconciles different aspects of the poem. From the Trojan point of view all is now set for victory, and the hostility of Juno, which has delayed it so long and made it cost so much in suffering, is now eliminated. From Juno's point of view she has achieved what she wanted. From the Roman point of view it establishes the fact of history in Virgil's time, that it was the Italians who constituted the strength and pride of Rome's empire. Paradoxically the hostility of Juno (who has been presented throughout the poem as harsh and hateful) has achieved a beneficial result for mankind.

These four patriotic passages which have been analysed in detail give beyond any question an optimistic, almost a panegyrical tone to the *Aeneid*, and there are many shorter ones scattered through the poem, mostly achieved by forward-looking prophecies or editorial comments. We have seen in the previous section how the seven-line proem to Book 1 gives a majestically proud opening to the theme of the 'walls of mighty Rome' and how the last line before the narrative begins (1. 33) stresses the immense task which was involved. In the second book, chronologically of course the earliest, occurs the first revelation to Aeneas of Rome's future greatness when the ghost of Hector appears to him on the last night of Troy and tells him that he must leave Troy, taking with him the household gods and sacred emblems, and found a mighty city for them after wandering over the seas – *his moenia quaere magna, pererrato statues quae denique ponto* (2. 294–5). This indication to Aeneas of a great future is reinforced by the ghost of his lost wife, Creusa, who tells him (2. 780–4) that he must endure long exile over the sea and then will come to a western land where the River Tiber flows through rich countryside: there he will found his kingdom (*regnum*).

Book 3 is rich in oracular prophecies of greatness (designed to hearten Aeneas through all his wanderings): the oracle of Apollo tells him to seek his ancient mother (meaning Italy, whence Dardanus originally came) and 'here the house of Aeneas will rule over all the lands, and the sons of their sons and those who will be born from them' (3. 97–8). When they mistakenly make for Crete, a vision of the *penates* corrects the mistake, and promises that they will raise Aeneas' descendants to the stars and give empire to the city (3. 158–9). The Trojans reach Buthrotum and receive detailed instructions from Helenus about the future perils of their journey and how to overcome them, and he ends by saying 'Forward you go, and extol Troy to the heavens, mighty in her achievements' (3. 462).

At this stage of the poem then, apart from the sonorous prophecy of Jupiter in 1. 257 ff, which the reader has heard but Aeneas has not, Aeneas himself has received promises of glory in ascending order of greatness: *moenia magna* (a mighty city), *regnum* (a kingdom), *cunctis dominabitur oris* (will rule all the world), will have empire (*imperium*), and his descendants will be raised to the stars; finally Troy will be extolled to the heavens.

Thus the poem so far is dotted with references to Rome's greatness, couched in proud patriotic and imperialist terms; and this continues to be the case as the poem unrolls. Examples may be found at 5. 600, 7. 98 ff., 7. 272 ff., 9. 642 ff., and elsewhere, but I concentrate on two other instances, one a short phrase and the other a much longer episode. Book 4 is by its nature not one which turns our attention constantly to Rome (we are too much concerned with the tragedy of Dido, part of the price paid for the triumph of Rome), but there is a very significant passage about the imperial mission when Jupiter sends down Mercury to remind Aeneas that his duty requires that he should no longer linger in Carthage but must proceed towards the foundation of his city. He says that Aeneas' task is to be the man who will rule an Italy teeming with empire and fierce in war, who will transmit a race from the noble blood of Teucer and bring the whole world under the sway of laws (*totum sub leges mitteret orbem*, 4. 231). This is one of the most direct indications in the whole poem of Rome's ultimate mission after military conquest and empire has been achieved, and it is certainly one which it fulfilled to a remarkáble extent in the then existing Mediterranean world. What inspired Virgil in his patriotic vision of the present and future of his country was first the idea of universal peace (which he and his contemporaries had good reason to desire passionately) and secondly the idea of a settled world, accepting a Stoic idea of universal law, and dignified by the marks of civilized living (roads, great religious buildings, literature and art etc.) which could be given by the Roman adaptation of Greek achievements plus their own special contributions.

The longer episode is in Book 8, when Aeneas visits Evander, an Arcadian immigrant settled on the site on the Tiber where later the massive buildings of Rome would arise. He finds the Arcadians engaged in celebrating a religious festival in honour of Hercules, who had freed them from the monster Cacus. The passage ends with reference to the priestly caste who were in charge of the ceremonies in Virgil's day, and the Ara Maxima where they were celebrated (8. 268–72); thus a strong religious bond of continuity between Aeneas' times and those of Virgil is set up. The poet makes a special point of the ancient and traditional religious basis of Rome's empire in his own day (cf. also 8. 281–8), and by selecting Hercules as his example renews the suggestion, hinted at from time to time in the poem, that the task of Aeneas in eliminating the threats to the growth of Roman civilization is comparable with that of Hercules in using his strength and determination to rid the world of mythical monsters which threatened the early growth of civilization. It also strengthens the links of Aeneas with Stoic ways of thought, as Hercules, was the patron or *exemplum* of Stoicism. More than this, it suggests that an ideal leader of Rome will have the qualities of Hercules, courage and rock-like determination to overcome opposition, and it recalls the memorable comparison of Augustus (6. 801 ff.) with Hercules. Virgil does no more than suggest indirectly: Augustus is not Hercules, nor is Aeneas, but certain qualities of the Stoic hero are called for in both men.

Next Evander prepares to show Aeneas round the site of his little city, first explaining that originally a hardy but uncivilized people lived there (*quis neque mos neque cultus erat*, 8. 316), living on berries and hunted animals. Then came Saturn from heaven, seeking refuge from Jupiter who sought to depose him (hence the word *Latium* from *latere* 'to hide'); he brought together the scattered mountain-dwellers into a community and taught them laws (*legesque dedit*), and founded the golden age, with its universal peace until it gradually declined into war and greed. It was Anchises' claim to Aeneas in the underworld (6. 792 ff.) that Augustus would again establish a golden age such as that over which Saturn had presided in these legendary days.

The tour of the site now proceeds with the Carmental Gate, Romulus' Asylum, the Lupercal, the Argiletum, the Tarpeian rock and the Capitol Hill. Here Virgil intervenes to break the time-scale by the authorial comment: 'Golden now, but in those days gone by rough with shrubby undergrowth' (8. 348). Evander says that it was already a religious centre for the worship of an unknown god, but his Arcadians believed that Jupiter himself was present there – a clear foreshadowing of the temple in Virgil's time to Jupiter Capitolinus, Jupiter Optimus Maximus. Next comes the Janiculum and the hill of Saturn, and then they enter 'the house of humble Evander' and see cattle lowing in the Roman forum and the elegant suburb ('elegant' again is an authorial comment) of Carinae (8. 359–61). The passage, and indeed the whole section, now ends with the entrance to Evander's simple home, and Evander's words 'Be brave enough, my guest, to despise wealth (like Hercules) and do not be contemptuous of my poor abode' (8. 364–5). And he gives Aeneas a bed of leaves and a bearskin.

In this whole passage Virgil has trodden a path between the glorification of Rome's present greatness and the glorification of her earlier simplicity and poverty. There is of course a paradox here, but it is one which Virgil's readers would easily accept. The beauty and brilliance of the capital of Augustus' empire was indeed dazzling, but at the same time the Romans prided themselves and loved to look back on the days of their simple origins, the peasant soldiery so sympathetically described in the early pages of Livy with their contempt for riches and wealth. Augustus greatly encouraged this link with tradition, living himself in a relatively simple dwelling on the Palatine, and Horace frequently in his *Odes* dwells upon the corrupting influence of wealth (for example, 3. 3. 49 ff.) and the character-forming qualities of poverty and the simple life (*angustam amice pauperiem pati robustus acri militia puer condiscat*; 'let our young men, toughened by fierce warfare, learn to endure gladly the straits of poverty' 3. 2. 1 ff.). This is a frequently recurring theme in literature of the Augustan age, and one which Virgil uses often in the *Aeneid*: Aeneas is condemned for his lapse in Carthage when he wears regal purple (4. 261 ff.); Camilla goes to her death because of her desire for golden ornaments (11. 768 ff.); the simple virtues of the Italians are praised throughout the catalogue at the end of Book 7; Numanus (9. 603 ff.) speaks movingly of the simple and hardy way of life of the Italians; Fabricius (6. 843–4) is praised as *parvo potentem* (great in poverty); Antony (as we have seen) is condemned at the battle of Actium for being associated with 'barbarian wealth'.

The paradox of the need for Rome to be properly splendid as a capital city should be and the desire to contrast her tough simplicity with the corrupt extravagance of the East runs through the *Aeneid*. It is very noticeable that these Roman ideal qualities are much more evident among the Italians in the *Aeneid* (they were very dominant throughout the *Georgics*, the poem of Italy) than among the Trojans, and three times Aeneas is accused by his enemies of effeminate eastern qualities (by Iarbas, 4. 215; by Numanus, 9. 617 ff.; and by Turnus, 12. 98–100). 'Be bold, my guest, to despise wealth,' Evander had said, and this traditional aspect of the Romans of long ago was one that Virgil and Augustus sought to emphasize. In the subsequent history of Rome such a view persevered perhaps less in practice than in theory.

The passages which we have considered at some length suggest that a major aim of the *Aeneid* is to link the past with the present and the future in a patriotic and optimistic way. In the next section we shall consider the elements in the poem which militate against – strongly against – such an optimistic view of the present and the future. But first we should discuss other ways, sometimes overlapping with the aspects already considered, by means of which Virgil sought to link the remote legend of Aeneas with the Rome of his own day.

A major method which Virgil used was to narrate the first origins of names, places, buildings, ceremonies, which were well known in his time. This aetiological method of explaining origins (much to the fore in the Evander episode which we have just examined) was very much favoured in Alexandrian literature (for example Callimachus' *Aitia*, parts of which survive) and arose from the academic curiosity of the scholar-poets of that time. In Virgil this aspect is present too, but it is often subordinated to the patriotic desire to reinforce Rome's long traditions by taking them back to Trojan days. A good example is the celebration of the Trojan game – *lusus Troiae* – at the end of the anniversary games in honour of Anchises in Book 5. Here Virgil takes advantage of an accidental verbal similarity (it is almost certain that the original meaning of *troia* was 'pageantry') to make a point of the Trojan link with the equestrian pageant which was very popular in his own time, having been revived by Julius Caesar and established under Augustus as a regular institution, performed by boys of noble birth (Suetonius, *Augustus*, 43). They formed a notable part in Augustus' campaign to encourage the young to take part in outdoor activities of all sorts. Virgil enters the narrative himself after the long and pictorial description of the manoeuvres of the horsemen, and says:

> *hunc morem cursus atque haec certamina primus*
> *Ascanius, Longam muris cum cingeret Albam,*
> *rettulit et priscos docuit celebrare Latinos,*
> *quo puer ipse modo, secum quo Troia pubes;*
> *Albani docuere suos; hinc maxima porro*
> *accepit Roma et patrium servavit honorem;*
> *Troiaque nunc pueri, Troianum dicitur agmen.*   (5. 596–602)

This tradition of riding and these mock battles Ascanius first revived, when he was enclosing Alba Longa with its fortifications, and he taught the Latins of old to celebrate it as he had as a boy with the young men of Troy; the Albans taught their people, and from these origins mighty Rome took it on and preserved their ancestral tradition, and now the boys are called 'Troy' and their formation is called Trojan.

Here we have a very careful and deliberate description of the tradition, moving from one stage to another in Rome's development, and ending up in the well-known ceremony of Virgil's own time.

More than this, it is evident that a major reason for Virgil's long description of the anniversary games for Anchises which are concluded by the *lusus Troiae* (as well as the Homeric precedent) was the recent establishment by Augustus of Actian games on the Greek model to be celebrated every fourth year in honour of his victory. An indirect reference to these Actian games had already been made in *Aeneid* 3. 280, when the Trojans stop at Actium (which did not figure in the traditional legend) and celebrate games on the beach there.

Another institution to which reference had already been made was the worship of Hercules at the *Ara Maxima*; another was the Roman festival of the *Parentalia* (5. 60); another the Roman habit of covering the face during sacrifice (3. 405 ff.); another, which occurs twice, was the Sibylline books, foreshadowed by Helenus (3. 444) and linked by Aeneas (6. 69 ff.) with a promise to build a magnificent temple in Apollo's honour into which the Sibylline books would be transferred (this actually happened while the *Aeneid* was being written (Suetonius, *Augustus*, 29).

A particular form of this aetiological method is the linking of ancient names with existing families. By far the most important of these was the linking of Iulus, Aeneas' son, backwards with Ilium (Troy) and forwards with the Julian *gens* into which Augustus was adopted (1. 288, referring to Augustus: *Iulius, a magno demissum nomen Iulo*; 'Julius, a name handed down from the famous

Iulus'). Another example (5. 568) is the mention of Atys in the *lusus Troiae* with the explicit comment 'from whom the Latin Atii derived': Augustus' mother was a member of the Atian family. Another is the list of the captains of the ships in the ship race, again with specific reference to the Roman families descended from them: 'Mnestheus from whom came the Memmii'; Gyas (without a specific mention of his descendants); Sergestus, ancestor of the Sergii; and Cloanthus of the Cluentii (5. 116 ff.).

Quite often this aetiological method associates characters in the *Aeneid* with famous place names of Italy and Sicily: for example Segesta is linked with Acestes (5. 718); Capua with Capys (10. 145); Caieta with Aeneas' nurse of the same name (7. 1–2); Cape Palinurus with Aeneas' helmsman Palinurus (6. 381); Mount Misenus with the Trojan whose death occurs just as Aeneas is preparing for his descent to the underworld (6. 234–5).

Thus Virgil uses all kinds of devices, large-scale or small-scale, to link his ancient legend with the world of his own day. Those which we have considered so far have been very specific; there is another which is far less specific but enormously important in that it concerns not only the Roman world but the universal world of human behaviour. It spans not only the distance from Homer to Virgil but puts the Roman world in the context of the great problems faced by mankind in the past, the present, and the future. This Virgil does by comparing the moral values and virtues and vices of the Homeric heroes with those of Roman times. He uses the Homeric world as a point of comparison for the evaluation of the proto-Roman qualities of Aeneas. Should a Roman hero show the same qualities as Achilles or Odysseus, and if not, in what ways should they be different? And further than that, is it in the power of human individuals under the pressure of circumstances to behave always according to their ideals? And if not, how nearly should they cling to them? Or should they abandon them if they seem incapable of dealing adequately with the harsh situations which so often beset people? These are the fundamental questions which the *Aeneid* explores, thus making it not merely a examination of the Roman world *vis-à-vis* the Homeric world, but *vis-à-vis* all human behaviour, past, present, and future. This essentially is why it is proclaimed as a universal poem, dealing with the sort of problems which have confronted and will confront the human race until it finds Utopia.

(iii) PATHOS AND SORROW – THE WAR SCENES

Perhaps the most striking aspect of Virgil's poem is what we may
call the tension between optimism and pessimism, between Virgil's
public voice extolling the greatness (actual and potential) of Golden
Rome and his private voice of sympathy and sorrow over the fate of
the lonely individual, the victim of the mighty force of destiny, the
outsider who does not fit into the great plan of fate (like Dido or
Turnus), or the warrior who loses his life fighting in a war which is
seen in the poem to have been, in the end, senseless. We have
examined in detail in the previous section the optimistic side of the
poem: we turn now to the other side, the sadness at human suffering
which Virgil presents so poignantly that certainly in the last few
generations he has been appreciated primarily as the poet of the
world's sorrows, the poet of *lacrimae rerum*. It is very typical of
Virgil's way of presenting this tension that each half of the poem
ends on a note of intense pathos immediately following a
triumphantly optimistic scene. The pageant of Roman heroes in
Book 6 has, at the end of Anchises' long speech, a proud expression
of the Roman mission of bringing peace and civilization to the
world, yet it is followed by the account of the tragic death of the
young Marcellus. The last book of the poem moves to its conclusion
with the removal of the remaining obstacles to the fulfilment of the
Roman mission, yet it finally closes with its focus not on Aeneas'
triumph but on the pitiless slaughter of the suppliant Turnus.

This sense of sadness for man's suffering is more dominant in
Virgil than in Homer or Milton. In Homer death on the battlefield,
grim and tragic though it is, is accepted as a part of the expected
circumstances of life, and the climactic horror of the *Iliad*, Achilles'
savagery towards Hector, is partially expiated in Achilles' meeting
with Priam and the ransoming of Hector's body with which the
poem ends. In Milton the sin of Adam is expiated by the redemption
of humankind by the Son of God. But Virgil's poem ends with an
act of savagery by Aeneas for which, however much it may be partly
justified, no expiation is given.

The first indication of Virgil's preoccupation with suffering
occurs, as we have seen, at the beginning of the poem with his
reference to Juno's hostility towards Aeneas, and his question:
tantaene animis caelestibus irae? ('Can there be such anger in the
minds of gods?', 1. 11). Much later in the poem he intervenes in the
narrative again to ask the same question, this time extended from
Aeneas himself to all the warriors of Troy and Italy:

tanton placuit concurrere motu,
Iuppiter, aeterna gentes in pace futuras? (12. 503–4)

Was it really your wish, Jupiter, that peoples destined to be
peaceful ever after should clash in such fierce conflict?

These two editorial interventions into his narrative by Virgil
illustrate the two kinds of apparently inexplicable injustice with
which the poem is filled. The first is the wreckage of human
happiness caused by tragic circumstances, for example suffered by
Aeneas himself, who has to undergo many traumatic experiences
(for which he often feels self-blame), and by Dido, whose ill-starred
love for Aeneas leads to her death. The second is the actual slaughter
on the battlefield which dominates Book 2 and Books 9–12. The
feeling of sorrow and bewilderment is concentrated on Dido and on
Turnus and (for the discerning reader) on Aeneas himself; these
three major characters in the poem will be discussed in later
sections. Here we should consider some of the innumerable other
characters whose suffering appears inexplicable and unacceptable.

Book 2, the earliest chronologically in the poem, is one of the
most intense and horrifying accounts of the destruction of a city that
could possibly be imagined. It was anticipated in Book 1 when
Aeneas in Carthage viewed the pictures of the Trojan War which
decorated Dido's temple to Juno (1. 453–93); and it was there that,
upon seeing the depiction of King Priam, Aeneas uttered the famous
words which have so often been quoted to summarize Virgil's sense
of sadness – *sunt lacrimae rerum*. The phrase has proved to be a
convenient one for summarizing Virgil's sensitivity towards human
suffering – what Tennyson referred to when he invoked Virgil as
'Thou majestic in thy sadness at the doubtful doom of human kind'
('To Virgil', 6. 2). There is of course no doubt that this sadness is
a major feature of the poem, but we should note that the common
usage of the phrase to mean that the world is full of sorrows, or a
'vale of tears', is not precisely what Virgil means in this passage.
Aeneas says to Achates as he looks at the pictures, 'What place,
what region in the whole world is not full of our sorrow? Look, there
is Priam'; and he continues:

sunt hic etiam sua praemia laudi;
sunt lacrimae rerum et mentem mortalia tangunt.
(1.461–2)

Here too glory has its special reward, here too there are tears for
what happens and mortal sufferings move men's hearts.

The meaning then is not that the world is a vale of tears (though indeed the *Aeneid* often suggests this), but that here too (in Carthage, a wholly unknown place for the Trojans) people react with sympathy for suffering and their hearts are moved.

The pictures on the temple wall all refer to events prior to the actual destruction of Troy, which is the subject-matter of the whole of Book 2. They concentrate on deeds of horror committed by the Greeks (Diomedes slaughtering the Trojan allies in their sleep, Achilles killing young Troilus, Achilles dragging Hector's body round the walls and then ransoming his dead body for gold to his aged suppliant father, King Priam). It is a foretaste of the much greater horror of Book 2, where Achilles' son Pyrrhus surpasses his now dead father in vicious cruelty. There is also a foretaste of the ruthlessness of fate in the decree that Troy shall be destroyed: Rhesus is killed before he can fulfil the oracle which would have saved Troy, Achilles prevents Troilus from growing to full manhood (which again would have saved Troy), the goddess Pallas Athena will not be placated by the suppliant maidens.

From the all-pervasive horror of Book 2 I pick just a few passages which illustrate the empathy of Virgil with the victims. The strong narrative guidelines of the book are first the trickery of Sinon, the tragic fate of Laocoon, and the entry of the wooden horse, secondly the mad fighting culminating in the death of Priam, and thirdly the final realization by Aeneas and Anchises that they must leave the stricken city. It is within the central section of the book that Virgil describes the violent deaths of the unknown and the famous alike. His method of battle description is very varied: there are general pictures of destruction and fire (2. 301–13) and general pictures of universal slaughter (2. 366–9, 383–5, 396–8, 440–50). These are interspersed with specific accounts of the deaths of Trojans who have been introduced to us briefly as Aeneas gathers his forces for a last-ditch resistance (2. 318, 330–41). Some of these (Hypanis and Dymas) are commemorated only by mention of their names, but others are given a little cameo description. Rhipeus dies 'he who was the most just of all the Trojans and the most righteous, but the gods willed otherwise' (2. 426–8). The last phrase, *dis aliter visum*, was a Stoic maxim suggesting that human expectation (i.e. that Rhipeus was too good a man to die like this) was often contrary to the inscrutable ways of providence, and must simply be accepted. The context here strongly suggests that Virgil cannot accept the conventional Stoic explanation of apparently undeserved disaster. Panthus dies, the priest of Apollo; he has been introduced to us fleeing from the Greeks carrying the sacred emblems and dragging his little grandson with him (2. 318–20). Now we learn (2. 429–30) that his religious office and his devotion to it (*pietas*) do not save him. Coroebus is the member of Aeneas' band who stands out most in the memory in this section. We meet him in 2. 341–6, hearing that he has come from Phrygia to help the Trojans because of his love for Cassandra, and Virgil anticipates his fate by the comment

> *infelix qui non sponsae praecepta furentis*
> *audierit!*   (2. 345–6)

Unhappy man not to have heeded the warning of the inspired prophetess, his bride-to-be.

In the general fighting Coroebus sees Cassandra being dragged from Minerva's temple by the hair, her arms bound, and he rushes to his certain death (2. 403–8); he falls at the hands of Peneleus right by Minerva's temple.

This method of battle description, sometimes general slaughter without names, sometimes simply with names and no more, often with a little cameo description, is taken by Virgil from Homer, and used, as we shall see, as a technique for variety and for vividness in the battle – scenes of *Aeneid* 9–12. Often, because of his extreme hatred of war, the cameos are even more poignant in Virgil than in Homer.

These are the methods which Virgil uses in the lead-in to the climax of the fighting in Priam's palace itself. There are other techniques too, again Homeric: short speeches from the warriors (*Aen.* 2. 322, 324–35, 348–54, 373–5, 387–91), and vivid similes (2. 304–8, 355–8, 379–82, 416–19) occurring more densely in the war scenes than elsewhere in the poem.

Aeneas climbs on to the battlements of the palace of Priam, trying to prevent the Greeks from occupying this position, and consequently is an eye-witness of the horrific events in the palace itself. Here Virgil spares us no detail of horror. He begins with the terrifying figure of Achilles' son Pyrrhus, comparing him in his flashing armour with a snake, its slough newly cast, rearing up threateningly with forked tongue. As he and his comrades force an entrance, the interior of the palace itself is revealed – *apparet domus intus* – and the sanctity of private life is profaned by violence (often a major theme in the *Eclogues* and *Georgics*): the women and children scatter in fear; we see Priam (uselessly attempting to resist) and Hecuba at the altar; we see Polites, one of Priam's sons, killed before his father's eyes and Priam himself savagely slaughtered in front of the altar itself, dragged by the hair, slipping in his son's blood, and murdered with a sword-thrust up to the hilt.

haec finis Priami fatorum, hic exitus illum
sorte tulit Troiam incensam et prolapsa videntem
Pergama, tot quondam populis terrisque superbum
regnatorem Asiae. iacet ingens litore truncus,
avulsumque umeris caput et sine nomine corpus.   (2. 554–8)

This was the end of Priam's destiny, this was the fate that came
upon him as he saw Troy ablaze, its citadel fallen, once with all
its peoples and lands the proud ruler of Asia. There lies a mighty
body on the shore, a head cut off from the shoulders, a nameless
corpse.

The last line-and-a-half of this passage is very strange. Virgil seems
to be conflating the account which he has given of the death of
Priam at the altar with an alternative version that Priam was taken
and beheaded at Achilles' tomb on the shore. Logically the two
accounts do not cohere, but the switch to the other version adds a
sense of desolation and perpetuity to the immediacy of the previous
description, and that Priam himself should be among the
unnumbered dead gives a culmination to the harshness of the
workings of fate.

The last passage of pathos in Book 2 is much more muted, yet
intensely poignant. In the departure of Aeneas' family from Troy his
wife Creusa is lost; for this it seems Aeneas himself was much to
blame, having inexplicably told her to follow a long way behind (2.
711). Aeneas is distraught and rushes in among the marauding
Greeks looking for her, when suddenly her ghost appears to him,
telling him gently that these things are fated, and that he has a new
destiny ahead of him. For herself, she will not be taken prisoner, but
is under the protection of Cybele, the great mother of the gods. She
concludes:

iamque vale et nati serva communis amorem   (2. 789)

And now farewell, and cherish your love for the son we had.

Aeneas seeks to embrace her for the last time, but the ghost is
unsubstantial, like a light breeze or a winged dream. These lines,
taken from Homer, are used again as Aeneas tries to embrace the
ghost of his father in the underworld (6. 700–2).

The note of suffering continues through Book 3 (Polydorus,
Andromache, Achaemenides), Book 4 (Dido), Book 5 (lamentation
for Anchises and especially the loss of Palinurus, the faithful
helmsman swept overboard by the god Sleep at the very point of

final arrival at their destined landing-point in Italy), and Book 6, with the hapless ghosts who may not cross the Styx (including Palinurus) and those in Limbo (especially Dido and Deiphobus). Book 7 has a happy beginning which is soon upset by Juno; and the outbreak of war, with the accidental killing by Ascanius of Silvia's pet deer, has a quite remarkable and almost lyrical poignancy of sadness in the way Virgil tells it. Book 8, the last before the full-scale battle scenes which occupy the rest of the poem, is conspicuous for its optimism; it is a brief pause before Virgil confronts again the problems of violent death.

Book 9

The ninth book begins with a powerful scene of impending violence as Turnus and his men move to attack the walls of the Trojan camp. Turnus hurls his javelin and rushes forward in all his might (9. 52–3); his men take up the battle-cry as they follow their commander (9. 54–5); the Trojans, terrified, stay behind their walls; Turnus is like a wolf hunting down lambs (9. 59–66). The mood is hard, military, relentlessly realistic, as the Italians determine to set fire to the Trojan ships.

Even now Virgil holds back from the battle description towards which the action is inevitably moving, and there follows the most astonishing scene in the poem – the supernatural transformation of the Trojan ships into nymphs. It is an episode highly appropriate for a mythological poem like Ovid's *Metamorphoses*, but it is most unexpected in the realistic battle scenes which Virgil has begun to set in train. Servius tells us that in his day it was adversely criticized (*notatur a criticis*), and many modern commentators have felt the same. It has an other-worldly serenity and beauty about it which contrasts sharply with the scenes of horror and bloodshed in the rest of the book. But it is Virgil's habit to put in juxtaposition moods of triumph and disaster, pathos and optimism, and here serenity and horror. The effect of the episode is to suggest that what we call the 'reality' of human life is somehow balanced, perhaps even negated, by things outside our ken. It is a vision of a pastoral imaginary world which defeats the hard facts of human existence.

Immediately upon this episode there follows the story of the bravery and death of the two Trojan friends, Nisus and Euryalus. Their story has often been among the most praised parts of the second half of the *Aeneid*: Heyne found it by far the most splendid episode of the whole *Aeneid*, displaying *summa suavitas, generosa indoles, praeclara laudis cupido,* and concluded that any student who did not react favourably towards it is unworthy of any further teaching (*Aeneid*, 9. 176). It is certainly unique, as we shall see, in

Virgil's subjective handling of the narrative, culminating with a personal invocation to the two friends:

> *Fortunati ambo! si quid mea carmina possunt,*
> *nulla dies umquam memori vos eximet aevo,*
> *dum domus Aeneae Capitoli immobile saxum*
> *accolet imperiumque pater Romanus habebit.*   (9. 446–9)

Happy pair – if my song can achieve anything, no day shall ever expunge you from the memory of time, as long as the house of Aeneas dwells on the everlasting rock of the Capitol, and the senators of Rome hold sway.

The episode recounts how Nisus and Euryalus volunteer to break out of the besieged camp in order to make contact with the absent Aeneas, and it is based closely on the account in *Iliad* 10 (the Doloneia) of the exploits of Odysseus and Diomedes, who go out on a night sally. But Virgil has made two significant changes: firstly, whereas Odysseus and Diomedes were highly experienced Greek warriors, Nisus and especially the young Euryalus were comparatively inexperienced and motivated by a sudden idealistic desire, a reckless heroic impulse to do something glorious. Secondly the Homeric pair are successful, as could well have been expected of those two mighty warriors; but the night sally of Virgil's pair ends in death for them both.

In this first episode of the war in Italy Virgil has, perhaps more intensely than anywhere else (apart from the brief description of the start of hostilities in Book 7), indicated his horror at the wastage of human lives. We have met Nisus and Euryalus only once before in the *Aeneid*, and that was in a much lighter context, when Nisus helped Euryalus to win the foot race (5. 315–38). Now Nisus is inspired by a sudden desire 'to do something big' (*aliquid magnum*), and Euryalus immediately insists on accompanying him. They go to the council of Trojan chieftains, and the aged Aletes and the youthful Ascanius vie in their praises of such valour and devotion, offering and giving prizes and trophies. What is particularly noticeable about Virgil's narrative style in this section is its extreme simplicity and direct subjective involvement with the characters. This subjectivity is indeed a general feature of Virgil's style, in contrast with Homer's, as Otis has well shown: but nowhere is it more evident than here. The characters are presented as naïve, too immature to appreciate the formidable dangers of their undertaking: the pathos and sympathy are thus greatly increased. Epic normally expects a somewhat distanced attitude: the events narrated are generally in some way sublimated, made universal; they may be none the less terrible for that, but they are seen as universal rather than personal. Here however Virgil has gone further than anywhere else in his personal identification with the characters.

The same tone continues right through the episode, which contains horrific deeds of blood by Nisus and Euryalus before concluding with the pathos of the death of both – first Euryalus, betrayed by the gleam of the helmet which he has unwisely taken as spoil from one of his victims, and then Nisus, rushing to his death when he sees Euryalus overwhelmed. The pathos is intense as Virgil describes the death of Euryalus with a flower simile based on Catullus (11. 21 ff.).

> *purpureus veluti cum flos succisus aratro*
> *languescit moriens, lassove papavera collo*
> *demisere caput pluvia cum forte gravantur.*   (9. 435–7)

Like a bright flower cut down by the plough when it fades and dies, or like poppies, their stalks bent and their heads hanging down when they are beaten by the rain.

The death of the two Trojans is followed by the invocation to them already quoted, the exhibition by the enemy of their severed heads on spears, and finally the wildly hysterical lamentation of the mother of Euryalus (9. 481–97). It is hard to imagine a more harrowing way of presenting death in battle: Virgil has spared no device for increasing the horror of this long opening action of the war.

The rest of the book is entirely different: it deals with the mighty deeds of Turnus (his *aristeia*) in a very Homeric manner. Of course it still has pathos and tragedy; but this time it is distanced, more traditional. Virgil signals the change in tone by means of reminiscences of Ennius (Catullus is left behind now).

At tuba terribilem sonitum procul aere canoro increpuit. (9. 503–4)

But the battle-trumpet with its fearsome call sounded in the distance its brazen notes.

Compare Ennius *at tuba terribili sonitu taratantara dixit* (*Annals*, 140). Soon afterwards in his new invocation Virgil uses the memorable phrase *ingentes oras evolvite belli* ('unroll the mighty frontiers of war', 9. 528), which is taken directly from Ennius (*Ann.* 174), and the phrase *opum vi* (9. 532), with its archaic monosyllabic ending, is from Ennius (*Ann.* 161).

These imitations of Ennius are clear signals of what is to be evident all through the remainder of the book — that Virgil is, for a time at all events, reverting from his personal agonized view of youthful death on the battlefield to the Homeric and Ennian methods of telling of the glory of prowess, the traditional literary way of presenting battles and great heroes. What is particularly noteworthy is that, before turning to the traditional style, he has begun with the long episode of Nisus and Euryalus in which glory is almost wholly overshadowed by the sense of futility and sorrow.

Turnus dominates the rest of the book as in the *Iliad* Diomedes and Hector and Idomeneus and Patroclus and Achilles (and others too) in their turn dominate parts of the poem. Virgil has many reminiscences of Homer, as Turnus' deeds correspond with those of Hector (especially in *Iliad* 12) when he drives all before him, and with those of Ajax (especially in *Iliad* 16.102 ff.) as he is finally forced to retreat. Many of the similes are from Homer, and Virgil presents the battle scenes in fast-moving narrative, sinewy and vigorous. Taunts are exchanged: particularly memorable is the long speech from Numanus (9. 598–620) in which he contrasts the simple virtues and hardy way of life of the Italians with the foppish effeminacy of the Trojans. The interchange between Pandarus and Turnus shows all the boastful confidence of the Homeric warrior. Pandarus closes the camp gates with Turnus inside and says to him:

> non haec dotalis regia Amatae,
> nec muris cohibet patriis media Ardea Turnum.
> castra inimica vides, nulla hinc exire potestas.　　(9. 737–9)

This is not the palace of Amata whose daughter you are wooing, nor does the safety of Ardea protect Turnus with the walls of the fatherland; what you see is the enemy's camp, and you cannot get out.

Turnus is no whit dismayed:

> olli subridens sedato pectore Turnus:
> 'incipe, si qua animo virtus, et consere dextram,
> hic etiam inventum Priamo narrabis Achillem'.　　(9. 740–2)

To him smiling and unperturbed, Turnus replied: 'Come on then, if you have any courage in your heart, and join battle with me; you will be able to tell Priam (in the underworld) that you encountered another Achilles here.'

Pandarus is killed and the Trojans fly from Turnus in all

directions, but typically he fails to take the opportunity of opening the camp gates for his own friends, overcome as he is by the desire to satisfy his personal prowess: had he opened the gates, Virgil tells us (9. 759), it would have ended the war on that very day.

The passage which follows may be taken as typical of the way in which Virgil, closely following the Homeric model, builds up a picture of slaughter on a massive scale.

> *principio Phalerim et succiso poplite Gygen*
> *excipit, hinc raptas fugientibus ingerit hastas*
> *in tergus, Iuno vires animumque ministrat.*
> *addit Halyn comitem et confixa Phegea parma,*
> *ignaros deinde in muris Martemque cientes*
> *Alcandrumque Haliumque Noemonaque Prytanimque.*
> *Lyncea tendentem contra sociosque vocantem*
> *vibranti gladio conixus ab aggere dexter*
> *occupat, huic uno deiectum comminus ictu*
> *cum galea longe iacuit caput. inde ferarum*
> *vastatorem Amycum, quo non felicior alter*
> *unguere tela manu ferrumque armare veneno,*
> *et Clytium Aeoliden et amicum Crethea Musis,*
> *Crethea Musarum comitem, cui carmina semper*
> *et citharae cordi numerosque intendere nervis,*
> *semper equos atque arma virum pugnasque canebat.* (9. 762–77)

First he caught Phalaris and Gyges, severing his hamstring; he snatched their spears and hurled them at the backs of his fleeing opponents; Juno gave him strength and courage. Next he sent Halys to join them and Phegeus, piercing his shield, and then Alcander, Halius, Noemon and Prytanis unaware that he was there as they fought from the walls. Then as Lynceus came to meet him, calling his friends to help, he attacked him with all his might from the rampart on the right with his flashing sword: Lynceus' head was severed with the one blow struck from so close and rolled away, still helmeted. Then he slew the hunter of wild beasts, Amycus, than whom no one was more successful at daubing his weapons and covering the tip with poison; then Clytius son of Aeolus and Cretheus, friend of the Muses, Cretheus the companion of the Muses, who always loved songs and the lyre and fitting tunes to the strings: he always used to sing of war-horses and the armour and battles of warriors.

We notice first the Homeric device of a line (767) consisting entirely of names of the dead. A little more detail is added in other cases by the description of the fatal wound (Gyges, Phegeus, Lynceus, in the last instance with gruesome detail). Sometimes a brief indication of the occupation of the victim is given (Amycus the hunter), and sometimes pathos and irony is added (Cretheus the war-poet, beloved of the Muses – notice the repetition (774–5) – who discovered to his cost the difference between literature and real life).

Having built up the magnitude of Turnus' prowess by the listing of so many of his victims Virgil is free to concentrate upon Turnus himself and his gradual retreat in the face of sheer numbers. For this he uses Homer's description of the retreat of Ajax (*Iliad* 16. 102 ff.), which itself was imitated by Ennius (*Ann.* 401–8) and is preserved for us by Macrobius (*Saturnalia* 6. 3).

The Homeric passage, as one can see even from translation, has about it the true note of massive grandeur:

> But Ajax no longer held firm, for he was beset with missiles. The will of Zeus was taming him, and the noble Trojans as they threw; and the shining helmet on his temples rang with a terrifying noise as it was struck and struck again on its well-wrought cheekpieces. And Ajax's left shoulder grew tired as he kept holding his flashing shield firmly, and they could not knock it back upon him, though they pressed him hard with their missiles. And he was beset with laboured breathing, and the sweat poured from his body everywhere in streams, and he could get no respite, and everywhere evil was heaped on evil.

The imitation by Ennius refers to a tribune in the Istrian War:

> Undique conveniunt velut imber tela tribuno:
> configunt parmam, tinnit hastilibus umbo
> aerato sonitu galeae, sed nec pote quisquam
> undique nitendo corpus discerpere ferro;
> semper abundantes hastas frangitque quatitque;
> totum sudor habet corpus multumque laborat,
> nec respirandi fit copia: praepete ferro
> Histri tela manu iacientes sollicitabant.

The weapons come from every side upon the tribune like a rain-storm. They pierce his shield; the boss rings with the sound of the spears, the helmets with the clash of bronze. But not one of them for all their efforts from every side can rend his body with steel. Constantly he breaks and shakes the showers of spears: sweat covers his whole body, he is in great distress and has no chance for rest; with the flying steel the Histrians pressed him hard as they hurled their weapons upon him.

This has a vigour and a robustness and well illustrates the power of Ennius' poetry which was so admired by many of the later Roman writers. Virgil has the vigour too, but with an extra elegance of rhythm and expression, particularly evident in the variety of the sense pauses and the frequent enjambement.

> *ergo nec clipeo iuvenis subsistere tantum*
> *nec dextra valet, iniectis sic undique telis*
> *obruitur. strepit adsiduo cava tempora circum*
> *tinnitu galea et saxis solida aera fatiscunt*
> *discussaeque iubae capiti, nec sufficit umbo*
> *ictibus; ingeminant hastis et Troes et ipse*
> *fulmineus Mnestheus. tum toto corpore sudor*
> *liquitur et piceum (nec respirare potestas)*
> *flumen agit, fessos quatit aeger anhelitus artus.* (9. 806–14)

And so the young warrior cannot hold out with shield or right hand, so overwhelmed is he by the weapons showered upon him from every side. His helmet round his curving temples rings with ceaseless clash, and the solid bronze is battered in by the stones; the crest is torn from his helmet, and the boss of his shield cannot withstand the blows. The Trojans, and Mnestheus especially like a thunderbolt, redouble their attacks with their spears. Then sweat flows all down his limbs, forming a black rivulet; he has no chance of respite, and as he gasps painfully for breath his whole weary body shudders.

Virgil ends the episode, rapidly and brilliantly, as Turnus leaps, as a later Roman of equally heroic qualities was destined to leap, fully armed into the Tiber:

> *tum demum praeceps saltu sese omnibus armis*
> *in fluvium dedit. ille suo cum gurgite flavo*
> *accepit venientem ac mollibus extulit undis*
> *et laetum sociis abluta caede remisit.* (9. 815–18)

Then at last he leaped headlong in full panoply into the river; the river welcomed him as he came in its yellow stream and held him up upon its gentle waters; it washed away the blood and returned him joyful to his companions.

These 300 lines of the *aristeia* of Turnus show Virgil as master of the robust and vigorous style, ready for a spell – but only for a spell – to shed all he had learned from Alexandria and to let the narrative speak for itself. Here for a change the traditional themes of epic are presented without subjective involvement of the kind often so characteristic of Virgil. The interest is literary and formal; the poet explores the potentiality of the epic form in description of prowess, death, valour, battle; the obligation upon the reader to identify himself with the characters and events is here at its minimum. We are invited to take our satisfaction from the excellence of the literary command of grandiose situations, related of course to human experience, but distanced and stylized.

Thus I think we could say that the two battle sections which make up Book 9 are of opposite kinds: with Nisus and Euryalus the poet aims to the greatest possible extent to join his characters inside the poem, and he invites us to do so too; with Pandarus and Bitias (9. 672 ff., 703 ff.) and Turnus he stands away and operates his skill as a narrator of events. This ability to fluctuate between the 'subjective' and 'objective' methods of narrative is one of the factors which contribute to what Macrobius called Virgil's *multiplex facundia*, his many-faceted command of literary expression.

Book 10

The battle scenes in Book 10 are postponed first by a council of the gods in Olympus, and then by a description of the return of Aeneas from Pallanteum and a short catalogue of his allies, followed by the supernatural appearance of the nymph Cymodocea, who tells Aeneas of the critical situation of his men in camp. At line 308 the fighting begins, and soon focuses on Pallas, the young son of Evander entrusted to Aeneas' care in this his first experience of battle. He performs great deeds, while on the other side young Lausus, son of Mezentius, distinguishes himself by killing Trojans and Etruscans. The war scenes so far have been in the style of the second half of Book 9, Homeric, rapid, staccato; but now (10. 435 ff.) Virgil signals a change towards his own subjective style of personal involvement. He links these two warriors as young men 'to whom Fortune had denied a return' from the battlefield; they were not permitted by Jupiter to meet each other – death awaited each of them at the hands of a mightier adversary (for Pallas, Turnus; for Lausus, Aeneas).

Immediately Virgil moves into the description of the confrontation of Turnus and Pallas. Turnus is proud, ruthless, justifiably self-confident against his inexperienced adversary; his arrogant behaviour in this crucial episode is analysed in the section discussing his character, and here I concentrate on Pallas. In many ways he is reminiscent of Euryalus, a young warrior under the spell of the heroic gesture, a character of truly tragic mould, sadly unequal to the task he so boldly undertakes. He is amazed at Turnus' mighty appearance, but he shows no sign of fear and speaks proud words in reply to Turnus' boasting challenge, proclaiming that he is ready for death or glory. Much of the pathos of the fate of the young warriors in Virgil (especially Euryalus, Pallas and Lausus) derives from their reckless, almost senseless, readiness to accept a challenge to which they are patently unequal. Virgil seems to admire the heroism of this attitude, and yet the intense pathos which their futile deaths generate must in some sense negate the glory of their self-sacrifice.

The outcome of the contest (which indeed we must have guessed already) is anticipated by the simile of Turnus like a lion attacking a bull (10. 454 ff.), and pointed specifically as Pallas tries to take the initiative *viribus imparibus* ('with unequal powers', 10. 459). Now Virgil's subjective involvement with Pallas is given full rein as the young man prays for victory to Hercules, patron god of his city Pallanteum. Hercules hears his prayer, but cannot grant it, and weeps that he cannot.

> *audit Alcides iuvenem magnumque sub imo*
> *corde premit gemitum lacrimasque effundit inanes*
>
> (10. 464–5)

Jupiter tries to console Hercules by telling him that the day of death must come to all, that he himself could not save his son Sarpedon at Troy, that Turnus too will soon reach the end of his allotted span. The task of valour, he says, is to extend one's fame by one's deeds. This is what Hector had said to himself as he faced Achilles: 'Let me not die without a struggle or ingloriously, but having done some great deed for future generations to hear of' (*Iliad* 22. 304–5). This is the Homeric way, the heroic way, and Virgil here presents it again – but the whole mood and tone of sorrow is so overwhelmingly strong that it seems to over-ride, or at least call in question, the heroic ideal.

Turnus proceeds to kill Pallas, to boast arrogantly over him, and to strip him of his sword-belt. At this point Virgil intervenes editorially in the narrative twice in rapid succession (10. 501 ff., 507 ff.), indicating once again a closeness of personal involvement which is at variance with the normally distanced tone of epic. First he reflects on man's inability to show moderation in victory, and how

Turnus will soon come to regret his deed, and immediately
afterwards he invokes Pallas (as he had invoked Nisus and Euryalus
in Book 9):

> o dolor atque decus magnum rediture parenti,
> haec te prima dies bello dedit, haec eadem aufert,
> cum tamen ingentes Rutulorum linquis acervos.
>
> (10. 507–9)

O hero destined to return to your father bringing great grief and
glory alike, this day first showed you to war, and takes you from
it too, yet you leave behind great piles of Rutulian dead.

It seems that Virgil as an epic poet admired (in a literary way, one
feels) the noble glory of youthful self-sacrifice, and yet as a sentient
human being felt the intensity of the tragedy and folly of it all. In
particular the last line quoted (10. 509) rings very untrue: this was
the traditional heroic compensation for death (that one had done
great deeds), but the diction of the line and the syntactical way in
which it is tacked on somehow reflect the poet's intense dislike of
it all.

The rest of the book describes the violent deeds in battle of Aeneas
on the one side and Mezentius on the other. The behaviour of
Aeneas here is unbelievably cruel: the death of Pallas drives him
berserk and he performs acts of savage fury which shock the reader.
They are matched by those of Mezentius, of whom however,
savagery is expected, to judge from the glimpses of his past career
which Virgil has given us. The tone throughout these scenes up to
the end of the book is hard and harsh, except for one brief passage
which has the typically Virgilian pathos, all the more notable and
moving because of the context of military might in which it is set.

This is the story of Lausus, young son of Mezentius, introduced
to us in the catalogue as a youth worthy of a less hateful father than
Mezentius. Aeneas has wounded Mezentius, and Lausus intervenes
to try to save him. Once again Virgil uses his favourite device of
invocation to concentrate our attention on Lausus:

> hic mortis durae casum tuaque optima facta,
> si qua fidem tanto est operi latura vetustas,
> non equidem nec te, iuvenis memorande, silebo –
>
> (10. 791–3)

And now I will not let pass in silence the story of your grim death
and your splendid deeds, if the passage of time will allow belief of

your great achievement, and I will tell your story, young man deserving of being remembered.

Lausus is at first successful in protecting his wounded father, and his companions rain showers of missiles upon Aeneas. But Aeneas resists the onslaught, and warns Lausus not to rush to his death against a greater warrior, adding the highly significant comment: *fallit te incautum pietas tua* ('your devotion to your father is leading you too far', 10. 812). This we may take as a signal that whatever slaughter Aeneas has committed since the death of Pallas he has no wish, unlike Turnus when he killed Pallas, to vent his anger against the father on the son. The use of the word *pietas* concedes and compliments Lausus' motive and strongly differentiates Aeneas' attitude here from that of Turnus, the Achilles figure whose sole concern on the battlefield is his own prowess and the death of his opponents.

But Lausus does not heed the warning – he madly persists in his attack (*exsultat demens*, 10. 813), and Aeneas' wish to spare him suddenly disappears under the provocation: 'fierce anger rises in him higher and higher' and he kills him with a single sword-thrust. Such is the ambivalence of Aeneas' character on the battlefield: generally he fights reluctantly and only when he must, but under provocation he kills savagely and is impervious to considerations which would normally affect him deeply. Lausus' acknowledged *pietas* to his father is over-ridden in Aeneas by a burst of furious anger, just as at the end of the poem Turnus' plea for mercy because of his old father Daunus is over-ridden by Aeneas' sudden fury at the sight of Pallas' belt.

Thus Virgil has aroused in us a sense of pathos and bewilderment very different from the heroic victories and defeats of the Homeric poems; he now proceeds to deepen this sense of sorrow by dwelling on it.

> *transiit et parmam mucro, levia arma minacis,*
> *et tunicam molli mater quam neverat auro*
> *implevitque sinum sanguis; tum vita per auras*
> *concessit maesta ad manes corpusque reliquit.*   (10. 817–20)

The blade cut through his shield, light armour for one so threatening, and through the tunic which his mother had woven of pliant gold, and the blood filled the folds. Then his spirit departed sorrowing through the breezes to the world below, and left his body.

This might seem to be the conclusion of the episode, but Virgil is ready to dwell on it longer yet.

> At vero ut vultum vidit morientis et ora,
> ora modis Anchisiades pallentia miris,
> ingemuit miserans graviter dextramque tetendit,
> et mentem patriae subiit pietatis imago.   (10. 821-4)

But when indeed the son of Anchises looked on the expression of the dying warrior, and his face – his face so wondrous pale – he groaned deeply in pity and held out his right hand, and there came into his thoughts a picture of his own love for his father.

Here the pathos and the remorse of Aeneas reach their peak. Line 821 begins with powerful alliteration of *v* and the next line uses the Alexandrian feature of repetition from the previous line (cf. 2. 405–6) and the memorable Lucretian phrase *modis . . . miris*. Across the middle of the line straddles the word *Anchisiades*, an epithet here most deliberately chosen for Aeneas, son of Anchises, to indicate that he would have done the same for his father as Lausus had for Mezentius. The point is hammered home in line 824 with the words *patriae . . . pietatis imago*, and by Aeneas' speech to the dying man in which he refers to himself as *pius Aeneas*, reinforcing the idea that he himself would equally have sacrificed his life for his father. The speech is a gentle one, with a promise of the returning of the body to his family, and after it Aeneas himself picks up the dead body and gives it back to Lausus' companions.

The episode forms a startling contrast to Aeneas' behaviour a short time earlier when, in his passionate anger over Pallas' death, he mowed down all who stood in his path, boasted cruelly over them when they fell before his onslaught, and took prisoners to sacrifice at Pallas' funeral. The same man in the same hour can show frenzied cruelty and gentle remorse.

The book ends with the death of Mezentius at the hands of Aeneas. This is told in detached and distanced style, with little personal involvement called for from the reader. Mezentius has been a hateful figure in the poem: in the acceptance of his death he shows a certain nobility, but no attempt is made to involve the reader's emotions. Only two short passages, the death of Pallas and the death of Lausus, have done that in this book of battles, but they are the ones which linger in the memory as most typically Virgilian.

Book 11

Virgil closed Book 10 in distanced heroic style with the death of Mezentius at the hands of Aeneas; now, before resuming the scenes of fighting, he begins Book 11 with a long passage of pathos, the most sustained pathos in all the battle narrative, as he describes the funeral of Pallas and the lamentation of Evander. There is a long build-up to the description of the actual ceremony, with universal lamentation and a speech by Aeneas filled with self-blame as he remembers the promises he gave to Evander, and pictures Pallas' father making prayers and sacrifices to the gods for the safe return of his son (11. 34–58).

The description of the funeral itself begins with an accumulation of words denoting sorrow: *deflevit, miserabile, supremum honorem, patris lacrimis, solacia luctus exigua ingentis, misero*. This is reinforced by the assonance of gentle sounds, and very markedly (11. 66–8) by three consecutive lines using a favourite rhythm of Catullus – a word of three long syllables to begin the second half of the line – which Virgil generally uses far more sparingly. The link with Catullan pathos is then reinforced by a flower simile (cf. Catullus, 62. 43 ff., 11. 22 ff.) very similar in its impact to the one which Virgil has used at the death of Euryalus (*Aen.* 9. 435 ff.):

> *qualem virgineo demessum pollice florem*
> *seu mollis violae seu languentis hyacinthi,*
> *cui neque fulgor adhuc nec dum sua forma recessit,*
> *non iam mater alit tellus virisque ministrat.*　　　　(11. 68–71)

Like a flower picked by a girl's hand, a tender violet or a drooping hyacinth; its brightness and beauty have not yet left it, but mother earth no longer nourishes it and gives it strength.

Immediately after the simile Virgil describes how Aeneas covered the body with a cloak which Dido had made for him. The poignant reference to Dido at this stage links the tragedy of her death with that of Pallas, and is intensified by the phrases used – it was a cloak which 'Dido had once made for him with her own hands, so happy to be doing it'. Next in the procession of mourners comes Acoetes, the now aged one-time squire of Evander, who had accompanied Pallas on the expedition, and behind him the horse Aethon, its trappings removed, 'weeping and bedewing its face with big tear-drops'. This links Pallas with Homer's Patroclus (to whom in many respects he corresponds in the plot of the *Aeneid*), whose horses weep at his death and are consoled by Zeus (*Iliad* 17. 426 ff.). This image fits more naturally into Homer's world than into Virgil's, but the accumulation of so many aspects of pathos already in this passage enables Virgil to add this final touch.

When the procession has been completed Aeneas speaks the last words:

> *nos alias hinc ad lacrimas eadem horrida belli*
> *fata vocant: salve aeternum mihi, maxime Palla,*
> *aeternumque vale.*(11. 96–8)

The same dread fates of war call us from here to further sorrows – for ever, mighty Pallas, I bid you hail and for ever farewell.

These brief words summarize the horror of warfare and its tragedies which Aeneas feels, and recall once more the pathos of the poetry of Catullus. His well-known poem (101) written at the tomb of his brother ends with the phrase *atque in perpetuum frater ave atque vale*. It is true that *ave* (or *salve*) *atque vale* was a formulaic phrase at funerals, but the use of it by Catullus in one of the most famous poems of antiquity undoubtedly lies behind Virgil's use of it here.

The note of the futility and horror of warfare continues unabated. Envoys come from the Latins asking for a truce to bury the dead: Aeneas immediately grants it, wishing that there could be a truce for the living too. The body of Pallas is returned to Evander, whose long speech of broken-hearted lamentation and self-blame (11. 152–81) contains the prayer (11. 177 ff.) that Aeneas should exact retribution from Turnus, thus putting Aeneas under an obligation which he fulfils at the end of the poem, to the horror and dismay of many modern readers.

Next follows a long account of funeral ceremonies for the dead Trojans and Etruscans (11. 182–202), and then a description of the similar activities on the Latin side. Some are buried, some are taken back to their homes, and

> *cetera confusaeque ingentem caedis acervum*
> *nec numero nec honore cremant.*   (11. 207–8)

The rest, a huge pile of mingled carnage, they burn uncounted and unsung.

Nec numero nec honore cremant: this simple and horrifying phrase sums up with the utmost clarity Virgil's essential feelings about warfare. However much he tries, and indeed succeeds, when it is appropriate, to present the heroic ideal of prowess, death and glory on the battlefield, it is the attitude to warfare presented here that is the dominant and convincing message of the *Aeneid*. A few lines later on (11. 215–7), as he continues his account of the lamentations of the Latins, he focuses on the bereaved families who 'curse the ghastly war and Turnus' marriage plans' (*dirum exsecrantur bellum Turnique hymenaeos*, 11, 217).

This opening of Book 11 has been a long and sustained reflection on the horrors of war, expressed most intensely and vividly, and undoubtedly it represents Virgil's innermost sentiments. But it is never reconciled with the glory of heroic sacrifice, the grandeur of Rome achieved by military might and warfare, which is also a dominant characteristic of the *Aeneid*. These two opposites are set in juxtaposition throughout the poem, and sometimes the one prevails, and sometimes the other. It is the most basic of all the problems which the *Aeneid* explores.

Now at last the mood begins to change, first by a transitional passage in which the gloomy news is brought to the Latins by Venulus that Diomede will not come to their help. Following Venulus' speech King Latinus formally urges that peace be made with the Trojans, and this leads to the altercation between Drances, who supports peace proposals, and Turnus, who does not. This is one of the finest pieces of writing in the *Aeneid*, and it is of a totally different kind from the rest of the book. Its mood is entirely rhetorical, and the enjoyment of it arises from the literary appreciation of the oratorical exchanges, the scoring of points, the use of irony and hyperbole. It is a clash of personalities in which both speakers are well able to look after themselves, and Virgil lets them get on with it, presenting us with a verbal firework display of the utmost brilliance.

When we return to the battle narrative, as the Trojans move to the attack, the whole focus of the rest of the book is on Camilla, the warrior-princess who is an ally of Turnus. Her deeds of prowess, her *aristeia*, are parallel to those of Turnus in Book 9; she shows the same exultation in battle, the same self-confidence, the same relentless ferocity: her attack on Ligus is like a falcon pursuing a dove and tearing it to pieces (11. 721–4). Only at the beginning of her story (11. 532 ff., when the goddess Diana tells of Camilla's pastoral upbringing and laments her destined death), and at the end (11. 799 ff., when she is shot by Arruns) is there a variation from the Homeric method of the description of deeds of bravery and glory on the battlefield. Book 11 has presented a parallel with Book 9 in its mood-structure: the first part powerfully coloured by Virgilian empathy and pathos, the second part traditional in its heroic presentation of individual military prowess.

Book 12

The last book is dominated by the confrontation on the battlefield
of Turnus and Aeneas in spite of all attempts to make peace between
the two sides. With typical Virgilian irony and ambivalence, our
disquiet at the ferocious battle-lust of Turnus is tempered by
sympathy for his dedication to his lost cause; and the dislike of
violence which is characteristic of Aeneas is twice totally over-
ridden by passionate fury. In this last book, as in all the battlefield
scenes, there is a mixture of admiration for heroic prowess and
sorrow for the futility and pathos of untimely death. The various
aspects of the final book of the *Aeneid* will be considered in detail
in the sections analysing the characters of Aeneas and Turnus; but
before we come to the final confrontation of the protagonists, we
may end this survey of the war scenes in the *Aeneid* with two last
examples of Virgilian pathos. Among Turnus' many victims is one
Menoetes, a fisherman:

> *et iuvenem exosum nequiquam bella Menoeten,*
> *Arcada, piscosae cui circum flumina Lernae*
> *ars fuerat pauperque domus nec nota potentum*
> *munera, conductaque pater tellure serebat.* (12. 517-20)

And Turnus killed Menoetes, a young man who hated warfare –
all in vain – an Arcadian whose skill had been in the rivers of
Lerna, good fishing places; his family was poor and knew nothing
of patronage from the rich; his father's crops were sown in rented
land.

A little later on Turnus kills the Trojan Aeolus:

> *te quoque Laurentes viderunt, Aeole, campi*
> *oppetere et late terram consternere tergo.*
> *occidis, Argivae quem non potuere phalanges*
> *sternere nec Priami regnorum eversor Achilles;*
> *hic tibi mortis erant metae, domus alta sub Ida,*
> *Lyrnesi domus alta, solo Laurente sepulcrum.*
>
> (12. 542-7)

You too, Aeolus, the Laurentian plains saw falling in death, your
body sprawling on the ground; yes, now you lie dead, though the
Argive hosts could not lay you low, not even Achilles, who
brought down Priam's kingdom. Here was the final end of life for

you; you had a lofty mansion beneath Mount Ida, yes, at Lyrnesus a lofty mansion. But your tomb is in Laurentian soil.

CHAPTER 6

The Characters of the Aeneid

(i) AENEAS

The character portrayal of Aeneas was the most difficult of all the aspects of the poem which Virgil undertook, and is the aspect which has most often been severely criticized. Charles James Fox regarded Aeneas, in a famous phrase, as 'always either insipid or odious' (Glover, *Virgil*, p. 208); T. E. Page says 'Virgil is unhappy in his hero; compared with Achilles Aeneas is a shadow of a man' (*Aeneid*, p. xvii); and Wight Duff comments that Virgil 'does not make him uniformly interesting (*A Literary History of Rome*, p. 338). It is true that in recent times sympathetic analyses of Aeneas have been presented (especially in Brooks Otis's important book), but there is still very strong opposition (e.g. Putnam and Boyle).

Over the centuries the objections to Aeneas' character have fallen into two main categories: (i) that he is unreal, puppet-like, a symbol rather than a real person; (ii) that his behaviour is on occasions unacceptable and unforgivable. Of these propositions the first is almost wholly untrue, and arises from the mistaken view that Virgil was trying to create a hero like Achilles or Odysseus and failed to do so. The second is largely true, but so far from diminishing interest in Aeneas' character it makes him a complex and convincing human person.

Virgil's problem was how to create an epic hero in an age that was very different from Homer's. Aeneas had to step out of the heroic world in order to found a proto-Roman world. What were to be the qualities of this new type of hero? In order to try to define them Virgil used characters in the Homeric poems as points of comparison, and nowhere is this clearer than at the beginning of the poem.

The structure and episodes of *Aeneid* 1 show a remarkable similarity to those of *Odyssey* 5–8. In both of them the hero of the poem is seen in dire distress because of a storm aroused by a hostile deity (Juno, Poseidon), and Aeneas' first words echo those of Odysseus (*Od.* 5. 306 ff.): 'Three times and four times blessed those Greeks who died in broad Troy bringing help to the sons of Atreus. Would that I had died then . . .'. Aeneas' words are

> o terque quaterque beati
> quis ante ora patrum Troiae sub moenibus altis
> contigit oppetere! o Danaum fortissime gentis
> Tydide! mene Iliacis occumbere campis
> non potuisse, tuaque animam hanc effundere dextra!
>
> (1. 94–8)

O three times and four times blessed those whose lot it was to fall before the eyes of their fathers beneath the lofty walls of Troy. Oh Diomede, bravest of the race of Greeks – could I not have fallen on the plains of Troy and breathed forth my life under your right hand.

This patent imitation in an identical setting immediately sets up in the reader's mind a powerful recollection of Homer's Odysseus, and prepares him for a comparison of the two heroes. This is very strongly encouraged by similarities throughout the rest of *Aeneid* 1; these have been summarized in Chapter 3 (i), and may be briefly repeated here. Both heroes reach land after the storm in dire distress; both are met by a goddess in disguise and escorted, concealed in a cloud, to a great city; both are welcomed hospitably by the ruler of the land, and at a splendid banquet are entertained by a minstrel; both are asked to tell the story of their past voyaging, and they do so, Odysseus in *Od.* 9–12 and Aeneas in *Aen.* 2–3.

This very close parallelism of structure has compelled us to think of Aeneas as a second Odysseus making his voyage westwards after the fall of Troy. But intertwined with all the correspondences of situation Virgil has two passages which have no parallel in Homer, both of them concerned with the gods. The first is Jupiter's majestic prophecy to Venus of the future of Rome; this has indeed a contextual relationship with Athena's request to Zeus (*Od.* 5.5) that he should help Odysseus, but Jupiter's speech is concerned not with the immediate needs of the situation but with the long process of history of which Aeneas is the servant. The second is the intervention of Venus to cause Dido to fall in love with Aeneas, with the result that (without intending it) Venus interposes a psychological and personal barrier, in addition to the external dangers of voyage and battle, between Aeneas and his mission.

We can now begin to realize how basically the voyage of Aeneas differs from that of Odysseus for all its external similarities. Odysseus' aim was to return home to resume in Ithaca the life he was leading before he sailed away, to return to Penelope and Telemachus and Laertes and the rest, and pick up where he left off. The remainder of his life would be personal, of no significance outside Ithaca. To achieve his return he had to show the most amazing qualities of endurance and resource. Not one of his companions could show these – all the other ships in his company were lost, and all the other members of the crew of his ship. His personal qualities were such that he could survive when no one else could. He stands out as perhaps the most vivid individual in Classical literature.

But Aeneas' voyage was not undertaken to return home; it was undertaken to leave his home, set on fire by the Greeks, when he would much sooner have stayed and died fighting. It was in pursuance of a divine mission which he saw only dimly, in order to found a new city he knew not where, and a new way of life different from the heroic and Trojan world he had left, and prefiguring and anticipating the Roman way of life with the special qualities on which the Romans prided themselves. To do this he had to sacrifice much of himself and his personal wishes; in particular he would have wished to stay with Dido had he been free to do so (and in fact did stay disastrously long enough to cause Dido to kill herself in despair when he left). This meant that he could not be a brilliant and breath-catching hero like Odysseus, but had to try to reject the heroic way of life for a more co-operative and self-denying attitude. He had to be the group hero, the social man, bringing his companions safely to their new city, following the ever-present dictates of the gods who governed his divine mission, showing in a word that quality of *pietas* (responsibility to others in preference to personal desires) which is his characteristic throughout the poem (though as we shall see he does not always live up to it).

If we now look back through the first book to evaluate Aeneas' attitude to this mission which so differentiates him from Odysseus, how do we find him tackling it? With unflinching courage, resolution, joyful acceptance of this tremendous role? No, we do not. He is frail, uncertain, even resentful. We see that he is no superman inspired by total conviction in the rightness of his cause and ready to accept all setbacks and disasters in a determined effort to fulfil what is required of him. Virgil is presenting to us a new kind of hero: a man of limited strength, limited resolution, who nevertheless seeing dimly what is required of him does not give up. He does not draw from his mission such inner strength that we know he will prevail: he can only grope step by step towards it. He has human weaknesses, human frailties and human failings, but against all the odds he keeps on going in order to fulfil what he feels is his mission. Whatever else he is or is not, he is a man of flesh and blood.

We have already seen how on his first appearance in the poem, during the storm instigated by Juno, he showed himself to be the opposite of a heroic commander of his fleet – he groaned and wished he had died at Troy. Mackail has called him a pathetic figure, and Glover refers to him as the most solitary figure in literature. A man with a calling to follow, who draws strength from his deep convictions and thus overcomes his human frailties, is not pathetic or lonely: it is when his task is so heavy and he does not see clearly why it is his to undertake that he must win our sympathy as he fights his inner battles.

The Trojans survive the storm, and their ships are driven to the coast of Africa. Aeneas addresses his men, urging them to take heart – they have survived worse perils than this:

> *O socii (neque enim ignari sumus ante malorum),*
> *o passi graviora, dabit deus his quoque finem.*
>
> (1. 198–9)

Friends, we have experienced disaster before now – you have endured worse than this; God will bring an end to this too.

It is a splendid speech – but at the end of it Virgil shows us Aeneas' inner feelings:

> *Talia voce refert, curisque ingentibus aeger*
> *spem vultu simulat, premit altum corde dolorem.*
>
> (1. 208–9)

So he spoke, and sick at heart with his fearful anxieties he made hope appear in his expression while keeping his anguish hidden deep in his heart.

He conceals his real feelings: this is also the key to his apparently heartless desertion of Dido.

At daybreak Aeneas goes forth with Achates to find out where they are. His mother Venus, in mortal form, meets them, and Aeneas suspecting her divinity prays to her to lighten their sufferings, for they are completely lost; his words have in them the sadness of despair and there is a catch in his voice as he speaks (portrayed by the hypermetric syllable):

> *et quo sub caelo tandem, quibus orbis in oris*

iactemur doceas; ignari hominumque locorumque
erramus, vento huc vastis et fluctibus acti.

(1. 331–3)

And tell us please under what sky and in what part of the world we
are storm-tossed: we are wanderers, knowing nothing of the people or
places, driven here by the winds and mighty waves.

Venus tells him that he has come to the land of Carthage, and
mockingly asks who he is: he replies that if he were to tell the tale of their
sufferings it would last till nightfall. He proceeds with the words *sum
pius Aeneas*, to which many critics have taken strong exception.
Now Virgil has already used the epithet *pius* of Aeneas twice; once
when he lamented the loss of Orontes' ship (1. 220), and once when
he lay awake wondering what to do to alleviate his comrades' plight
(1. 305); and the noun *pietas* in connection with Aeneas twice, once
in the invocation when the poet asks why a man *insignis pietate*
should suffer as Aeneas has done (1. 10), and once when Venus in
heaven indignantly asks: *hic pietatis honos?* ('Is this the reward for
doing one's duty?', 1. 253). Virgil has very strongly impressed on the
reader that Aeneas is trying to carry out his mission and do what he
is required by the heavenly powers to do. In the present passage the
adjective is used with intentional force: 'I am Aeneas', he cries, 'and
I am trying to carry out my mission', and he implies what Virgil has
already twice made explicit – why should such suffering come
upon him and his companions when they are doing all they can to
carry out the divine will? He ends his speech thus:

ipse ignotus, egens, Libyae deserta peragro,
Europa atque Asia pulsus.   (1. 384–5)

I myself, unknown, without resources, am wandering through the
deserts of Libya, driven out from Europe and Asia.

Venus breaks in on his complaints – *nec plura querentem passa
Venus.* A good Stoic does not complain of the will of heaven: a
puppet, an abstraction of righteousness, would not complain.
Aeneas is human enough, weak enough if you like, to cry out in
protest to the gods. And when Venus leaves him, and he recognizes
her as she goes, he angrily reproaches her for mocking him:

quid natum totiens, crudelis tu quoque, falsis
ludis imaginibus?   (1. 407–8)

Why do you so often mock your son with false phantoms: to think that you too are cruel to me!

There is a strong protest against his treatment at the hand of destiny in *crudelis tu quoque*. It is sometimes suggested of Aeneas that he is a prototype of the Christian hero, having true humility towards the gods, and never being defiant. This is an overstatement: he differs from the Christian hero in the degree of his self-abandonment to his mission, and therefore in the degree of strength and resolution which he can bring to it.

X

The flashback of Aeneas' narrative in Books 2 and 3 shows the stages by which he has managed to get this far on a mission which he did not ask for (cf. 11. 112) and only very slowly comes to accept and then to understand. The first indication of any such thing comes to him on Troy's last night, when the ghost of Hector appears to him telling him to escape, for Troy cannot be saved. Hector's speech ends:

> *sacra suosque tibi commendat Troia penates;*
> *hos cape fatorum comites, his moenia quaere*
> *magna, pererrato statues quae denique ponto.*
>
> (2. 293–5)

Troy commends to you its sacred emblems and its native gods; take these as companions of your destiny, and for them seek out a city, a mighty city which you will at last establish after long voyaging over the sea.

How does Aeneas react to this first indication of a new and glorious destiny? He disregards it altogether: like a true Homeric warrior he is agog to make the heroic gesture and when all is lost to die fighting along with his fellow warriors. The sight and sounds of fighting come to him and he seeks the glory of death in battle.

> *arma amens capio; nec sat rationis in armis,*
> *sed glomerare manum bello et concurrere in arcem*
> *cum sociis ardent animi; furor iraque mentem*
> *praecipitat, pulchrumque mori succurrit in armis.*
>
> (2. 314–17)

Madly I seize my weapons: there was no reason in it, but my heart was on fire to collect a band for battle and rush to the citadel with my comrades. Frenzy and fury ruled my intentions, and I thought, 'How glorious to die fighting':

He collects a band of followers and in a few words spoken to them reiterates his determination to die: the gods have deserted Troy, the city is on fire; therefore

> *moriamur et in media arma ruamus.*
> *una salus victis nullam sperare salutem.*
>
> (2. 353–4)

Let us die, charging into the midst of the fighting. The one hope for the conquered is to have no hope.

As Aeneas' band rush into the hopeless battle, they are compared with wolves, a simile of savagery used again in the fighting scenes in the second half of the *Aeneid*, but never again of Aeneas. Furious fighting takes place, and Aeneas swears by the ashes of Troy and the death of his comrades that he did not try to avoid danger but constantly courted death. What of Hector's message? Aeneas has ignored it in the face of his overwhelming desire to show himself a warrior in the true Homeric style, a brave and valiant leader who when all is lost will discharge his responsibilities by accepting a glorious death. It is true that Virgil may have been led to this Homeric presentation of his hero by the versions of the legend which regarded Aeneas' departure as cowardly, and he wished to avoid this aspect; but what is much more important is that Aeneas, as he begins his quest to found Rome, is depicted as an absolutely typical Homeric hero, and that in the course of the quest he slowly and uncertainly begins to learn that his new civilization will require new ideals of behaviour.

The ideal that so often hovers in the background of the poem is the need to control impetuous and wild, irrational behaviour such as instinctive and emotional reactions may lead to. *O cohibete iras* ('control your fury'), says Aeneas to his men when the truce is broken (12. 314); this is what Homer's Achilles had failed to do, with disastrous consequences, and it is what Virgil's Aeneas, for all his efforts, also on occasions fails to do. Here in Book 2 he does not try to do so. On his way back home to protect his family he comes across Helen, the ostensible cause of it all. Rage seizes him (*exarsere ignes animo*, 2. 575), and he is about to kill her, rushing at her in mad anger (*furiata mente*, 2. 588), when Venus restrains him, telling him that the doom of Troy is sealed, and that he must escape. The genuineness of this passage (2. 567–88) has been much disputed: it is not in the major MSS, but is preserved for us by Servius as one of the passages deleted by the *Aeneid*'s posthumous editors. It certainly has some imperfections, and the most likely conclusion seems to be that Virgil wrote it, but left some signs in his manuscript indicating his dissatisfaction with it.

The divine intention for Aeneas to escape is indicated again when Anchises refuses to leave, but is convinced by an omen of flames encircling Iulus' head, immediately confirmed by the appearance of a shooting star. As the family seek to escape, Aeneas' wife Creusa is lost. When he suddenly realizes she is not there, all thoughts of his own obligation to escape are forgotten: he calls down curses upon gods and men (2. 745) and wildly rushes through the midst of the slaughter seeking to find her, avoiding no dangers (2. 751). He is still, under the pressure of intense personal grief, completely unmindful of what Hector had told him of his divine mission. The ghost of Creusa now appears to him, tells him that these things do not happen without the divine will, and prophesies that after long wandering he will come to a western land where the river Tiber flows through rich countryside: there he will find prosperity and a kingdom and a princess to be his queen. Creusa disappears and finally Aeneas leaves Troy and with a band of followers makes for the mountains.

Thus in this tragic book we have seen Aeneas frustrated in his innate desire to make the heroic gesture and fight to the last, a frustration which is echoed when (6. 494 ff.) he meets the ghost of his comrade Deiphobus, who died on Troy's last day; Aeneas speaks to the ghost in tones of guilt and remorse because he did not fight side by side with him. He has as yet no feelings of justification for quitting Troy, and his reluctance to do so is still dominant in his thoughts when he tells Dido that had he been permitted to live his life the way he wished (*meis auspiciis et sponte mea*) he would have stayed in Troy and rebuilt it (4. 340 ff.).

The dominant note of Aeneas' account of his wanderings in Book 3 is by no means one of steady and resolute progression towards a destined goal, but rather of the toil and pain of ever striving onwards. His experiences at his first landfall in Thrace are horrific, with the gruesome tale of Polydorus, and his attitude is summed up by his words as he leaves Helenus: in tears he envies those whose destiny is already achieved in contrast with his own lot, which is to wander from place to place (3. 492–4). This is reminiscent of his feelings in Book 1 when (much later) he envies Dido:

> *o fortunati quorum iam moenia surgunt!*   (1. 437)

Lucky indeed are those whose city is already being built.

This lack of resolution and verve, this inability to draw inner

strength from the grandeur of his destiny, is not greatly dispelled by
the various divine prophecies which he receives indicating the glory
of the ultimate achievement; for example Apollo's oracle tells him
that his descendants will rule over all the world (3. 97–8); the vision
of the *penates* says that his descendants will be raised up to the
heavens, and his city will have empire over the world (3. 158–9);
even the Harpy Celaeno tells him he will eventually reach Italy and
found his city (3. 254–7); and the prophet Helenus gives him many
instructions and ends by urging him to press onwards and by his
deeds raise mighty Troy to the heavens (3. 462). In spite of this
progressive revelation of his goal and the greatness of his destiny
Aeneas shows few signs of being heartened or feeling pride in what
he is doing: it is all almost too much for him. This is underlined by
the fact that nearly all the decisions in moments of crisis are taken
by his father Anchises (see the following section on Anchises); and
the death of his father at Drepanum, right at the end of Aeneas'
story to Dido, might well seem to have put the task beyond him.

When the story of Dido's love for Aeneas resumes in Book 4 we
are now in a much better position to understand why her kindness
to him finds a ready response. Although he must know in his heart
that he will have to leave her, the battering which he has undergone
at the hands of fate makes him grasp at the fleeting chance of
happiness. The two have much in common: Dido as a leader of her
people has been through exile and wanderings similar to those of
Aeneas, and has surmounted them and established her city. She has
greeted Aeneas as a kindred spirit, and he responds: he helps in the
building of Carthage (4. 260 ff.), and wears the robe and the sword
which she has given him; he lingers in Carthage when he should be
continuing on the mission which has already caused him such toil
and unhappiness.

This is the point at which the king of the gods intervenes, by
sending his messenger Mercury with severe and imperious
instructions to the effect that Aeneas must resume his mission.
Aeneas realizes with a terrible shock what he should have realized
long before, and he instantly decides that he must obey. There is no
hesitation, no thought any more of his personal happiness with
Dido:

> At vero Aeneas aspectu obmutuit amens,
> arrectaeque horrore comae et vox faucibus haesit.
> ardet abire fuga dulcesque relinquere terras,
> attonitus tanto monitu imperioque deorum.

> (4. 279–82)

But Aeneas was utterly struck dumb and bemused by the apparition. His hair stood on end in horror, and his voice stuck in his throat. He was wildly anxious to get away, and leave the land he loved, thunder-struck by such a warning and such a command from the gods.

His first thought, naturally, is how to tell Dido – meanwhile he gives instructions to his men to prepare for departure. They are all delighted to leave (4. 294–5); among his rejoicing companions Aeneas has little cause for joy.

The decision to leave Dido represents a very sudden shift in Aeneas' attitude towards his mission. Until now he has often been hesitant, often uncertain; now the divine admonition instantly has its effect. Virgil presents this sudden change in the mythological terms of epic: a speech of instruction by Jupiter to Mercury, the flight of Mercury – made very visual – down to Carthage, the speech of Mercury and his visually described departure. If we remove the imagery and rationalize the episode, we may say that all of a sudden Aeneas hears inwardly the voice of God (like Paul on the road to Damascus), or that his guilty conscience suddenly prevails over his selfish wishes. What is perhaps most remarkable is the sudden and total decision that he will obey; he has no uncertainties on that, his uncertainties centre (as well they might) on how he can best tell Dido. He thinks of her as *optima* (4. 291), and he knows that she does not believe that such love as theirs can be shattered (4. 292).

During their confrontation Virgil focuses all the sympathy on Dido, and Aeneas' reply to her pleas is cold and heartless in the extreme. He presents his reasons logically, and clearly is wholly convinced that he must not diverge from Jupiter's commands. Virgil makes it clear both before Aeneas speaks, and also at the end of their last meeting, that for all his refusal to show it Aeneas is deeply unhappy to be forced to leave his lover:

> *Dixerat. ille Iovis monitis immota tenebat*
> *lumina et obnixus curam sub corde premebat.*
>
> (4. 331–2)

She had finished speaking; he, because of the commands of Jupiter kept his eyes unmoving, and with a struggle hid his love in his heart:

> *At pius Aeneas, quamquam lenire dolentem*
> *solando cupit et dictis avertere curas,*
> *multa gemens magnoque animum labefactus amore*
> *iussa tamen divum exsequitur classemque revisit.*
>
> (4. 393–6)

But Aeneas, following his destiny, in spite of his longing to soothe her sorrow with words of comfort and to say something to take away her grief, with many a groan, shattered to the heart by his deep love, nevertheless followed out the orders of the gods, and went back to his fleet.

In this second passage the narrative reinforces the words with which Aeneas ended his reply to Dido: *Italiam non sponte sequor* ('It is not at my own wish that I am making for Italy', 4. 361). The use of the epithet *pius* strongly reinforces the reason why Aeneas, apparently so heartlessly, decides to leave Dido: in the mental conflict between his own personal wishes and his sense of duty towards his mission, duty prevails in spite of all. We are only allowed glimpses of what it has cost him, but these glimpses are specific enough: Virgil in his narrative has revealed the love and affection which Aeneas did not dare to show to Dido at this decisive moment.

Twice again in the next fifty lines Virgil shows the conflict in Aeneas. He listens to no pleas from Anna, for 'fate prevents it, and heaven makes his ears deaf to entreaty, though as a mortal he would have listened': (*fata obstant, placidasque viri deus obstruit aures*, 4. 440). The juxtaposition of *viri deus* portrays with the utmost clarity the conflict between his human wishes and the divine purpose. A little later he is likened in a simile to an oak tree buffeted by the winds, which yet holds firm, and the simile ends:

> haud secus adsiduis hinc atque hinc vocibus heros
> tunditur, et magno persentit pectore curas;
> mens immota manet, lacrimae volvuntar inanes.
>
> (4. 447–9)

Even so the hero was buffeted on all sides by endless appeals, and he felt all the time his deep emotion in his mighty heart. But his purpose remained unshaken; the tears fall in vain.

It has been much debated whether the tears are those of Aeneas (as well as of Anna and Dido herself); it seems clear from the context of the previous line that they are indeed Aeneas' tears too. The fulfilment of Rome's mission involves suffering not only from Rome's opponents but from Rome's champions.

Two things are evident from Virgil's portrait of Aeneas in Book 4: the first is the sacrifice of personal emotional desires which he is forced to make, and the second is the resolution with which he makes it. The message from Jupiter has a total effect upon him: it is a divine revelation whose power is such that it completely overwhelms other considerations. The frailty and uncertainty of Aeneas in the first three books is banished in this one blinding conversion. It does not mean that it is easy for him to reject all other considerations, but it does mean that he knows for certain that he must. So true is this that later we are told *iam certus eundi carpebat somnos rebus iam rite paratis* ('now resolute on departure, with everything prepared, he was enjoying sleep', 4. 554–5). Many readers find this unacceptably heartless (it contrasts very strongly with the preceding passage, 4. 522–32, in which the sleeplessness of the wretched Dido is described). But it indicates that in spite of everything the resolution of Aeneas at this stage is no longer in question: he has fought his inner battle, and decided that whatever it involves he must and will carry out the message he has received from Jupiter. Whether this resolution can last is another question.

In the fifth book, at the anniversary games at his father's tomb, Aeneas seems still to be in a mood of confidence in his decisions and actions. For a while we see him with the weight off his shoulders, organizing the athletic events, awarding the prizes, apparently ready for the final stages of his destined journey. But the traumas of what he has been through have left their mark. At the news that the women have set the ships on fire he is cast into despair, and he appeals on the grounds of his own *pietas* to the *pietas* of the gods: let them save him now or hurl down to death what little remains of Troy. Jupiter quells the fire, saving all but four of the ships, but Aeneas is deeply downcast by this blow, and for the first and only time in the poem he deliberately and consciously considers whether to abandon his mission.

> *At pater Aeneas casu concussus acerbo*
> *nunc huc ingentes, nunc illuc pectore curas*
> *mutabat versans, Siculisne resideret arvis*
> *oblitus fatorum, Italasne capesseret oras.*

(5. 700–3)

But father Aeneas, shattered by this bitter blow, turned his heavy anxieties over in his heart, shifting his thoughts one way, and then the other: should he settle in the fields of Sicily and forget the fates, or should he press onwards to the shores of Italy?

This passage presents starkly the two vital aspects of Aeneas and his mission which Virgil has illustrated throughout the poem thus far: first that the mission imposes burdens and strains which seem again and again almost too much for Aeneas to bear; and secondly that it is only through the resolution and will of Aeneas that destiny can be fulfilled. At this moment of sudden and unexpected disaster Aeneas consciously formulates and considers the option of abandoning his mission and (unlike his immediate decision about leaving Dido) this time he finds himself unable to make a decision. Nautes attempts to comfort him with Stoic platitudes and urges him to continue, but by nightfall he is still profoundly depressed and undecided.

Again Jupiter intervenes with a direct message, this time conveyed (most significantly) by the ghost of Aeneas' father Anchises, who did so much to bring him through the initial long years of voyaging. Anchises tells Aeneas that he has been sent by Jupiter, and gives him instructions to leave some of his party behind but to take the bravest onwards to Italy: before that he must visit the underworld so that Anchises can give him further instructions. Now Aeneas hesitates no more.

Virgil has here given us a character study of the hero of the poem facing, without mortal aid, the toils and dilemmas into which his mission has led him. Here, as with Dido, it is from supernatural sources that he draws strength to make his decision. He is not strong enough without the gods; but because he has devoted his life to the gods he gets spiritual help at the moment that he needs it most. The Homeric heroes, too, get help from the gods, but they have more certainty and confidence about themselves than Aeneas has; they are in a way more self-sufficient, less dependent on their spiritual resources. We see indeed in Aeneas a new kind of epic hero, one closer to our own understanding of the nature of human endeavour.

But even after the two direct interventions by Jupiter Aeneas is not yet proof against discouragement, and he has to undergo further traumatic experiences in the land of the ghosts before he reaches his father in Elysium. The first part of Book 6, prior to the actual entrance into the underworld, is designed to build up an atmosphere of supernatural awe: it begins with Aeneas' visit to Apollo's temple and a description of the pictures on the door of the temple, pictures of the grim story of the Minotaur and the labyrinth symbolic of the wandering in the underworld for which Aeneas is preparing. It continues with the Sibyl's prophecy about the events which await him, a highly discouraging prophecy:

> o tandem magnis pelagi defuncte periclis
> (sed terrae graviora manent), in regna Lavini
> Dardanidae venient (mitte hanc de pectore curam),
> sed non et venisse volent. bella, horrida bella,

et Thybrim multo spumantem sanguine cerno.
non Simois tibi nec Xanthus nec Dorica castra
defuerint; alius Latio iam partus Achilles,
natus et ipse dea; nec Teucris addita Iuno
usquam aberit, cum tu supplex in rebus egenis
quas gentes Italum aut quas non oraveris urbes!
causa mali tanti coniunx iterum hospita Teucris
externique iterum thalami.
tu ne cede malis, sed contra audentior ito
qua tua te fortuna sinet. via prima salutis,
quod minime reris, Graia pandetur ab urbe.

(6. 83–97)

O you who have at last finished with the great perils of the ocean (but worse await you by land), the Trojans will come into their kingdom of Lavinium (put that anxiety away from your thoughts), but they will not be glad to have come into it. I foresee wars, grim wars, and the Tiber foaming with much blood. You will not be without a Simois, a Xanthus, Greek war-camps; a new Achilles is already there in Latium, himself born of a goddess; and Juno will ever be present to dog the Trojans, while you as a suppliant in dire straits will beseech for help all the peoples and cities of Italy. The cause of this great suffering for the Trojans will once more be a foreign bride and alien wedlock. Do not yield to disasters, but rather go on more boldly along the road which fortune permits. The first road to safety, little do you imagine it, will be shown you from a Greek city.

Aeneas puts a brave face on this grim prophecy, and begins his response by saying, in very Stoic phrases, that he is prepared to face what he must. He continues by making his request to be accompanied to the underworld: the Sibyl responds by telling him to find the Golden Bough and expiate the death of one of his companions. In this context of death the final sacrifices are made and Aeneas enters the underworld.

Virgil now uses the traditional geography and inhabitants of the underworld (monsters, Charon, Cerberus, Aloidae, Ixion etc.) as a background for Aeneas' meeting with ghosts of his past – Palinurus, Dido, Deiphobus. He has to experience again the tragic events in which his mission had involved him, and in these encounters we see that the psychological wounds are still very deep: we see him involved with guilt and regrets about the past, unable to wrench his thoughts away from those tragedies or to focus on the future.

First Aeneas meets the ghost of his unburied helmsman, Palinurus, and in speaking to him throws blame on Apollo for prophesying falsely that Palinurus would come safely to Italy. It is a measure of Aeneas' feelings of self-blame and guilt that he tries to put the blame elsewhere. Palinurus explains that Apollo's prophecy was not false, and begs to be taken across the Styx, a prayer which Aeneas cannot fulfil.

Worse is to come: after crossing the Styx Aeneas reaches the region of the untimely dead, and here in the Fields of Mourning he comes face to face with Dido's ghost. At this he is overwhelmed with sorrow and guilt, and we see perhaps more of the depth and sincerity of his feelings for Dido than we (or Dido) were allowed to in Book 4. Three times within the twenty-five lines describing their meeting Aeneas is shown in tears (*demisit lacrimas*, 6. 455; *lacrimasque ciebat*, 6. 468; *prosequitur lacrimis longe*, 6. 476). His words to her arise from his deep love and affection for her (*dulcique adfatus amore est*, 6. 455). He tries to explain, as he had tried to in Book 4, that he did not want to leave her but was forced to by the dictates of heaven:

> *invitus, regina, tuo de litore cessi.*   (6. 460)

Unwillingly, O queen, I left your shore.

His speech ends in broken rhythm:

> *siste gradum teque aspectu ne subtrahe nostro.*
> *quem fugis? extremum fato quod te adloquor hoc est.*
> (6. 465–6)

The phrases recall his words to the ghost of Anchises

> *quem fugis? aut quis te nostris complexibus arcet?*(5. 742)

They stress the loneliness of Aeneas, bereaved of both his father and his beloved, who are now unsubstantial ghosts, vanishing after a brief moment.

There is a further point to make about Aeneas' last words to Dido: the phrase *quem fugis?* returns us with grim irony to Dido's plea in Book 4 when she hears Aeneas is leaving – *mene fugis?* ('Is it from me you are running away?', 4. 314). The wheel has gone full circle: in the course of its circuit Dido has lost her life and Aeneas his chance of peace and personal happiness.

Aeneas' unhappy journey through the tragedies of his past is not yet completed. Farther on in the region of the untimely dead he meets his Trojan companions who died in the war against the Greeks, and the spotlight is turned on Deiphobus, Aeneas' colleague in arms who died on Troy's last night when Aeneas escaped. Aeneas is again filled with guilt and remorse that he has not been able to help or even to find Deiphobus' body to bury him. Deiphobus consoles him and exonerates him from blame, and finally urges Aeneas to press onwards:

> *i, decus, i, nostrum; melioribus utere fatis.*   (6. 546)

Press on, glory of our race, press on: enjoy happier fates.

Thus far the journey of Aeneas through the underworld has been in every way traumatic for him, and we have seen him guilt-laden and filled with remorse at the tragedies of the past in which he has been involved. He has been backward-looking, obsessed with the miseries which his mission has involved. But this is all changed when he finally reaches Elysium and the ghost of his father Anchises. Anchises' first words to Aeneas are:

> *venisti tandem, tuaque expectata parenti*
> *vicit iter durum pietas!*   (6. 687–8)

Have you come at last, and has your devotion, awaited by your father, conquered the hard journey?

These words are to be interpreted on two levels. On the surface level they mean that Aeneas' sense of duty, expected by his father, has conquered the hard journey down to the underworld, and they refer to Anchises' instructions (5. 731 ff.) that Aeneas should visit him in the underworld. But on another level they sum up the whole of the events so far in the poem: it is Aeneas' devotion to his mission which has conquered all the dangers and disasters of his journey from Troy towards his new city in Italy. Anchises ends by referring to the most crucial danger of all to the mission:

> *quam metui ne quid Libyae tibi regna nocerent!* (6. 694)

How I feared that the kingdom of Libya might bring you harm. Aeneas tries to embrace his father, but all in vain.

> *ter conatus ibi collo dare bracchia circum,*
> *ter frustra comprensa manus effugit imago,*
> *par levibus ventis, volucrique simillima somno.*
>
> (6. 700–2)

Three times then he tried to put his arms around his neck, three
times the ghost vainly clasped eluded his embrace, like the light
breezes, most like to a winged dream.

These are the same lines that were used to describe, long ago,
Aeneas' attempt to embrace the ghost of his lost wife Creusa (2.
792–4). Their use again here serves to emphasize the length of
Aeneas' weary quest and above all his loneliness.

Aeneas now catches sight of the ghosts of those waiting to be
born, and when he asks who they are Anchises replies that they are
the future Romans and that he has long been wanting to reveal them
to Aeneas 'so that you may rejoice the more with me now that Italy
has been found': (*quo magis Italia mecum laetere reperta*, 6. 718).
For the reader this line is full of irony; Aeneas has had little enough
cause for rejoicing all through his wanderings, and particularly in
the underworld thus far he has had no cause at all. This is reflected
in his reply:

> o pater, anne aliquas ad caelum hinc ire putandum est
> sublimes animas iterumque ad tarda reverti
> corpora? quae lucis miseris tam dira cupido?
>
> (6. 719–21)

Father, am I to think that some ghosts go from here aloft to the
upper world, and enter again into a frail body? What is this
dreadful desire for the light of life which the poor wretches feel?

The last few words are a very grim expression of what Aeneas has
suffered in life.

But what Anchises has to tell him totally changes Aeneas' mood
of despair. First he explains the secrets of the afterlife and the hope
of everlasting bliss for the virtuous; and then he gives a long
description of the future heroes of Rome who will be born if – and
only if – Aeneas fulfils his mission. In the midst of this description,
after the vision of the future emperor Augustus, he breaks off to ask
his son:

> et dubitamus adhuc virtutem extendere factis,
> aut metus Ausonia prohibet consistere terra?
>
> (6. 806–7)

And do we still hesitate to enlarge our valour by deeds, or does
fear prevent us from making our settlement in Ausonian land?

Aeneas does not reply, but we can reply for him: surely now that the great prospect is before his eyes he will not hesitate any more. The prospect is reinforced and generalized as Anchises ends his speech with his definition of the Roman mission to bring peace and civilization to the world. The optimism is indeed modified by the vision of young Marcellus, destined to die in early manhood, but when the time comes for Aeneas to depart Anchises has 'fired his heart with love for the glory to come' (*incenditque animum famae venientis amore*, 6. 889). This is the true turning point of the poem: the fuller understanding of his mission gives Aeneas the confidence, resolution and positive passion to succeed which he has lacked so far. His problem from now on will not be whether he can summon the strength and energy to continue (we know that he will) but how he is to cope with the violent opposition that he is destined to meet.

In the second half of the poem Aeneas is seen to be basically peace-loving, fighting only because he has to, unlike Turnus who fights because he welcomes the opportunity of showing his prowess on the battlefield. Aeneas is at heart like King Latinus, a man of peace, but unlike Latinus he is also a warrior determined to carry out his mission, and at times of extreme pressure he is savage and brutal on the battlefield. For the most part, and in the essence of his true character he is like the statesman in the simile in Book 1 (148 ff.) who because he is known to be thoughtful and responsible can calm the fury of others: but three times in the poem, as we shall see, he loses his temper and behaves wildly and cruelly.

Aeneas' desire for peace is seen in the serene and friendly scenes with King Latinus in the early part of Book 7, and very clearly in the beginning of Book 8, after the war has broken out. Turnus is all agog to fight: Aeneas on the other hand is deeply worried and cannot sleep, and the uncertainty of his thoughts is compared in a memorable simile (8. 22 ff.) to the flickering reflexion of sunlight from a cauldron of water. Phrases used of him are *magno curarum fluctuat aestu* ('he tosses on a great tide of anxiety', 8. 19), and *tristi turbatus pectora bello* ('his heart distressed by the grim war', 8. 29). But when he actually enters battle on his return from his visit to Evander (10. 310 ff.) he shows himself to be a most formidable warrior, killing many opponents and calling on Achates for more weapons. When he learns of the death at Turnus' hands of his protégé Pallas all thoughts of the horror of war leave him and he goes berserk on the battlefield:

> *proxima quaeque metit gladio latumque per agmen*
> *ardens limitem agit ferro,*   (10. 513–14)

He mows down with his sword everything around him, and in hot anger cuts with steel a broad path through the battle line.

He captures eight youths to sacrifice alive on Pallas' pyre. This must not be dismissed as an unhappy imitation of Achilles' behaviour in Homer, nor will it do with Mackail to deplore Virgil's 'single lapse into barbarism' and to hope that the passage would later have been cancelled (*Aeneid*, p. lxvi). It is very deliberate on Virgil's part, and very unexpected: wild grief has overcome a man who could so often show self-control. He brings Magus low, and in spite of his offer of ransom and his pleas for mercy in the name of his father and young son (pleas which would normally weigh with Aeneas) he is mercilessly despatched by Aeneas with the comment − reminiscent of Achilles after Patroclus' death − that all such bargaining in war has been eliminated by the death of Pallas. The slaughter continues − the priest Haemonides, the brothers Lucagus and Liger, and many more. His vaunting speeches over his defeated victims are savage in the extreme: he rages victoriously over the battlefield when once his sword-point has grown warm with blood (10.569–70). The word *furit* has been used of him near the beginning of this episode: it is used again at the end after nearly a hundred lines devoted to his uncontrollable rage and deeds of blood:

> talia per campos edebat funera ductor
> Dardanius torrentis aquae vel turbinis atri
> more furens.   (10. 602–4)

. Such were the deaths which the Trojan leader inflicted on the plains, raging madly like a torrent of water or a black whirlwind.

The scene shifts to Olympus, and when we return Mezentius is causing havoc on the battlefield among the Trojans. Aeneas moves to meet him, wounds him, and gladdened at the sight of his blood (*viso Tyrrheni sanguine laetus*, 10. 787) presses on to kill him. Lausus, Mezentius' young son, comes with his companions to try to save his father; Aeneas for all his rage is forced to take shelter (10. 802). Then suddenly for the first time on the battlefield, we see a revulsion of feeling in Aeneas. He warns Lausus, who takes no heed, and angry again he kills him: then a wave of pity comes over him and as we have seen in detail in Chapter 5 (iii) he feels intensely the pathos of it all, groaning in sorrow and thinking of his own filial devotion. So little a margin is there between lust for blood and overflowing pity. The nature of Aeneas' character is such that he cannot be consistently ruthless like Turnus nor consistently gentle like Latinus.

Book 11 opens with deep sorrow and pathos as the funeral of Pallas is described, and Aeneas in his closing words at the ceremony shows his horror of war (in which he had so recently revelled) as he says:

> *nos alias hinc ad lacrimas eadem horrida belli*
> *fata vocant:*   (11. 96–7)

These same dread fates of war call us from here to further sorrows.

This is immediately followed by the arrival of Latin envoys seeking a truce to bury the dead, and here we have the fullest statement of Aeneas of his basic hatred for war (provided he is not on the battlefield). He asks:

> *pacem me exanimus et Martis sorte peremptis*
> *oratis? equidem et vivis concedere vellem.*   (11. 110–11)

Do you ask me for peace for the dead, those taken off by the fate of war? I would have liked to grant it to them when alive.

He goes on to explain that it is fate, and Turnus' hostility that is responsible for the war:

> *nec veni, nisi fata locum sedemque dedissent.*
> *nec bellum cum gente gero: rex nostra reliquit*
> *hospitia et Turni potius se credidit armis.*
>
> (11. 112–14)

I should not have come unless fate had apportioned me this place of abode. I have no war with the people: it is the king who has abandoned his friendship with us and rather put his trust in Turnus' forces.

The feeling of the unnecessary futility of it all continues through the following episodes, the lament of Evander, the burial of the dead Trojans, the burial of the dead Latins, the hostility of the Latin peace-maker Drances to the warmongering of Turnus.

Virgil has presented in the most powerful manner the two contrasting sides of Aeneas – the angry warrior and the rational and merciful peace-maker. This he does again very strikingly in the last book of his poem. Single combat is arranged in order to settle the matter without further mass bloodshed, and Aeneas in his solemn oath agrees that in the case of defeat the Trojans will withdraw, while in the case of victory they will not seek dominion over the Italians but an equal alliance with them.

non ego nec Teucris Italos parere iubebo
nec mihi regna peto: paribus se legibus ambae
invictae gentes aeterna in foedera mittant.
sacra deosque dabo; socer arma Latinus habeto,
imperium solemne socer; mihi moenia Teucri
constituent urbique dabit Lavinia nomen.

(12. 189-94)

I will not order the Italians to obey the Trojans, and I seek no dominion for myself: under equal laws both peoples, unconquered, must enter eternal alliance. I will be responsible for the religious rites and divinities: my bride's father Latinus shall keep his army and his power as before; the Trojans shall build my city, and Lavinia shall give it her name.

Latinus makes a similar solemn oath promising peace between the two peoples, and all seems set fair.

The Rutulians, however, fearing the almost certain defeat of Turnus, break the truce. Aeneas' reaction is what we should like to expect of him: he tries to prevent the bloodshed from beginning again, and the epithet *pius* is used of him, as it has been at the beginning of the oaths (12. 175).

at pius Aeneas dextram tendebat inermem
nudato capite atque suos clamore vocabat:
'quo ruitis? quaeve ista repens discordia surgit?
o cohibete iras! ictum iam foedus et omnes
compositae leges, mihi ius concurrere soli . . .'

(12. 311-15)

But Aeneas, thinking of his men, held out his weaponless hand, with head unhelmeted, and loudly shouted to his comrades: 'Where are you rushing to? What is this sudden confusion among you? Control your fury! The treaty is already struck and all the agreements made − it is right for me alone to go to battle . . .'

But all this changes when Aeneas is wounded by a chance arrow: he reverts to being the cruel and ruthless warrior which he showed he could be after the death of Pallas. When he is healed by divine intervention he is greedy for battle (*avidus pugnae*, 12. 430) and cannot bear to be delayed (*oditque moras*, 12. 431) and he sweeps on like a tempest which will wreak terrible destruction (12. 451 ff.). When Messapus hits his helmet with a spear-cast, then indeed fury rises up in him: *tum vero adsurgunt irae* (12. 494). He re-enters the battle and

terribilis saevam nullo discrimine caedem
suscitat, irarumque omnis effundit habenas.

(12. 498–9)

A frightening figure, he deals slaughter indiscriminately, and gives
full rein to his fury.

The use of the word *irae* twice within half-a-dozen lines inevitably
recalls his words just a brief while ago when the truce was broken
– *o cohibete iras.* Where now is Aeneas' control of his own fury?
    In the battle scenes which follow, the deeds of Aeneas and Turnus
are described alternately as they each demonstrate their relentless
valour in war. Most remarkably they are given a joint simile (where
now is the difference between them which was so carefully built up
by Virgil?)

> *ac velut immissi diversis partibus ignes*
> *arentem in silvam et virgulta sonantia lauro,*
> *aut ubi decursu rapido de montibus altis*
> *dant sonitum spumosi amnes et in aequora currunt*
> *quisque suum populatus iter: non segnius ambo*
> *Aeneas Turnusque ruunt per proelia; nunc, nunc*
> *fluctuat ira intus, rumpuntur nescia vinci*
> *pectora, nunc totis in vulnera viribus itur.*

(12. 521–8)

Just like two fires coming from different directions upon a tinder-
dry wood and upon the rustling laurel undergrowth, or like
foaming rivers speeding wildly down from lofty mountains,
roaring and rushing seawards, each causing destruction in its
path: just as fiercely did the two of them, Aeneas and Turnus, go
rushing through the fray. Now indeed their passions burn within
them, their unconquerable hearts beat to bursting point, they go
with all their strength to the deadly combat.

    The general mêlée eventually becomes a single combat as Aeneas
goes in pursuit of Turnus. After a long pursuit Turnus is wounded
and begs for mercy. We have been reminded constantly during these
scenes of the single combat between Achilles and Hector in *Iliad* 22
(see the section on Turnus), and now we remember how Achilles
rejected Hector's plea for mercy in a brutal and savage speech. We
expect Aeneas to behave otherwise, to show in this moment of
victory that clemency which Anchises picked out as a characteristic
of the Romans – *parcere subiectis et debellare superbos* (6. 853).

Turnus has indeed been *superbus*, but now he is *subiectus* (*ille humilis supplexque*, 12. 930). It comes therefore as a savage shock when Aeneas' inclination to show mercy is in an instant destroyed by the sight of the sword-belt which Turnus has taken as spoils from the dead Pallas.

> *ille, oculis postquam saevi monimenta doloris*
> *exuviasque hausit, furiis accensus et ira*
> *terribilis: 'tune hinc spoliis indute meorum*
> *eripiare mihi? Pallas te hoc vulnere, Pallas*
> *immolat et poenam scelerato ex sanguine sumit.'*
> *hoc dicens ferrum adverso sub pectore condit*
> *fervidus; ast illi solvuntur frigore membra*
> *vitaque cum gemitu fugit indignata sub umbras.*
>
> (12. 945–52)

When he had caught sight of these spoils, reminders of his cruel grief, then fired by frenzy and terrible in his fury he said: 'Are you to be saved from me when you are wearing spoils taken from my loved ones? It is Pallas who sacrifices you with this blow I deal, Pallas I say, exacting vengeance on your accursed life.' As he spoke he plunged his sword into his breast as he faced him, in hot fury. Then Turnus' limbs were loosened in the chill of death, and his life with a groan fled complaining to the shades below.

The words used to describe Aeneas' final act in the poem (*furiis accensus et ira terribilis*) are those which the *Aeneid* has taught us to regard as contrary to man's better nature, contrary to the self-control which is proper to the human character. And who would have thought that we would take our leave of the hero of the poem with the word *fervidus*?

Virgil has left us in no doubt whatever of the motive of Aeneas in killing Turnus. There may be other reasons why Turnus must die; but the reason Virgil gives is vengeance. The repetition of the word Pallas, the use of the sacrificial term *immolat* (Turnus is an offering to the dead Pallas), the phrase *poenam sumit*, all make this absolutely clear. We should remember that Evander, on hearing of his son's death, sent a solemn message to Aeneas demanding vengeance, so that Aeneas is bound by an obligation. But this is not how his action is described – it is clearly presented as an uncontrollable impulse of emotion and violence. Is it justified? If we think back to Turnus' behaviour in Book 10 when he killed Pallas so brutally, we shall remember that Virgil invited us then to feel that Turnus must pay for such brutality. But now that he does pay, the poetic treatment of the scene makes Aeneas' action seem unacceptable, and that this is how the whole poem ends leaves an impression of deep disquiet. This could easily have been avoided if Virgil had described Turnus' death differently – if Aeneas' spear-cast instead of wounding Turnus had killed him, the poem could have ended more comfortably. But it is not meant to be a comfortable poem.

(ii)   ANCHISES

The importance of Aeneas' father, both on the divine and on the human level, is a crucial feature of the main themes of the *Aeneid*. He is a link, through Aeneas' mother Venus, with the religious intentions of fate, and when after his death a vision of him comes to Aeneas at a time of great crisis he tells his son: 'I come here on the instructions of Jupiter' (5. 726). He provides a link between the past (before Troy was destroyed) and the future (which his ghost outlines to his son at the end of Book 6). On the human level he exemplifies the Roman concept of the *paterfamilias*, and by the comfort and help and guidance which he gives to Aeneas during his lifetime he sets a standard for Aeneas to follow in his relationship with his son Iulus. His importance to Aeneas, especially in the early faltering stages of his mission, is much greater – old and frail though Anchises is – than that of any of Aeneas' contemporaries. In Homer's *Iliad* Agamemnon had many stout warriors and wise counsellors around him; in Virgil's *Aeneid* Aeneas has none. The 'faithful Achates' is a most shadowy figure, Ilioneus has little impact upon events; there is no one to whom Aeneas can turn except his father – and to him, all through the seven years' wanderings, he turns again and again.

The special religious importance of Anchises is seen on his first appearance in the poem, when Aeneas on Venus' instructions goes back out of the fighting to rejoin his family and take them away with him from the burning city. Anchises refuses to leave (2. 634 ff.), believing that the end of Troy is also the end of his destiny. Jupiter convinces him otherwise by the omen of flames around Iulus' head. Anchises now directly addresses Jupiter, asking for confirmation of the omen, and this is promptly given by thunder and a shooting star. Anchises immediately consents to the divine directive, and recognizes because of this intervention of Jupiter that Troy does have a future as well as a past. Thus it is only through divine motivation, conveyed to Anchises, that the Roman mission starts at all.

The old man who has to be carried out of Troy on his son's shoulders plays a dominant role in leadership during the wanderings described in Book 3 (and described, it must be remembered, by Aeneas himself, showing how completely aware he was in retrospect of the dominant part played by his father). At almost every one of the many stages of the journey Anchises takes the decisions. The actual departure from the Troad is arranged by Anchises (3. 9). The horrific experience, at their first landing, when the voice of the dead Polydorus is heard from the reed-bed, is immediately referred by Aeneas to a council of elders, and especially to his father. At the next stop, in Delos, King Anius recognizes Anchises as an old friend and welcomes the Trojans accordingly. When they consult the oracle of Apollo there for instructions about where they are to go, the riddling reply ('seek your ancient mother') is referred to Anchises, who wrongly interprets the answer as meaning Crete. Here they are confronted by plague, and the *penates* appear to Aeneas in a vision, telling him that Italy – not Crete – was meant. He immediately informs his father of this, and Anchises recognizes his mistake, and recalls that Cassandra spoke to him of Italy. To Italy then, he says, they must go: the Trojans obey his instructions.

During these opening episodes it is not an exaggeration to say that Anchises rather than Aeneas has been the leader; during the rest of the journey it is the same. Two most significant aspects of the *Aeneid* are highlighted by this: one is the tremendous importance which the Romans (much more than the Homeric heroes) attached to the family as a unit and the father, however aged, as the head of it; the other is that the death of Anchises leaves Aeneas in a position of sole authority which he only gradually learns to assume successfully (witness his despair at the storm in Book 1, shortly after his father's death, his subsequent delay in Carthage, his deep depression at the burning of the ships).

The next episode in Book 3 is the strange encounter with the Harpies, ending with Celaeno's sinister prophecy that the Trojans will not be successful in founding their city until hunger makes them eat their tables. In the general panic Anchises makes a move and sacrifices to the gods, calling upon them to avert such a catastrophe and be propitious to the god-fearing Trojans. Perhaps the most striking of all the indications of how much Aeneas owed to Anchises is the mistake made by Aeneas (or Virgil) on the occasion of the fulfilment of the prophecy about eating the tables (7. 122 ff.), where Celaeno's prophecy is attributed to Anchises. In recollection it seems to Aeneas that all of the early guidance was given by Anchises, as in fact nearly all of it was.

After the long prophecy by the seer Helenus (3. 374 ff.) it is Anchises who gives the order to resume the journey (3. 472 ff.), and it is to him that Helenus gives instructions about the route, stressing both Anchises' own special position as *coniugio Veneris dignate superbo* ('thought worthy of the proud privilege of marriage with Venus') and as *cura deum* ('object of the gods' concern'), and also as *felix nati pietate* ('happy in the devotion of your son').

At the joyful moment of the first sight of Italy it is Anchises who makes thank-offerings to the gods. The first thing they see in Italy is a group of four white horses: Anchises recognizes the omen and interprets it as indicating first war and then peace (the horse signifying both the war-horse and the beast of burden).

As they voyage on, Anchises recognizes the distant sound of Scylla and Charybdis, and gives instructions to change course to avoid them. They land near Etna and are met by the Greek castaway Achaemenides who begs for help. Anchises gives him his hand and calms his fear.

We have seen in detail that throughout all these years of voyaging the Trojan leader is nominally Aeneas but in reality Anchises. The Roman father–son relationship is illustrated at its very strongest, and it is destined to continue supernaturally after the death of Anchises.

Aeneas relates the death of Anchises at Drepanum briefly, as if he could not bear to dwell on it. He speaks of his father as having been *omnis curae casusque levamen* ('the comfort in all my anxieties and misfortunes'), and continues:

> *hic me pater optime fessum*
> *deseris heu tantis nequiquam erepte periclis!*
> (3. 710–11)

Here it was, best of fathers, that you left me, tired and weary, when you had been saved from such great dangers, alas all in vain.

Aeneas now is left alone to contend with the ravaging of his fleet by the storm which drives the Trojans to Carthage, and with the weakening of his resolution to continue which is caused by Dido's love for him and his for her. The need for Jupiter's intervention to remind Aeneas of his mission, and the tragic ending for Dido, would have been avoided had Anchises still been alive. Indeed Aeneas tells Dido as he tries to justify his intended departure, that he has been visited in his sleep by visions of his father warning him and frightening him and reminding him of his own paternal obligations to his son Iulus who is being deprived, through Aeneas' delay in Carthage, of his destiny of a kingdom in Italy (4. 351 ff.).

In the next two books the influence of the dead Anchises upon the action is all-pervasive. The greater part of Book 5 is taken up with funeral games held in Sicily on the anniversary of Anchises' death. More important in the themes of the poem than the games themselves are the religious ceremonies which Aeneas performs in honour of his dead father. These are clearly to be seen as the origin of the annual Roman *Parentalia*, a festival regularly and scrupulously celebrated in Virgil's time at the tomb on the anniversary of a father's death. The description with its speeches is a long one: it stresses the filial devotion of Aeneas, and also the more than human status of his father. The Hellenistic idea of the deified hero is behind much of the narrative: Anchises is called *divinus* and *sanctus* and Aeneas vows he will found a temple in his honour. It is emphasized that it was the will of the gods that Aeneas should return to Sicily for the anniversary of Anchises' death, and the appearance of the snake at the tomb adds a further touch of the supernatural.

After the games are completed there is a further, most powerful, indication that Anchises is still a crucial figure in the success of Aeneas' mission. Aeneas is in despair after the burning of the ships, and the advice of the seer Nautes does not help him. During the night a vision of his father Anchises appears to him, sent on the instructions of Jupiter himself; he gives Aeneas advice, and in particular motivates the visit to the underworld in Book 6 by saying that Aeneas must come to meet him in Elysium and learn of all his descendants and the city which will be granted to him. Two things stand out here: the first is that this occurs at the time of Aeneas' deepest despair during the whole mission; and the second that, as Anchises in life had helped Aeneas decisively during the voyage, so now in death he provides the motivation for the transformation of Aeneas' attitude from irresolution to confidence.

During his journey through the underworld to reach Elysium Aeneas' experiences, as we have seen, are gloomy and grim: but from the moment that he meets the ghost of his father all this changes. The main events in the last part of Book 6 have been discussed elsewhere: here it will suffice to stress that Anchises is responsible for all of them. He welcomes his son with great relief that his *pietas* has conquered the difficulty of his journey, and that his sojourn in Carthage was not disastrous, and he it is who delivers the great speech about life in the hereafter (6. 724–51; see Chapter 7). Immediately afterwards he describes to Aeneas the pageant of Roman heroes waiting to be born (see Chapter 5 (ii)). In the middle of it he breaks off to ask whether there is still any doubt or lack of resolution to found a city in Italy. He it is who pays the sorrowful

tribute to Marcellus (6. 808–86). In fact, of the last 200 or so lines
of the book more than four-fifths are spoken by Anchises. At the end
he explains to his son the wars and future events which await him,
and finally sends him forth having 'fired his heart with love for the
glory to come'.

In the first half of the poem, up to its turning-point at the end of
Book 6, the part played by Anchises, both in life and after death, has
been absolutely decisive in the fulfilment of the Roman mission.
Virgil makes us feel that Aeneas could not have won through on his
own: the support of his father was completely crucial. Filial
devotion to one's father, and paternal devotion to one's son, were
aspects of *pietas*, ideals in family life, that were especially
characteristic in Roman society and they are vividly and powerfully
depicted as vital in the *Aeneid*.

(iii) DIDO

The story of Dido has always been the most widely read part
of the *Aeneid*, and she has nearly always been favourably
portrayed by the many authors and musicians who have been
inspired to retell her story, being betrayed by malevolent powers
(like the witches in Purcell's opera) or by the heartless Aeneas,
though (as Quinn well points out, *Latin Explorations*, p. 35)
'those who think ill of Aeneas for deserting Dido are often the
same people as those who think ill of Antony for not deserting
Cleopatra'. She is very much Virgil's own creation: the legend
about her before Virgil seems to have been shadowy in the
extreme.

There are some traces in the Greek historian Timaeus (third
century BC) of the story of how her husband was murdered by
Pygmalion, and she fled to Libya and founded Carthage (no mention
of Aeneas). She certainly figured in Naevius' *Bellum Punicum* (late
third century), and so did Aeneas, but there is no firm evidence of
any conflict between them (emotional or otherwise). The prose
writers of the Aeneas legend (such as Virgil's contemporaries Livy
and Dionysius) make no mention of any visit to Carthage by
Aeneas. It can be said with certainty that Virgil's full-scale
description of this episode is very largely original.

When we consider on what other famous heroines of past
literature Virgil could have based this addition to the legend we find
again that his presentation of the love-story is very largely original.
Aeneid 4 is the most un-Homeric book in the *Aeneid* – the story
of Odysseus and Nausicaa in *Odyssey* 6 is as different as could be.

Nausicaa wins our affections, Dido torments herself and us. Dido has more in common with the Homeric witches, Circe and Calypso, both of whom delay Odysseus on his voyage. But this is purely a structural similarity: they are not real humans and they inspire no pity when Odysseus succeeds in leaving them, nor any fear of vengeance in the future.

As we have seen in the chapter on Virgil's literary sources, there were two poets to whom he was indebted to some extent in the Dido story. Apollonius Rhodius, in Book 3 of his *Argonautica*, set a precedent for the ultimate portrayal of the emotion of love in epic, and there are some verbal and structural similarities between his Medea and Dido (they are ensnared by scheming goddesses, they cannot sleep when all the rest of nature sleeps, they both have recourse to magic). But the Medea of Apollonius is a girl, confused by her emotions, wavering in her attitude: Dido is a mature queen who knows well enough the issues involved, and when she has made up her mind she does not waver from her purpose.

In Catullus 64 is told the story of the desertion of Ariadne by Theseus, and again Virgil has used some verbal similarities, especially in the passages of highest pathos (see Chapter 3). But Ariadne is a gentle and pathetically sad heroine, who in her devoted love for Theseus would, if he had wished not to marry her, have been his servant and washed his feet. She has no dimension of character like the pride and slighted anger of the queen of Carthage. Indeed the contrast of Dido with Apollonius' Medea and Catullus' Ariadne brings into sharp relief the richness of Virgil's character portrayal. Dido when we first meet her is the serene and beloved queen of her people; she changes to the pathetically rejected lover, and then to a majestically terrifying figure of vengeance, a symbol of Carthage and of war. Her pride, her knowledge of power – these are the things that compel her: she is a monarch scorned. Greek tragedy knew well the intense effect of focusing on grandeur in disaster, and it is in this primary sense that *Aeneid* 4 is 'tragic'.

Our interest in Dido and our sympathy for her are first aroused by Venus' account of her story to Aeneas (1. 338 ff.), in which we hear of her love for her husband Sychaeus, and of how he was murdered by Pygmalion. Warned in a dream, Dido left Tyre to found a new city – *dux femina facti*. When Aeneas reaches her city he is amazed at its extent and at the activity going on; she is achieving what he is still far away from. Clearly there is much in common between these two leaders of their people. He looks at her temple to Juno and sees pictures of the Trojan war – here is a link between Trojans and Carthaginians. Dido herself appears, majestically beautiful like Diana among her nymphs, and sets to work on the tasks of government: *instans operi regnisque futuris* (1. 504); *iura dabat legesque viris* (1. 507). While Aeneas is still hidden, the rest of the Trojans under Ilioneus appear, complaining about rough treatment on the shores and begging Dido's help. Her reply is gracious and generous in the highest degree: she bids them banish their fears, she is impressed at their being Trojans, of whom she has heard much, and she offers them a share in her kingdom (*urbem quam statuo vestra est*, 1. 573). Aeneas reveals himself to her, and in terms which have a deep latent irony in the light of later events, says that he will never be able to thank her enough; if justice and righteousness exist, if the gods have thought for the good (*si qua pios respectant numina*, 1. 603), then they will reward her. He will always hold her in honour, whatever lands call him. How very far away from these happy prospects is the ultimate fate of Dido.

She is astonished to learn that this is Aeneas himself, of whom she has heard so much, and she recalls ancestral links with Troy. She invites them to her palace with the memorable words: *non ignara mali miseris succurrere disco* ('Myself not unacquainted with suffering I am learning to help the unfortunate', 1. 630). A banquet is prepared and things could not be happier.

In these opening scenes Virgil has portrayed a woman whom there is every reason to admire. The first of her qualities revealed to us has been her energy and courage – *dux femina facti*. Secondly her beauty is like that of a goddess. Thirdly she is a capable and beloved ruler, whose people happily accept her leadership. Fourthly she is warm-hearted and helpful to those in distress. It does not seem that such a person could be brought to such a point of despair as to take her own life.

But the serene human situation which these first scenes have depicted is shattered by the intervention of the goddess Venus: *At Cytherea novas artes . . .* (1. 657). Venus has other plans: in order to frustrate any schemes of Juno on behalf of her two-tongued Carthaginians, she substitutes Cupid for Ascanius so that her son may shoot his arrows of desire into Dido's heart. This is an outstanding example of the *Aeneid*'s exploration of the interrelationship of the divine and the human action. At first sight it might seem that Venus is entirely responsible for subsequent events, and that Dido is a puppet of irresistible forces. But this determinist view is not Virgil's. The humans are subject to pressures from outside themselves of all kinds – sometimes the will of providence (as when Mercury is sent by Jupiter to remind Aeneas of his destiny), sometimes the forces of hostile circumstances (as when Juno persecutes Aeneas, or as here when Venus assails Dido). But at each and every moment in the poem the humans are free to resist. True, they may not be successful – the forces may be too great for them – but they are free to try.

Dido is brought to disaster by her own desire for Aeneas, which she might have resisted more strongly than she did. Under this pressure to yield to a love which – as we shall see – she knows is both wrong and impossible, she gives in. Had she resisted we do not know what would have happened; all we know is what did happen when she yielded. Initially, indeed, Venus was to blame for bringing this about (or in non-mythological terms, a situation fraught with disaster developed); but how Dido dealt with this situation was up to her. Much later Virgil breaks off his narrative to exclaim:

> *improbe Amor, quid non mortalia pectora cogis!*
>
> (4. 412)

Tyrant love, to what do you not force mortal hearts?

In the face of this tyranny, whether exercised upon her by Venus from without, or by her own passions from within, Dido has at every moment to decide how to act. The circumstances which have arisen are not her responsibility, but her reaction to them is.

In the rest of the first book the mood of the banquet is joyful and merry, but there are undertones of impending disaster as Virgil takes the reader behind the narrative.

> *praecipue infelix, pesti devota futurae,*
> *expleri mentem nequit ardescitque tuendo*
> *Phoenissa,*   (1. 712–14)

Especially the unhappy Phoenician queen, victim of disaster to come, cannot satisfy her heart, and her passion burns more strongly as she gazes on him.

> . . . *gremio fovet inscia Dido*
> *insidat quantus miserae deus.*   (1. 718–19)

Dido fondles him (Ascanius) in her lap, little knowing – alas – how mighty a god was sitting there.

Consequently there is an intense sense of tragic irony behind Dido's happy words of welcome:

Iuppiter . . .
hunc laetum Tyriisque diem Troiaque profectis
esse velis, nostrosque huius meminisse minores.

(1. 731–3).

Jupiter, grant that this be a day of joy for the Tyrians and those who have come from Troy, and that our descendants may remember it.

At the end of the story she asks her descendants to remember in a quite different way – *pugnent ipsique nepotesque* (4. 629).

After the banquet Dido asks Aeneas to tell the story of the fall of Troy and his subsequent wanderings, and during his long account it must be very evident to her that because of his quest to found a new settlement in Italy he is not free to stay with her. Nevertheless when the narrative resumes in Book 4 her passion is unchecked; she nourishes the wound that Cupid has dealt, and her love-lorn frame of mind is described in a way reminiscent of the Medea of Apollonius. As Medea pictured Jason after he had gone (Apollonius, *Argonautica*, 3. 451 ff.), what he had looked like, what he had said, so with Dido:

multa viri virtus animo multusque recursat
gentis honos; haerent infixi pectore vultus
verbaque, nec placidam membris dat cura quietem.

(4. 3–5)

The bravery of the hero, the nobility of his race, come back again and again to her mind; his face, his words are for ever present in her thoughts, and her love gives no sweet repose to her limbs.

She speaks to Anna of her love and its problems, as Medea spoke to her sister Chalciope; she says that she cannot and will not yield because of her promise to Sychaeus – she will not violate *pudor*. Anna replies with a series of arguments proposing that Dido should break her promise, and these arguments are wholly and immediately successful:

His dictis incensum animum flammavit amore
spemque dedit dubiae menti solvitque pudorem.

(4. 54–5)

With these words she added fuel to the fire of her love, and gave hope to her uncertain heart, and destroyed her scruples.

Dido seeks religious sanction for the decision to yield, and though there is no indication that she gets it, she now yields totally: she is ablaze with the fire of love, in her frenzy she roams one way and another through Carthage; she is as helpless as a wounded doe, and when Aeneas is away she holds Ascanius in her lap, trying to assuage a love which cannot be spoken. Carthage is forgotten and the work comes to a full stop:

> *non coeptae adsurgunt turres, non arma iuventus*
> *exercet portusve aut propugnacula bello*
> *tuta parant: pendent opera interrupta minaeque*
> *murorum ingentes aequataque machina caelo.*
>
> (4. 86–9)

The towers they have begun to build rise no higher, the young men no longer practise their manoeuvres or prepare harbours or strong military defences; all the work is broken off and hangs fire, and the mighty threatening walls are deserted and the cranes that tower to the heavens.

Dido becomes entirely oblivious of all other considerations than the satisfaction of her love for Aeneas, and it is with full justice that Anna says to her as she lies dying:

> *exstinxti te meque, soror, populumque patresque*
> *Sidonios urbemque tuam.*   (4. 682–3)

You have brought to destruction, sister, yourself and me and your people, and the fathers of Sidon and your city.

The scene shifts to heaven, where the goddesses Venus and Juno scheme, each with different intention, to turn the situation to their advantage by what Juno calls 'marriage' in the cave. As we have seen, Dido's mind had already been made up – the goddesses provide the *occasion* for the final step. The scene in the cave is daemonic and supernatural: elemental powers of Nature perform functions analogous to a marriage ceremony, and Dido in her deluded state 'calls it a marriage' (*coniugium vocat*). We know that it is not, and should not be surprised later to find Aeneas denying that he has entered into any compact.

Up to this point we have seen how Dido has become wholly possessed by her love for Aeneas and her desire to win him – all other aspects of her personality are eliminated, and she yields totally to what she knows is guilt. At the beginning she used the word *culpa* (4. 19); at the end of this section Virgil uses it – *coniugium vocat, hoc praetexit nomine culpam* ('she calls it marriage, under this name she conceals her guilt' 4. 172). The terms used of her love have been those of fire, illness, wounding, frenzy, madness: *saucia, vulnus, carpitur igni, male sana, flammavit, furentem, flamma, uritur, furens, demens, pestis,* and finally *ardet amans Dido traxitque per ossa furorem* (4. 101).

Thus the reason for disaster is that Dido has given up everything for Aeneas, and her pride can know no retreat. She has burnt all her bridges. We have watched with pity and sorrow as she allows herself to be swept into a position which we know (and does not she know too?) is impossible, and from which we fear she will find no way back. She has allowed herself to become trapped in a net of circumstances; we do not know what would have happened had she tried to resist these circumstances, we do not know whether she could have done so. All we know is what happened when she yielded.

Now for the first time the action centres upon Aeneas; he, like Dido, has abandoned his responsibilities (4. 193–4), but unlike Dido he can be recalled to them. Mercury, sent down by Jupiter to remind him of his mission, finds him busied with Carthage, even wearing Carthaginian clothes (4. 260 ff.); his stern rebuke immediately brings Aeneas back to reality. *Ardet abire fuga* (4. 281), and he makes his plans to escape from the disastrous situation into which he has so culpably got himself. Dido hears of the intended escape; her frenzy is intensified to the level of Bacchic madness (a comparison used again by Virgil, in *Aen.* 7. 385 ff., to mark the desperate madness of Amata goaded by the Fury Allecto), and she launches into an unrestrained series of emotionally moving pleas. She tells Aeneas that she has given up everything for him – the good will of her people, the friendship of neighbouring peoples, her own *pudor*, and her *fama prior*, and on this account she begs for pity and protection. Aeneas cannot yield to her pleas – because of Jupiter's instructions (*Iovis monitis*), he cannot yield – and he replies with a series of ineffective and tactless logical arguments. His efforts to make her see the inevitability of his decision, and his determination to conceal his emotion, make his speech seem harsh and unfeeling; but in fact it make no difference now what he says. There is no dialogue, there is no longer any communication possible with the unhappy Dido; she is now transmuted from the human plane to an archetypal figure of hatred and vengeance. She swears that she will haunt him after her death with her black torches – she has become a Fury of Vengeance, a cosmic personification of hatred and revenge, another Juno, more terrifying than Juno because she was once so kind and gracious.

This speech – *nec tibi diva parens* . . . (365 ff.) – is highly rhetorical, filled with all the effects of the orator's trade: the commonplace about the Caucasus and tigresses; the rapid rhetorical questions with anaphora – *num . . . num . . . num . . .*; the *quae quibus anteferam*? Commentators have seen a special Virgilian skill here, in that the poet can write like Lucan and yet not seem unnatural, still be in tune with the human heart. On the contrary the human heart is out of it now: Dido has become an unreal figure, stylized, grandiose, terrifying, a hyperbolical symbol of hate who will not allow herself to suffer defeat (cf. Euripides, *Medea*, 44–5). Up to this point our moral judgements have been involved; now praise and blame melt away before an awe-inspiring literary spectacle. The elements of pathos which remain in the rest of the book are all based on the backward glance at what she was before; she herself has now passed beyond pathos, except for the moment of death itself. The tragedy is that she should have been driven – or should have driven herself – to a point where her human qualities are entirely submerged in a sweeping torrent of frenzy, hatred and despair.

An analysis of the methods and intention of Dido's last long speech will illustrate these points.

> *et iam prima novo spargebat lumine terras*
> *Tithoni croceum linquens Aurora cubile.* 585
> *regina e speculis ut primam albescere lucem*
> *vidit et aequatis classem procedere velis,*
> *litoraque et vacuos sensit sine remige portus,*
> *terque quaterque manu pectus percussa decorum*
> *flaventisque abscissa comas 'pro Iuppiter! ibit*
> *hic', ait 'et nostris inluserit advena regnis?*
> *non arma expedient totaque ex urbe sequentur,*
> *diripientque rates alii navalibus? ite,*
> *ferte citi flammas, date tela, impellite remos!*
> *quid loquor? aut ubi sum? quae mentem insania mutat?* 595
> *infelix Dido, nunc te facta impia tangunt?*
> *tum decuit, cum sceptra dabas. en dextra fidesque,*
> *quem secum patrios aiunt portare penatis,*
> *quem subiisse umeris confectum aetate parentem!*
> *non potui abreptum divellere corpus et undis*
> *spargere? non socios, non ipsum absumere ferro*
> *Ascanium patriisque epulandum ponere mensis?*
> *verum anceps pugnae fuerat fortuna. fuisset:*
> *quem metui moritura? faces in castra tulissem*
> *implessemque foros flammis natumque patremque* 605

cum genere exstinxem, memet super ipsa dedissem.
Sol, qui terrarum flammis opera omnia lustras,
tuque harum interpres curarum et conscia Iuno,
nocturnisque Hecate triviis ululata per urbes
et Dirae ultrices et di morientis Elissae, .
accipite haec, meritumque malis advertite numen
et nostras audite preces. si tangere portus
infandum caput ac terris adnare necesse est,
et sic fata Iovis poscunt, hic terminus haeret,
at bello audacis populi vexatus et armis,
finibus extorris, complexu avulsus Iuli
auxilium imploret videatque indigna suorum
funera; nec, cum se sub leges pacis iniquae
tradiderit, regno aut optata luce fruatur,
sed cadat ante diem mediaque inhumatus harena.   620
haec precor, hanc vocem extremam cum sanguine fundo.
tum vos, o Tyrii, stirpem et genus omne futurum
exercete odiis, cinerique haec mittite nostro
munera. nullus amor populis nec foedera sunto.
exoriare aliquis nostris ex ossibus ultor   625
qui face Dardanios ferroque sequare colonos,
nunc, olim, quocumque dabunt se tempore vires.
litora litoribus contraria, fluctibus undas
imprecor, arma armis: pugnent ipsique nepotesque.

(4. 584–629)

And now first dawn was beginning to dapple the world with the new day's light as the goddess Aurora left the saffron bed of Tithonus. The queen, when from her watchtower she saw the first light whitening and the Trojan fleet sailing onwards in ordered array, and the shores and harbours deserted of sailors, three times and four times struck against the beauty of her breast, tore her fair hair and said, 'Great king of heaven, shall he leave me? Shall an intruder mock my power? Will my people not arm themselves, stream out in pursuit, launch the boats from the slipways? Quick, off, bring fire, bring weapons, drive the oars!

'What am I saying? Where am I? What madness affects my thoughts? Poor Dido, do your wicked deeds come home now? They should have done so long ago, when you were giving him your power. Is this the honour and faith of the man of whom people tell that he carried with him the household gods of his fatherland, and once bore on his shoulders his weary old father? Could I not have seized him, torn him to pieces and scattered his limbs on the sea? Could I not have killed his companions, yes, and his Ascanius and served his flesh up at a banquet for his father? But the upshot of the struggle would have been uncertain. Let it have been. Whom had I to fear, destined to die? I could have taken fire into their camp, I could have filled their ships with flames, I could have blotted out son, father and people, and I could have flung myself upon the burning wreckage.

'O Sun, you who survey all the works of the world with your fires, and you, Juno, mediator and witness of sufferings like these, and Hecate, whose name is wailed at night at the cities' crossroads, and avenging Furies and gods of dying Elissa, receive these words, turn upon my wrongs the divine sympathy which I must deserve, and hear my prayers. If the cursed villain must reach harbour and come safely to land, and thus the fates of Jupiter require, and this outcome cannot be changed, yet, harassed by the martial opposition of a bold people, torn from his home, snatched from the embrace of Iulus, let him beg for help and see the cruel deaths of his friends, and then, when he has accepted the terms of a harsh peace, may he not enjoy his kingdom or the life he longs for, but fall untimely dead, unburied in the far-stretching sand.

'This is my prayer, these my last words which I utter as I die. And then you, my Tyrians, harass with hatred his people and all his race to come; make this your offering to my ashes. Let there be no love and no agreement between our peoples. Arise unknown avenger from my bones to pursue the Trojan settlers with fire and sword, now, one day, whenever strength offers. I call on shore to fight with shore, wave with sea, weapons with weapons; let the peoples fight, now and to the last generation.'

The passage begins with two calm and sonorous lines describing dawn in phrases partly borrowed from Lucretius (2. 144 ff. *primum aurora novo cum spargit lumine terras et variae volucres . . .*), and adding the formalized mythology of the goddess Aurora and her husband. It is very lovely and serene – but its serenity is broken with the abrupt beginning of the new sentence: *regina* – there is to be no new dawn for Dido. With the words *e speculis* the idea of her isolation is impressed on us; she is alone and watching the last act of the wreckage of her hopes. What she sees is the ordered rhythm of the Trojan departure (*aequatis . . . velis*), smooth and organized in contrast with the total disorder of her own thoughts. As her hatred now defiles her personality, so she physically defiles her beauty in violent gestures of abandonment as she bursts into a wild series of angry questions. Above all she feels humiliated, her queenly power has been mocked and scorned by a chance intruder. She gives commands that she knows are inaudible, and the violence of her speech is conveyed metrically by the rare pause after the fifth foot in 593 (echoing that in 590), and the intense alliteration of *t*. Realization comes and the tone changes, briefly to self-blame and then to violent scorn. As she speaks her own name (596) she gives herself, for the first time, the epithet which Virgil has often given her in the earlier narrative, and the slow spondees convey the recognition of *facta impia* – too late.

Scorn and sarcasm now burst from her as she speaks with bitter irony of the traditional virtues of Aeneas – a man who rescued his country's gods, saved his old father, and now gives *this* indication of his care for other people. The ellipse of the antecedent (*eius*) of the doubled relative clauses (*quem . . . quem*, 598 – 9) and the alliteration of *p* and *s* heighten the impact of her words and prepare for the final violence of the ghastly acts of vengeance which she thinks she could have, should have, inflicted. The alliteration of *p* and *s* continues in these lines until finally the harsh *f* sounds echo the climax of frustrated rage. Her thoughts of tearing Aeneas limb from limb powerfully and inevitably recall the deeds of Medea in dismembering her brother Apsyrtus (cf. Cicero, *Pro Lege Manilia*, 22; in Apollonius the less harsh version is used); there have already been elements in Dido of this most terrifying figure from Greek literature (for example in her use of magic), and now the connection is made explicit. To the gruesome barbarity of Medea Dido now adds an even more horrible and primitive reference to Greek legend; she could have served up Ascanius' flesh at a banquet for Aeneas, as Atreus served up to Thyestes the flesh of his sons (Euripides, *Electra*, 699 ff., *Orestes*, 995 ff.). As Dido is carried away on the tides of her frenzy, Virgil now uses every device of rhetoric and sound to heighten the expression of her rage: the imaginary objection of soliloquy ending (603) with a pause after the fifth trochee (a rare rhythm) and answered with repetition and alliteration; again a trochaic pause in the next line with alliteration and then a series of four climactic clauses of what might have been – attack, fire, murder, then suicide – with four rhyming verbs of unfulfilled vengeance.

After the unfulfilled violence in the past follow Dido's prayers for vengeance in the future. The movement changes entirely; it becomes predominantly spondaic, and the first four lines (607 ff.) all begin with spondees, as in measured tones Dido invokes the powers who can bring to fruition the desires of her hatred. First the all-seeing Sun; then her special goddess Juno, goddess of marriage, goddess of Carthage, enemy of Aeneas; then the deity of the underworld, the goddess of magic and spells, patron goddess of

Medea, Hecate; then the avenging Furies (this reminds us of Dido's dream in 4. 471 ff. where the same words – *ultrices Dirae* – were used of the Furies who hounded Orestes in vengeance for Clytemnestra). The list is closed with an appeal to all her gods (whoever they may be) and a strange assonance between *et Dirae* and *et di*.

Dido's prayers for vengeance are of two kinds, the first (612 – 20) concerned explicitly with Aeneas. She accepts that he is fated to reach Italy, but she asks for disasters to befall him there. All of these prayers in one way or another come true. He is opposed in warfare by Turnus and his Rutulians, he has to leave the Trojan camp and the embraces of Iulus to seek Evander's help; he sees the death of many of his men (especially Pallas); he does accept peace terms which are more favourable to the Italians than to the Trojans (12. 834 ff.); and, according to varying forms of the legend, he did not rule his people for long but was killed in battle or drowned in the Numicius and his body not recovered. In this final curse upon Aeneas we are reminded of the fate of Priam, king of Troy: *iacet ingens litore truncus, avulsumque umeris caput et sine nomine corpus* (2. 557 – 8).

But Dido has more to say yet. From her particular curses upon Aeneas she turns to the longer vista of history and undying hatred. The transition to the years ahead is made in a line framed with *tum* and *futurum* (622), emphasized by the doublet *stirpem et genus omne*; the key word *odiis* gains great stress from its position after the verb. *Munera* is grimly ironical; the offering on her grave is to be not a conventional gift but a promise of never-ending hostility. The simple short sentence which follows (624) contrasts horribly with the hospitality and friendship which her people showed to the Trojans when they landed in Carthage after the storm, and with her speech at the banquet when she hoped that both peoples would remember the joyful first day of their meeting (1. 731 – 3).

Her last appeal for vengeance (625 ff.), made vivid by its hissing *s*'s and its second-person verbs in apposition with the normally third-person *aliquis*, is the seed of the Punic wars and the dreaded person of Hannibal; thus the Carthaginians will use against Dido's foes that fire and sword which she herself might have used but did not (604 ff.). It was not for nothing that Virgil chose as the last figure of all in his pageant of heroes in Book 6 the Roman general Fabius Cunctator, who saved Rome from Hannibal (6. 845 – 6): he exorcizes the memory of Dido's curse. Then finally in her last words Dido calls on the waves and shores of Nature herself to take part in the hostility of the peoples, the never-ending hatred of the generations, symbolized in the never-ending rhythm of her last words with the hypermetric elision that cannot actually be made because the speech ends. Of the twenty hypermetric elisions in Virgil only three others occur before a heavy stop, and no others at the end of a speech.

Here then, at the climax of Dido's tragedy, all the previous pity and pathos is purged away, and her speech is a grandiose and formalized imprecation, arising from thwarted power, injured pride, and the uncontrollable passion for revenge. Its great impact is due to the variety of ways in which her hatred is conveyed – first a useless plea for action, then a moment of self-blame, followed by a violent and inhuman outburst dwelling on the horrors which she might have committed; then the recognition that she herself can do nothing, and the prayer to other powers to bring about the destruction which she cannot, the destruction first of Aeneas himself and his people, and then of his Roman descendants. The particularized fury and despair of Dido turns into the generalized hostility and violence of two great peoples.

Upon this speech follows the suicide of Dido; her last words depict the two aspects of her story. The first eight lines (4. 651 – 8) briefly review the achievements of the life which she is now leaving and end with these phrases based on Catullus:

> *felix, heu nimium felix, si litora tantum*
> *numquam Dardaniae tetigissent nostra carinae'.*

Happy, ah only too happy, if only the Dardan ships had never touched our shores.

This is the aspect of the generous queen brought piteously to tragic disaster; the unhappy woman for whom St Augustine and many since shed tears. But these are not her very last words – she goes on:

> *'moriemur inultae*
> *sed moriamur' ait. 'sic, sic iuvat ire sub umbras.*
> *hauriat hunc oculis ignem crudelis ab alto*
> *Dardanus, et nostrae secum ferat omina mortis.'*
>
> (4. 659 – 62)

'We shall die unavenged,' she said, 'but die we must. Thus, thus, it is my pleasure to pass beneath the shades. Let the cruel Trojan gaze from the deep upon the fire of this my pyre, and carry with him the curse of my death.'

This is the other aspect: the spirit of vengeance. She cannot have vengeance in life, but after death she must and will. This is the Dido whose anger still burns in the underworld when Aeneas meets her – *ardentem et torva tuentem* (6. 467) – and who is no more moved by his words than if she were flint or Marpesian rocks. By what sorry process of human error, folly and pride is the heart turned to flint?

The book ends gently, as a Greek tragedy does, with its final choral song after the suffering and disaster is over. Juno sends Iris down to release Dido's soul from her body (4. 693 ff.); this is necessary because Dido is not dying in accordance with fate or by a death which she has earned – *nec fato merita nec morte peribat* – but unhappy, before her time, set on fire by sudden frenzy – *sed misera ante diem subitoque accensa furore*. To the reader of her long-drawn-out tragedy, the frenzy does not seem sudden – but in the time-scale of her life's achievement it was. Against this background it was sudden indeed – like the wreckage of the lives of virtuous heroes in Greek tragedy, brought in a moment to madness and self-destruction. Virgil, like the tragedians, makes us ask what was, what could have been the cause. Her own faults and folly, or the too heavy pressure of accidental and potentially disastrous circumstances, or a tragic mixture of both?

After her suicide Dido is mentioned in the poem four times, always in situations which evoke profound pathos. The splendid pageant of the *lusus Troiae* in Book 5 has in the place of honour Aeneas' son Iulus riding on a horse which 'Dido had presented as a token and pledge of her love' (5. 571 – 2). In the underworld Aeneas meets her ghost (6. 450 ff.), and her silent rejection of his attempt to explain why he had to leave her confirms that her love has turned irrevocably to bitter and uncompromising hatred. In the ninth book, when Nisus and Euryalus make their courageous offer to break out of their besieged camp (an exploit which ends in their death), Iulus promises to them as a prize for their valour an antique mixing bowl which Dido gave to the Trojans (9. 266). The very last mention of all is at the funeral of Pallas, the young warrior whose death caused the most bitter grief to Aeneas (*saevus dolor*, 12. 945) of all the events of the war. After his corpse has been placed on its leafy bier Aeneas covers it with one of two gold-embroidered cloaks which Dido 'had made for him with her own hands, so happy to be doing it':

> quas illi laeta laborum
> ipsa suis quondam manibus Sidonia Dido
> fecerat . . .   (11. 73 – 5)

(iv) TURNUS

Thematically Turnus plays in the last four books the part which Dido has played in the first four. He represents opposition to the Roman mission; he is an obstacle to the divine will; he becomes involved in a net of circumstances from which, because of traits in his personality, he cannot or will not escape. Like Dido he wins much of our sympathy; like Dido he is a 'tragic' figure in the full sense of the word, who recklessly pursues his own course contrary to the decrees of fate and pays for it with his life. By true tragic irony it is his excessively arrogant behaviour as he kills Pallas which leads to his own destruction, for in the moment of victory Aeneas is about to spare him until he catches sight of the sword-belt of Pallas which Turnus is wearing as spoils. Virgil indicates in an authorial comment, like the chorus in a Greek tragedy, that disaster will follow this hubristic behaviour:

> nescia mens hominum fati sortisque futurae
> et servare modum, rebus sublata secundis!
> Turno tempus erit . . .   (10. 501 – 3)

How mindful are men's hearts of fate and destiny to come, and of showing moderation when uplifted by success. There will come a time for Turnus . . .

One aspect of Turnus' character which is always apparent is his inflexible determination to display his personal prowess. He is a young nobleman of immense ambition and energy. He is brave, impetuous, unthinking in his constant preoccupation with his honour, irrational in his total self-confidence and the certainty of his unassailable excellence in warfare. The word *violentia* is used of him alone in the *Aeneid*, and other words applied to him include *audax, turbidus, furor, insania, fiducia, superbus*. He is portrayed as a man who is most truly himself on the battlefield, one to whom warfare brings fulfilment. He is thus set in contrast with Aeneas who (as we have seen) hates the prospect of war although (again as we have seen) he is a formidable warrior and he fights most savagely on occasion. Turnus relishes battle as a means of enhancing his own glory and honour: Aeneas fights only because he must. It was the task of the Romans to subdue the proud, *debellare superbos*, and Turnus was one of the *superbi*.

Many passages in the *Aeneid* illustrate the immeasurable self-confidence and pride of Turnus. On his first appearance in the poem

(7. 413 ff.), when Allecto comes to him in sleep in the form of the priestess Calybe with words of advice, he mocks and ridicules her for offering warnings of which he is in no need, and we see his boastful self-confidence even before she hurls her torch at him and maddens him. Then indeed he rages in frenzy:

> *arma amens fremit, arma toro tectisque requirit;*
> *saevit amor ferri et scelerata insania belli,*
> *ira super:* (7. 460 – 2)

Madly he roars for his weapons, on his couch and through the house he searches for his weapons; passion for steel rages in him, and the accursed madness of war, and anger above all.

He is arrogantly proud:

> *se satis ambobus Teucrisque venire Latinisque* (7. 470)

Indeed he would be enough and more than enough for Trojans and Latins put together.

In the first simile applied to him he is most appropriately compared with a seething cauldron of water boiling over (7. 462 ff.). Similes form a large part of Virgil's characterization of Turnus. There are sixteen altogether, almost all expressing fierceness and energy: three times he is compared with a lion (9. 792 ff., 10. 454 ff., 12. 4 ff.); twice with a bull (12. 103 ff., 12. 715 ff.); twice with a wolf (9. 59 ff., 9. 565 ff.); and once each with an eagle (9. 563 ff.), a tiger (9. 730), a war-horse (11. 492 ff.), Mars (12. 331 ff.), the north wind (12. 365 ff.), fire and torrent (12. 521 ff.), a landslide (12. 684 ff.), and finally, when all is lost, with the helplessness of a dream (12. 908 ff.).

In the catalogue of Italian forces at the end of Book 7, Turnus' helmet is decorated with a chimera, belching forth fire which glows hotter as the fight becomes fiercer (7. 785 ff.); this is a symbol of archaic violence and lust for battle. At the transformation of the Trojan fleet in Book 9 all are dismayed except Turnus, who tells them he cares nothing for omens:

> *at non audaci Turno fiducia cessit;* (9. 126)

But the self-confidence of bold Turnus did not desert him.

The characteristic line is repeated a little later on (10. 276).

When Turnus bursts into the Trojan camp and wreaks havoc all round, he does not pause to think of his plans or to let his comrades in:

> *sed furor ardentem caedisque insana cupido*
> *egit in adversos.*   (9. 760 – 1)

But his frenzy and his mad lust for slaughter drove him, all ablaze, against the enemy.

His behaviour at the death scene of Pallas is wild and cruel, and he wishes Evander were there to see his son's death – *cuperem ipse parens spectator adesset* (10. 443); Servius gravely comments *aspere et amare dictum* ('a harsh and bitter phrase'). At the end Turnus sends a message to Evander that he is returning Pallas as he deserved to have him back – *qualem meruit Pallanta remitto* (10. 492). We are reminded of the arrogant cruelty of Pyrrhus killing Polites in Book 2.

At the beginning of Book 12 Turnus sees that all eyes are upon him, and he blazes up in confidence and courage like a wounded lion raging with blood-stained jaws – *fremit ore cruento* (the same phrase which Virgil used of *Furor impius* in 1. 296).

> *haud secus accenso gliscit violentia Turno.*
> *tum sic adfatur regem atque ita turbidus infit:*
> *'nulla mora in Turno . . .'*   (12. 9 – 11)

Even so violence swelled up in Turnus' blazing heart. Then thus he spoke to the king and wildly began in these words: 'There is no delay in Turnus. . . .'

Latinus tries to dissuade him, but

> *haudquaquam dictis violentia Turni*
> *flectitur: exsuperat magis aegrescitque medendo.*
> *ut primum fari potuit, sic institit ore:*
> *'Quam pro me curam geris, hanc precor, optime, pro me*
> *deponas letumque sinas pro laude pacisci . . .'*   (12. 45 – 9)

The violence of Turnus was not altered at all by his words: it became more dominant still, and more inflamed by the efforts to soothe it. As soon as he could speak, thus he began: 'The anxiety which you have on my behalf, honoured king, I beg you put aside on my behalf, and let me bargain death for glory . . .'.

And as he arms himself for the battle his eyes sparkle in anticipation (12. 101 ff.).

We have considered some of the aspects of Turnus' part in the poem which give power and impetus to the second half of the *Aeneid*: he is indeed a formidable obstacle to the Roman mission; his role is destined to be that of a tragic hero who pursues a path which must lead to disaster; he is in himself a most courageous but an impetuous, over-confident opponent. There is a further aspect to his character which is of the utmost importance, and this is his similarity to Achilles in the *Iliad*. Turnus is the new Achilles whom the Trojans have to face, but this time it is the new Hector who prevails.

The first mention of Turnus in the poem is in the prophecy of the Sibyl in 6. 83 ff. 'I foresee wars', she tells Aeneas, 'grim wars, and the Tiber foaming with blood. And you will not be without a Simois or a Xanthus or a Greek camp; another Achilles is produced for you in Latium, himself born of a goddess (*alius Latio iam partus Achilles, natus et ipse dea*) . . . the cause of this woe for the Trojans is again an alien bride, again a foreign marriage . . . the path of safety, little do you imagine it, will first be revealed from a Greek city.'

This theme, the similarity between the old war and the new, the old opponent and the new, so explicitly stated by the Sibyl, continues with frequent emphasis in the second half of the poem. Amata complains at Latinus' decision that Lavinia must marry Aeneas because the oracle said she must marry someone of foreign descent: Turnus too is of foreign stock, Greek stock, Mycenaean stock:

> et Turno, si prima domus repetatur origo,
> Inachus Acrisiusque patres mediaeque Mycenae.
>
> (7. 371 – 2)

In the case of Turnus too, if the first beginnings of his line were traced, Inachus and Acrisius were his ancestors, and midmost Mycenae.

As if to support this claim, the shield of Turnus in the catalogue (7. 789 ff.) is described as decorated with pictures of Io and her father Inachus.

Turnus thinks of himself in these terms too. When battle is imminent in Book 9 he compares the situation of the Italians with that of the Greeks – Lavinia has been stolen just as Helen was; the Italians like the Greeks are justified in going to war:

sunt et mea contra
fata mihi, ferro sceleratam exscindere gentem
coniuge praerepta, nec solos tangit Atridas
iste dolor, solisque licet capere arma Mycenis.

(9. 136 – 9)

I too have my fates to oppose his, namely the destruction by the
sword of a criminal people who have stolen my wife from me; it
is not only the sons of Atreus [i.e. Agamemnon and Menelaus] who
are affected by such suffering, and it is not only Mycenae that may
resort to war against them.

A new people of Mycenae are marching to battle, he says, and he, their
leader, needs no armour from Vulcan, such as Achilles had had, no
thousand ships; the Trojans need not this time fear a wooden horse. In
broad daylight he, Turnus, will surround their walls with fire; they fight
now against a deadlier enemy than the Greeks whom they kept at bay
until the tenth year. Later in the same book Numanus mocks the Trojans
for being once more enclosed behind besieged ramparts (9. 598). It is the
Trojan War all over again, but this time, it is 'not the sons of Atreus nor
the eloquent Ulysses' (9. 602) who oppose the Trojans, but a hardy
Italian stock. Finally in this book Turnus confirms the Sibyl's words
when he tells the Trojan Pandarus that he will be able in the underworld
to tell his king, Priam, that he found another Achilles here:

hic etiam inventum Priamo narrabis Achillem. (9. 742)

We have already observed how Turnus is seen at his wildest and
cruellest when he meets and kills Pallas. The similarity between
Pallas and Patroclus in the plot of the two poems is very marked,
and as the death of Patroclus leads directly to Hector's death, so that
of Pallas leads to Turnus'. The new Achilles figure is destined this
time to be the loser: Turnus, who thinks of himself as Achilles, is
increasingly seen in the situation of Hector. His *aristeia* in Book 9,
performed in the absence of Aeneas, is similar in setting to that of
Hector in *Iliad* 15, performed in the absence of Achilles; now the
Hector situation closes in more tightly around the would-be
Achilles.

A little later in the poem the Italians hear that the Greek
Diomedes, now settled in Italy, will not join them. He says (11. 282
ff.) that he has experienced Aeneas' might before, formidable and
terrifying; if there had been two others like him, the Trojans would
have stormed Greece, the fates would have been reversed, and
Greece would have been mourning: *et versis lugeret Graecia fatis.*

Thus Virgil intensifies the feeling that the story he has to tell corresponds in reverse with one we already know: it is the Trojan War again, *versis fatis*. This theme is very dominant in Book 12, and with it are mingled other aspects of Turnus which we have already seen – the theme of *violentia*, the theme of the opponent of destiny, the theme of the tragic hero brought to utter downfall by the gods. All these themes, which contribute to the rich complexity of the last book, are embodied in an often sympathetic portrayal of the young Rutulian warrior.

At the beginning of Book 12 the dauntless Turnus, with the eyes of all upon him, seems to himself and to the reader as irresistible as Achilles was; yet it is of Hector that we are reminded in the opening scenes, when Latinus and Amata try to dissuade Turnus from fighting, as Priam and Hecuba tried to dissuade Hector at the beginning of *Iliad* 22. The scene moves to Olympus, where Juno plans to save the destined loser for a brief time, as Zeus in *Iliad* 22 wished to save Hector.

When the oaths are sworn before the single combat Turnus, at this supremely solemn time, loses for a moment his impetuous self-confidence; the Rutulians feel that the contest is unequal, and this feeling is heightened by Turnus' humble demeanour:

> adiuvat incessu tacito progressus et aram
> suppliciter venerans demisso lumine Turnus
> pubentesque genae et iuvenali in corpore pallor.
>
> (12. 219 – 21)

Turnus increased this feeling among them as he came forward without speaking and worshipped at the altar humbly, with downcast gaze; his face was so youthful and all his young body so pale.

Some commentators find difficulty with this passage, speaking of inconsistency of character. It is rather complexity of character; for all his youthful *élan* Turnus momentarily blanches at this supreme moment. Basically, for all his fierce words, he lacks the deep resolution of the mature Aeneas. Our sympathy is aroused for him as it was for Hector, when afraid and yet determined he persuaded his heart to face Achilles (*Iliad* 22. 98 ff.).

The moment of Turnus' supreme test in single combat is postponed by the violation of the treaty and the wounding of Aeneas; in the general fighting Turnus achieves great deeds, but on the return of Aeneas Turnus comes to feel that his end is near. He realizes as Hector had done (*Iliad* 22. 300 ff.) that the gods are against him and he now shows the same courage in facing death:

> *terga dabo, et Turnum fugientem haec terra videbit?*
> *usque adeone mori miserum est? vos o mihi Manes*
> *este boni, quoniam superis aversa voluntas.*
> *sancta ad vos anima atque istius inscia culpae*
> *descendam, magnorum haud umquam indignus avorum.*
>
> (12. 645 – 9)

Shall I turn my back, shall this land see Turnus running away? Is it indeed so terrible to die? Shades of the underworld, be kind to me, for the will of the gods above is hostile. I shall come down to you an unsullied soul, free of such a sin [as cowardice], never unworthy of my great ancestors.

The picture of the brave young Rutulian warrior facing his death is enriched as Hector's words ring in the ears: 'Let me not die without a struggle and ingloriously, but having done some great deed for future generations to hear' (*Iliad* 22. 304 – 5); and more faintly but still unmistakably we hear again those words of Dido in her last moments of life:

> *vixi et quem dederat cursum Fortuna peregi*
> *et nunc magna mei sub terras ibit imago.*
>
> (4. 653 – 4)

I have lived, and the course Fortune allotted I have completed, and now my ghost in majesty will pass to the underworld.

Turnus and Hector, Turnus and Dido.

Now Saces rushes up to Turnus – all is lost unless he can save them. Turnus' mind is utterly perplexed; the tragic hero, under adverse fate, victim of the gods, is in utter confusion.

> *obstipuit varia confusus imagine rerum*
> *Turnus et obtutu tacito stetit; aestuat ingens*
> *uno in corde pudor mixtoque insania luctu*
> *et furiis agitatus amor et conscia virtus.*
>
> (12. 665 – 8)

Turnus stood amazed, confounded by the shifting picture of events, and he halted, gazing and not speaking; in one human heart there seethed deep shame, madness mingled with grief, love driven on by frenzy, and the knowledge of his prowess.

And as the shadows disperse, and light returns to his mind, he
departs in search of Aeneas, to the doom to which his *virtus* now
forces him.

The last two hundred lines are crowded with reminiscences of
Homer, including some of the most famous lines of *Iliad* 22. The
similes of 12. 684 ff. and 12. 701 ff. are from *Iliad* 13. 137 ff., and
13. 754 ff.; the scales of Jupiter (12. 725 ff.) are from *Iliad* 22. 209
ff. Aeneas pursues Turnus as a hound pursues a stag (12. 749 ff.), as
Achilles had pursued Hector (*Iliad* 22. 188 ff.). In Virgil as in Homer
the onlookers are prevented from joining in (*Aen.* 12. 760 ff.; *Iliad*
22. 205 ff.); the chase continues round the walls, not for a prize in
the games but for the life of the loser ('their contest was for the life-
blood of Turnus', *Aen.* 12. 763 ff.; 'the race was for the life of
Hector, tamer of horses', *Iliad* 22. 158 ff.).

Now the scene shifts in Virgil, as in Homer, to Olympus, and the
conflict is resolved on the divine plane; as Apollo was forced to
desert Hector, so now Juno and Juturna must desert Turnus. The
will of Jupiter is made known to Juturna and to Turnus in the
daemonic scene of the Fury, in the shape of an owl, beating in
Turnus' face. Our thoughts go back to the lonely, terrified Dido,
whose nightmare visions and torments of conscience were
accompanied by the long-drawn hooting of an owl (4. 462 ff.). There
follows the lament of Juturna, as the sister says farewell to her
brother; the situation recalls Anna's farewell to her sister Dido, and
there are unmistakable echoes: 12. 871, describing Juturna's wild
gestures of grief, *unguibus ora soror foedans et pectora pugnis*, is
exactly the same line as that describing Anna in 4. 673; both sisters
lament their empty future, and wish they had died too (12. 880 – 1,
4. 677 – 9). The last scenes of the tragedy of Turnus are thus linked
with the tragedy of Dido.

So Juturna departs; Aeneas threatens Turnus, and, magnificent in
his hopeless defiance, he replies:

> *non me tua fervida terrent*
> *dicta, ferox: di me terrent et Iuppiter hostis.*
>
> (12. 894 – 5)

Your hot words do not frighten me, fierce though you may be; the
gods frighten me, and Jupiter my enemy.

Yet he still fights on. He seizes a mighty stone too great for ordinary
men to move, as Hector once did (*Iliad* 12. 447 ff.), but, unlike

Hector then, he is not strong enough to hurl it to its mark; it is as if he were not himself, but a man in a dream – *non corpore notae sufficiunt vires* (12. 911 – 12). In *Iliad* 22 Homer described the chase with this simile: 'as in a dream a man cannot pursue the man who flees, the one cannot escape nor the other pursue, so Achilles could not catch Hector nor Hector escape' (22. 199 ff.). The confusion of the dream world persists in Turnus: *tum pectore sensus vertuntur varii* (12. 914 – 15), and there is nothing he can do. Aeneas' spear-cast wounds him, and he begs for mercy for himself or his dead body (as Hector did, unavailingly, *Iliad* 22. 338 ff.). the opening words of Turnus' plea are not in Hector's speech:

> 'equidem merui, nec deprecor', inquit,
> 'utere sorte tua . . .'   (12. 931 – 2)

'I have deserved it', he said, 'and I ask no forgiveness. Use your advantage.'

This is not a recognition by Turnus that he is in the wrong; it is merely a statement that he has accepted a contest to the death and is prepared to abide by the consequences. It is a last splendid gesture of heroic defiance which he cannot sustain, and he ends with his plea for mercy.

Aeneas is inclined to spare Turnus (as we naturally expect of him) until he sees the belt of Pallas, and then, terrible in his anger, he kills him. Aeneas, who throughout the poem has tried – with intermittent success – to control violence and passion now, in an instant, yields to his impulse for vengeance – *furiis accensus et ira terribilis* (12. 946 – 7). And Turnus? Did he deserve it? Was it essential, as Otis argues (*Virgil: A Study in Civilised Poetry*, esp. p. 381), that his type of flawed heroism should be eliminated to make way for the new proto-Roman way of life? Or is he, as Quinn says, the agent of his own destruction through the fatal slip of tragedy – 'his death is no *punishment*, it is merely the way things worked out' (*Virgil's Aeneid: A Critical Description*, p. 327)? Or does Virgil intend us to feel the intense injustice of it, as Putnam argues (*The Poetry of the Aeneid*, ch. 4, esp. pp. 192 ff.)? The poetic brilliance of this last scene arises because Virgil has forced upon us in the most compelling way all these aspects of the situation; the result is that our thoughts at the end are focused not on the triumph of Aeneas but on the tragedy of Turnus, as 'his life with a groan fled complaining down to the shades below' (*vitaque cum gemitu fugit indignata sub umbras*).

CHAPTER 7

Religion and the Gods

The *Aeneid* is essentially a religious poem. Its whole scheme depends on the unquestioned assumption that there exists a power outside the world of men, and that this power directs and influences mortal actions in accordance with a far-reaching plan of its own, extending over the centuries as far as history can reach, and concerned with the long destiny of nations and mankind. This power may be called *fatum* (fate, destiny, providence), or it may be called 'God' or 'the gods', or it may be presented anthropomorphically in the form of Jupiter, Juno, Venus, Apollo and the other Olympian deities.

The basic theme of the *Aeneid*, as we have seen in previous chapters, is the fulfilment by Aeneas of a divine mission laid upon him by fate: the poem is heavy-laden with fate, but never becomes fatalistic. Aeneas has the free will to continue or not, and it is through his own free will that all the decisions he takes, sometimes it seems by a narrow margin, are that he should continue (see especially 5. 700 – 3).

The due performance of ceremony, ritual and prayer is evident throughout the poem, particularly in Book 3, at the various stages of the Trojans' journey; in Book 5, in the commemoration of the anniversary of Anchises' death; in Book 6, in the preparations for the descent, with Aeneas' long prayers to Apollo and to the Sibyl, with the full-scale description of Misenus' funeral, and with the final sacrifices before the entrance. Book 8 has a long account of Evander's worship of Hercules; Book 11 opens with the funeral ceremonies for Pallas; Book 12 has the solemn oaths of Aeneas and Latinus. The point need not be laboured: it is quite obviously a part of Aeneas' character to make the appropriate prayers and thank-offerings and perform the appropriate ceremonies, and it is clear that Virgil took pleasure in the full description of these external aspects of religious belief.

But what of the spiritual basis for these religious rituals? What is the theology of the *Aeneid*? We know that in his early life Virgil was much influenced by Epicureanism, a philosophical school which totally denied the involvement of gods in mortal affairs. It is very obvious that the whole concept of the *Aeneid* as a divine mission rejects the Epicurean view of the world – is it then a Stoic poem? In many respects its main framework does resemble Stoicism: the key Stoic belief was that men should live *secundum Naturam*, in accordance with God's plan, and should devote their lives to following this plan, standing firm like a rock against misfortune and disaster and never questioning why the divine plan involves human suffering. To a limited extent Aeneas does show Stoic traits, for example in his response to the Sibyl's speech – which has prophesied grim suffering but urged him to stand up against it – when he says:

> *non ulla laborum*
> *o virgo nova mi facies inopinave surgit;*
> *omnia praecepi atque animo mecum ante pereqi.*
>
> (6. 103 – 5)

Maiden, no shape of disaster comes before my eyes as something new or unexpected: I have anticipated all, and thought it over in my mind in advance.

But as we have seen in analysing Aeneas' character and behaviour in the poem he is very far from the Stoic *sapiens*: he shows in the first half of the poem a frailty of purpose very different from the Stoic ideal described for instance in Horace, *Odes* 3. 3: *iustum et tenacem propositi virum*: worse, he expresses (especially in Book 1) resentment at what he is suffering; finally, in the battle scenes he gives way three times to passionate anger, a quality which – as Seneca never tires of saying – the true Stoic must eradicate from his character. Stoicism is not the answer to Virgil's search for religious enlightenment. What of the anthropomorphic gods and goddesses who figure so largely in the poem?

The presence in the *Aeneid* of Olympian deities, major and minor, is of course a piece of epic technique which Virgil took from Homer. In Homer the anthropomorphic concept of deity was very real in religious thought: the Homeric warrior might indeed believe that Athene or Apollo could intervene in person to save him from death. In Virgil's time a more sophisticated concept of deity prevented this belief except in a symbolic sense, and the much stronger idea of fate as a long-term process necessarily diminished the power of individual deities. Yet Virgil decided to adopt the Homeric convention in a poem written in a different religious environment – why?

In the first place the presence of the Olympians serves to elevate and dignify the human scene. The mortal action takes place against

a background of cosmic forces, made more real to the reader by their
being personified. Secondly, they give an extra dimension to the
story by their interaction with each other, as well as with the
mortals. They are people in their own right, less vividly so than
Homer's Olympians but still with strong characters of their own.
Thirdly, and very importantly for the kind of poetry which Virgil
loved to write, they serve to enlarge the range of the poet's
imagination. The visualization of shapes not seen by mortal eyes
fascinated him, and he could paint pictures in words of the world
beyond the clouds as if with brush on canvas. We see this at the very
beginning of the poem with the image of Juno sweeping majestically
through the halls of heaven (1. 46); with Aeolus and his mountain
of the winds (1. 52 ff.); with Neptune calming the storm as he
sweeps over the waves in his chariot accompanied by his retinue of
sea deities (1. 142 ff.). Haunting pictures of the gods and goddesses
are frequent in the poem: we read of the beauty of Venus as she puts
off her disguise and appears as her true self to Aeneas (1. 402 – 5),
or again when she appears undisguised to him to warn him to leave
Troy (2. 589 ff.); there is the radiant loveliness of Iris as she descends
to earth by her own rainbow (4. 700 – 2); there is the swooping flight
of Mercury to Carthage as he pauses on Mount Atlas and then wings
his way like a bird just above the waves (4. 245 ff.); there is the
serene majesty of Jupiter as he replies to Venus (1. 254 – 6). These
supernatural scenes captured Virgil's visual imagination, imbued as
he was with the Greek art and literature which so constantly
portrayed them. With them he could transport his readers into
another world of fancy and beauty, and achieve for them what
Venus achieved for her son when she revealed to him, during the
destruction of Troy, what the gods could see, but mortals not:

> aspice (namque omnem, quae nunc obducta tuenti
> mortales hebetat visus tibi, et umida circum
> caligat, nubem eripiam . . .   (2.604 – 6)

Look, for I will remove from you all the cloud which now veils
and dims your mortal sight, and casts damp shadow around
you . . .

But above and beyond their anthropomorphic impact on the poem
the Olympian deities also have a symbolic significance, and in some
ways they can be regarded, as the Stoics regarded them, as different
aspects or manifestations of the single, universal God. Their king
Jupiter, as the agent of fate, represents the concept of an ordered
universe moving in a way mysterious to mortals towards the

fulfilment of the divine purpose for mankind. Jupiter's speech to Venus (1. 257 ff.) unrolls the secret book of fate (*fatorum arcana*); he supervises the destruction of Troy (2. 617 – 8); he intervenes through Mercury when Aeneas is dallying in Carthage (4. 220 ff.); he quenches the fires which are destroying Aeneas' fleet (5. 687 ff.). Like Zeus in Homer he sometimes has his purpose temporarily frustrated by others of the Olympian hierarchy, notably Juno. At the beginning of Book 10 he is provoked to call a council in heaven, and upbraid the other divinities for frustrating his plans:

> *abnueram bello Italiam concurrere Teucris.*
> *quae contra vetitum discordia?*   (10. 8 – 9)

I had forbidden the Italians to make war on the Trojans. What is the meaning of this fighting contrary to my decree?

He ends by ordering them to cease their discord and allow the peace treaty which he has approved to be observed. Venus and Juno both make indignant speeches, and Jupiter's decision in council is an unexpected one. He accepts that they will neither of them yield, and says that he will not intervene, but leave the upshot to fate.

> *rex Iuppiter omnibus idem.*
> *fata viam invenient.*   (10. 112 – 13)

King Jupiter will be impartial: the fates will find a way.

This seems a very strange temporary abdication of responsibility, a remarkable shift from what he said at the beginning of the council. It is made all the more remarkable by his decisive action at the very end of the poem, when he specifically forbids Juno to intervene any further, and she yields, as she knows she must. It seems that in this ambivalence of Jupiter's exercise of his power Virgil is once again indicating his perplexity at the way that providence works in human affairs. Jupiter may sometimes intervene to guide events, and sometimes not; if he does not, unnecessary and futile suffering occurs, but the destined march of events will not be permanently altered.

If Jupiter is an ambivalent figure in the *Aeneid*, Juno is not. As a character in her own right she is formidable, relentless, brilliantly rhetorical in expressing her anger or her guile (1. 37 ff., 4. 93 ff., 7. 293 ff., 10. 62 ff.); on another level she is the main cause of mortal suffering throughout the poem. As we have seen (Chapter 5 (i)), Virgil gives some reasons for her opposition to the Trojans in mythological and personal terms, reminiscent of the motivation of the Homeric divinities: she was angry because of her support for the Greeks, whom the Trojans had opposed for ten years; because of the judgement of Paris; because of Electra; because of Ganymede (1. 23 – 32). More significant than these reasons for her anger is the historical aspect: Juno is the guardian deity of Carthage (1. 12 – 22), and therefore opposes the Trojans by whose descendants her favourite city was destined to be destroyed. This historical aspect is an undertone throughout the story of Dido, as Juno schemes to divert the kingdom of Italy to the shores of Libya (4. 105). In a broader sense Juno is used by Virgil as a symbol of apparently inexplicable human suffering: he makes this clear at the very beginning of his poem when he invokes the Muse to explain why Juno brought such suffering, and asks whether it can be true that the gods harbour such anger (1. 8 ff.). His Juno symbolizes the hostile environment, the apparently senseless disasters that befall the good and the bad alike. Everywhere and implacably she schemes to bring calamity upon the Trojans (1. 36 ff., 5. 606 ff., 7. 285 ff., 9. 2 ff., 12. 134 ff.), and she is in fact directly responsible for much of the suffering in the poem, not only brought upon her Trojan enemies but upon her Italian friends. Her relationship with the fates is a paradox which Virgil sensitively explores; she cannot change the immutable purposes of destiny, but in all kinds of ways she can delay its fulfilment, cause such difficulty that the fulfilment may be less glorious, less complete. She does not in fact seriously impair the purpose of the fates, but she does – even more paradoxically – modify it to the great benefit of the future Romans by her requests to Jupiter in 12. 791 ff. (see Chapter 5 (ii), where this passage is fully analysed). She achieves for the Italians their dominance over the Trojans in the future history of Rome.

In perpetual opposition to Juno is Venus, the supporting goddess of the Trojans. Virgil's portrayal of her is a strange mixture of the protective mother-goddess (*alma Venus*), caring for her children, for Aeneas and for all his Trojans, and of the reckless Greek goddess Aphrodite, rejoicing in her power over mortals. We see her in her first guise as she appears to Aeneas in Book 2 (589 ff.), urging him to leave Troy with his family; in Book 1, as she guides him after the ship-wreck to the city of Carthage; in Book 8, as she secures new armour for him from Vulcan; in Book 10, as she argues the Trojan case against Juno; and in Book 12, as she heals Aeneas' wound and intervenes to help him in the single combat. Her 'Aphrodite' role is seen in 4. 105 – 128, as she schemes against Juno for her own ends; in 1. 314 ff., where she mocks her son; but particularly in 1. 657 – 94, where she boasts of her power as she plans to substitute

Cupid for Ascanius, in order to make Dido fall madly in love with Aeneas. There is a Hellenistic atmosphere in this episode reminiscent of the scheming goddesses at the beginning of Book 3 of Apollonius' *Argonautica*: it accords ill with the more dignified role which Venus plays in the rest of the poem, and as things turn out her scheming is most ill-considered. It leads to near-disaster for the Roman mission, and Jupiter has to intervene, through his messenger Mercury, to negate for Rome's benefit the consequences of her plotting.

The other chief deity in the *Aeneid* is Apollo. He was the main guardian god of the Trojans in Homer's *Iliad*, and in addition to this he was traditionally the god who presided over hazardous journeys and the foundation of colonies. Consequently he plays a dominant part in *Aeneid* 3, as the Trojans sail onwards in search of their new city: it is noteworthy that Venus does not appear or intervene to help in the course of the seven years of wandering. But more than this Apollo was the special patron of Augustus: the temple which Augustus had dedicated to him on the Palatine is promised by Aeneas in 6. 69 ff., and in the description of the battle of Actium at the end of Book 8 he is given the epithet *Actius* and portrayed as directing the victory in the battle (8. 704 ff.). Finally it is he who praises Ascanius' first exploits in battle (9. 641 ff.) but prohibits him from taking any further active part in the war.

We have seen that the Olympian deities play a part in the *Aeneid* as characters in their own right on a different plane from mortals, and that they also represent support for or opposition to the fate of nations. In addition to this, of course, they bring to mind the traditional religious ceremonies of Virgil's time – the annual festivals, the sacrifices, the processions. They are directly connected with the temples and the statuary of Augustan Rome, in fact with the whole contemporary panoply of hallowed and time-honoured religious imagery. It remains to consider how far it is legitimate to see them as externalizations of the qualities of humans. Can we say that their interventions are Virgil's way of representing what human characters were likely to do by themselves? Is it as if humans were to say: 'It was some irresistible force within me which caused me to do what I did'? This same question is properly asked about Homer's Olympians: it can be asked with greater force about Virgil's.

When the fiend Allecto, at Juno's instigation, hurls a torch at Turnus in order to inflame him with fury against the Trojans, we already know from Virgil's narrative (7. 435 ff.) that he has in his character a highly inflammatory streak; we are not surprised that her torch fires him to burning fury. When Beroe, at Juno's instigation, causes the Trojan women to set fire to the ships, we can easily see their human motivation, namely to be finished with the endless weary voyage. When Venus sends Cupid to make Dido fall in love with Aeneas, we see how easily she yields to the divine scheme which corresponds with her own personal desires. We are tempted to conclude, in our pity for her, that she herself is not to blame for the tragic results; that Venus is to blame. But if we rationalize the mythology we may well view Dido's predicament as the result of powerful forces latent in her own character which she allows to become dominant. When Mercury comes down to Aeneas at Jupiter's behest to order him to leave Carthage and pursue his mission, it is less helpful to say that our respect for Aeneas is diminished by the need for divine aid than to say that from somewhere within his own character he finds the sudden determination to abandon the land and the queen whom he has grown to love, because he realizes that it is his duty.

These are some instances of many in the poem in which Virgil explores the relationship between inner human motivation and the action upon it of external forces, whether we like to think of them as temptations, or as the force of circumstances, or as divine promptings. The problems of human motivation are vividly portrayed in Nisus' question to Euryalus, when he feels a sudden determination to do great deeds (*aliquid . . . invadere magnum*) in the Trojans' hour of trial:

> *Nisus ait: 'dine hunc ardorem mentibus addunt,*
> *Euryale, an sua cuique deus fit dira cupido? . . .'* (9. 184 – 5)

Nisus said: 'Do the gods put such enthusiasm in our hearts, Euryalus, or is each man's fierce passion his own god?'

There is one passage in the *Aeneid* in which the exposition of a religious belief is presented in specifically didactic fashion: this is when the ghost of Anchises in the underworld explains to Aeneas the nature of life after death. This systematic account of the afterlife does indeed serve the plot, because it is needed to explain the presence of the ghosts of future Roman heroes at the river of Lethe, but it is primarily a religious message to the Roman reader, in some places reminiscent in style of the didactic method of Lucretius, and strongly coloured with the Stoic ideas which Virgil had come to find more acceptable than Lucretius' Epicureanism. Here is the passage:

> *Principio caelum ac terras camposque linquentis*
> *lucentemque globum lunae Titaniaque astra*
> *spiritus intus alit, totamque infusa per artus*
> *mens agitat molem et magno se corpore miscet.*

inde hominum pecudumque genus vitaeque volantum
et quae marmoreo fert monstra sub aequore pontus.
igneus est ollis vigor et caelestis origo
seminibus, quantum non noxia corpora tardant
terrenique hebetant artus moribundaque membra.
hinc metuunt cupiuntque, dolent gaudentque, neque auras
dispiciunt clausae tenebris et carcere caeco.
quin et supremo cum lumine vita reliquit
non tamen omne malum miseris nec funditus omnes
corporeae excedunt pestes penitusque necesse est
multa diu concreta modis inolescere miris.
ergo exercentur poenis veterumque malorum
supplicia expendunt: aliae panduntur inanes
suspensae ad ventos, aliis sub gurgite vasto
infectum eluitur scelus aut exuritur igni.
quisque suos patimur manis; exinde per amplum
mittimur Elysium et pauci laeta arva tenemus
donec longa dies perfecto temporis orbe
concretam exemit labem, purumque relinquit
aetherium sensum atque aurai simplicis ignem.
has omnis, ubi mille rotam volvere per annos,
Lethaeum ad fluvium deus evocat agmine magno,
scilicet immemores supera ut convexa revisant
rursus, et incipiant in corpora velle reverti.

(6. 724 – 51)

First of all an inner spirit nurtures the sky and the lands and the watery expanses and the shining globe of the moon and Titan's stars, and a mind pervading the parts sets the whole mass in motion and mingles with its mighty frame. From this mind comes the race of men and cattle, and the lives of the birds and the strange shapes which the sea bears beneath its smooth surface. Those life-seeds have a fiery strength and a heavenly origin in so far as their harmful bodies do not slow them, and their earthly frame and mortal limbs clog them. Because of their bodies men feel fear, desire, grief, joy, and they do not see the air of heaven, shut in as they are in the gloom of their dark prison. Indeed when life leaves them at the last light, it is still not the case that all evil or all their bodily taints disappear completely from wretched mortals, and it needs must be that many stains which have grown up with them over long years must be deeply ingrained in wondrous wise. Therefore they are disciplined with penalties, and they pay the price of their misdeeds of old: some are hung up and spread out to the empty winds, others have the stain of their crime washed out by a vast whirlpool or burned out by fire. We all endure our own ghosts; then we are sent through wide Elysium and a few of us stay in the happy fields until the long passage of time, as the cycle of the years is complete, removes the ingrown taint and leaves all unsullied the heavenly soul and the fire of pure spirit. All these others, when they have rolled the wheel of time through a thousand years, God calls forth in a long array to the River Lethe, so that they may again visit the vaults above, and begin to want to revert to bodily form.

The content of Anchises' speech is based on Orphic and Pythagorean ideas as refined by later Greek thinkers, especially Plato; and the essence of it is that this life is merely a preparation for a richer life to come, and that this richer life – here identified as Elysium – is ultimately available to all whose virtuous life on earth has earned it. This has already been seen in Virgil's comment (6. 660 – 4) on those who are living with Anchises in Elysium: there are not only those who suffered wounds for their country, or were virtuous priests or poets, or enriched life by their discoveries, but also 'those who made some others remember them by their service' (*quique sui memores aliquos fecere merendo*). Thus, in some way only dimly seen, virtue in this world is rewarded in the next. Throughout the *Aeneid* Virgil presents scenes in which the events seem inexplicable and unjust: it is fair to say that he offers the only answer to the confusion and sorrow of mortal life as being found in the world to come. It is not a confident answer: it is presented as the groping hope of a poet wrestling with the incomprehensible, not giving up in despair, but not able to proclaim with religious certainty a solution for the suffering with which his poem is so constantly preoccupied.

CHAPTER 8

The Influence of
the *Aeneid*

(i) THE ROMAN EMPIRE

During Virgil's lifetime and in the period immediately following his death the *Aeneid* had already become well known and famous as the national epic of Rome's resurgence under the new regime which Augustus had inaugurated. The story is told by Donatus (*Vita Vergilii*, 11) that when Virgil made visits to Rome he was pointed out and followed and had to seek shelter; and Tacitus (*Dialogus*, 13) records that on hearing a quotation from Virgil in a play at which he was present the audience rose to its feet and applauded him as it would have applauded Augustus himself.

Parts of the *Aeneid* had been read during the time of its composition to audiences including Augustus himself, and well before its publication after Virgil's death in 19 BC it was known to, and exercised an influence upon, the leading literary figures of the time, for example Livy, Horace, Propertius and Tibullus. Propertius refers to it specifically in terms of high praise:

> *cedite Romani scriptores, cedite Grai!*
> *nescio quid maius nascitur Iliade.*
>
> (2. 34. 65 – 6)

Bow down, you writers of Rome and of Greece.
There is something coming to birth greater than the *Iliad*.

Livy, especially in the early books of his history, used poetic phrases based on the *Aeneid* (for example, in his account of the sack of Alba Longa, 1. 29). Horace was a close friend of Virgil (*Satires*, 1. 5. 40 ff., 1. 6. 54 ff.) and knew his poetry well (*Satires*, 1. 10. 45; compare *Epodes* 16 with *Eclogues* 4); *Odes* 3. 3 is explicitly reminiscent of Juno in the *Aeneid*. Tibullus, who died in the same year as Virgil, was much influenced by the *Eclogues* and the *Georgics* and has sometimes, because of his gentle sensitivity, been called a lesser Virgil. Quotations from Virgil by leading orators, contemporary or near-contemporary, are attested by the elder Seneca (for example, *Suasoriae*, 3. 4 ff.).

A few years later than Virgil's own generation Ovid, a poet of a totally different outlook, was greatly influenced in many ways by Virgil. The movement of his hexameter, though much lighter and less varied than Virgil's, owed a great deal to Rome's greatest master of metre and poetic diction. Echoes of Virgil are everywhere to be found (for example, cf. *Tristia*, 1. 3, with *Aen.* 2), and Ovid pays explicit tribute a number of times:

> *Tityrus et fruges Aeneiaque arma legentur*
> *Roma triumphati dum caput orbis erit*
> (*Amores*, 1. 15. 25 – 6)

Tityrus and corn crops and the wars of Aeneas will be read as long as Rome shall be head of the conquered world.

See also *Ars Amatoria*, 3. 39 – 40, and *Remedia Amoris*, 396.

Like many subsequent readers Ovid was particularly moved by the story of Dido, and *Heroides* 7 is an Ovidian adaptation – with totally different emphasis – of *Aeneid* 4. Indeed in his attempts to defend himself to Augustus against the charge of writing too freely on the subject of love (which had led to his exile) Ovid says:

> *et tamen ille tuae felix Aeneidos auctor*
> *contulit in Tyrios arma virumque toros.*
> (*Tristia*, 2. 533 – 4)

And yet the glorious author of your *Aeneid* brought his 'Arms and the man' to bed in Carthage.

It is not possible here to describe in detail the enormous influence of Virgil during the remaining centuries of the Roman Empire, but some indication can briefly be given of the all-pervading effect which his poetry, most especially the *Aeneid*, had in many different areas. His poems immediately became school textbooks, thumbed and learned by heart by generations of Roman children (Suetonius, *De Grammaticis*, 16; Juvenal, 7. 227), even at a very early stage (Quintilian, *Institutes of Oratory*, 1. 8. 5). Domitius Afer is quoted by Quintilian as placing Virgil second only to Homer and 'much nearer to first than third' (10. 1. 86), while Quintilian himself puts Homer and Virgil together as representing the peaks of poetry (12. 11. 26). Grammarians and scholiasts, such as Asper and Probus, wrote commentaries on his poems, and his impact on Roman education at every level, from the correct usage of language to literary appreciation of the highest qualities of poetry, was immeasurable.

All of the outstanding Latin authors of the Silver Age reveal the influence which Virgil had over them, most obviously the four epic poets of the first century AD. In their different ways, and in different degrees, they try to match the movement of the Virgilian hexameter either directly or as modified by Ovid; they use Virgil's epic devices and techniques and very often his actual phrases. A partial exception to this generalization is the earliest of the four, Lucan (AD 39 – 65). His unfinished poem *De Bello Civili*, on the civil war between Caesar and Pompey, was in some sense an anti-*Aeneid*, designed to show not the glory of Rome's past history but the utter corruption and vicious power-seeking of the leading figures. Lucan was a Stoic and was one of the conspirators against the excesses of the emperor Nero; he paid with his life for his anti-imperialist views. His poem is filled with cynicism and horror, and this is expressed in terse epigrammatical form which makes the movement of his hexameter and the perpetually rhetorical impact of his diction very different from Virgil's. Nevertheless such was Virgil's influence upon the techniques of using the Latin language that there are in fact innumerable verbal reminiscences of Virgil in a poem which is very unlike the *Aeneid*.

Valerius Flaccus (*fl. c.* AD 90) wrote an unfinished epic entitled *Argonautica* in which he did his utmost to be Virgilian in every possible aspect. The diction and the metre are quite successful, sometimes highly successful, imitations of Virgil. Whole episodes and characters are based on his model; his most successful section, on the love of Medea and Jason, owes much to Virgil's story of Dido and Aeneas, but lacks the power and depth of his original. The surface of Valerius' poem is, thanks to Virgil, attractive; but beneath the surface of the story there is nothing to correspond with, or even to emulate, the exploration of the human condition with which the *Aeneid* constantly struggles.

Statius (*fl. c.* AD 90) wrote various occasional poems (the *Silvae*) and a completed epic (the *Thebaid*), and began a second epic (the *Achilleid*). His theme in the *Thebaid* – the horrors of the Oedipus saga – is not a Roman one (in this he is like Valerius, unlike Lucan and Silius), but he aims to use the methods of the *Aeneid* to explore the nature of human behaviour in times of crisis, and the poem has a penetration which Valerius and Silius lack. Statius' command of the Virgilian hexameter, modified by the influence of Ovid, is of a high quality, and some of his descriptive passages are very memorable. His influence on antiquity and on the Middle Ages and afterwards (on Dante, Chaucer, Spenser, for example) was much greater than that of Valerius or Silius. His use of Virgilian epic techniques is all-pervasive (funeral games, descent to the underworld, catalogues of forces, Olympian deities, etc.), and he acknowledges his debt to his master (which has been evident all the way through) at the end of the last book, when he invokes his poem and says:

> *nec tu divinam Aeneida tempta,*
> *sed longe sequere et vestigia semper adora.*
> (*Thebaid*, 12. 816 – 7)

And do not rival the divine *Aeneid*, but follow far behind, and always revere the footsteps you tread in.

Silius Italicus (*fl. c.* AD 90) was the most imitative of all Virgil's followers. His *Punica*, an epic about the Second Punic War in seventeen books, is perhaps the least read of surviving Classical Latin poems. It consists of an earnest patchwork of Virgilian and Ovidian diction, with all the traditional epic machinery; his Olympian deities mingle most inappropriately with the historical subject-matter. There are some successful descriptive passages, but when Pliny commented that the *Punica* was written *maiore cura quam ingenio* ('with more diligence than talent') he was certainly not unfair. Silius' devoted admiration for Virgil is reflected not only in his literary efforts at emulation, but in his life itself: he is said to have celebrated Virgil's birthday with more ceremony than his own, and to have worshipped at Virgil's tomb as if at a shrine (Pliny, *Epistles* 3. 7).

It is interesting to reflect on these epigoni of Virgil, whose whole attitude (with the exception of Lucan, whose 'imitation' was different) was to aim to do the same again and to come second to Virgil. The contrast of the Roman Silver Age in this respect with the Greek Alexandrian poets of the third century BC is notable. The poets of both periods felt that they were successors to a heritage in which everything outstanding that could be done in the major genres had already been done. The Romans in many cases reacted by trying to do the same again in a second-rate way; the Greeks (for the most part) determined to seek new forms and a new spirit, and in various ways they succeeded – Theocritus originated the kind of poetry which we call pastoral, and Callimachus with his epigrams, elegies and epyllia produced something very different from the Classical Greek achievements. But the Roman epic poets wished to continue the Virgilian heritage although they knew that they could not equal it, and their survival for two thousand years indicates that their lack of originality was counter-balanced to some extent by other positive poetic qualities, mostly inspired by Virgil.

It was not only the epic poets who were influenced by Virgil: the didactic *Astronomica* of Manilius has echoes of him, and the light-hearted epigrammatist Martial has imitations of phraseology and references to Virgil's fame (including a terse suggestion that Virgil was luckier in his patrons than Martial himself was). The brilliant satirist Juvenal quotes and parodies Virgil, and assumes in his readers a familiarity with the *Aeneid* which he can take for granted. His training in the effective and rhetorical use of language, in which Virgil would have figured predominantly, helps to account for the fact that in Juvenal's hands the genre of satire was raised to an almost epic tone and dimension (so utterly unlike the informal and chatty style which Horace had preferred).

The prose writers of the Silver Age, too, were deeply imbued with Virgil's poetry, both because of the educational system in which Virgil played so large a part (as is frequently indicated, with total approval, by Quintilian) and because individually they admired his work for a variety of reasons. He is quoted again and again (much more often than any other author) by the younger Seneca in order to illustrate his religious and moralizing tracts; he is regarded by the elder Pliny as a vital source for much of the scientific information offered in the *Natural History*; he is cited often by the younger Pliny in his elegantly artificial letters; the *Georgics* are used extensively in the prose books of Columella's *Res Rustica*, and the single verse book of this work is inspired by Virgil's statement (*Geo.* 4. 147 – 8) that he leaves the subject of gardens for someone in the future to write about. Finally, the greatest prose writer of the age, the historian Tacitus, has echoes of Virgilian phrases, and his style is often influenced by Virgil's diction (for example, cf. *Annals*, 2. 23 – 4, with *Aen*. 1. 102 ff.).

When we look back over the first three or four generations after Virgil's death it is hard not to be astonished at the enormous dominance which he (far more than other distinguished Latin writers) exercised over all literature. The only figure in Classical literature comparable with him in reputation was Homer: but the very early period at which Homer wrote, and the artificial Greek which he employed, made him generally a subject for admiration, not imitation (except in so far as epic poets, especially Virgil himself, used techniques and episodes originating with Homer). But Virgil provided a basis of grammatical structure and rhetorical expression from which the Romans learned to handle their own language; and he presented national and moral sentiments and attitudes of which his successors were proud to be the inheritors.

During the remainder of the Classical period, from the second to the fifth century AD, Virgil's supremacy in Roman education and literature remained unchallenged. We hear of isolated criticisms of him from the earliest days (Donatus, *Vita Vergilii*, 43 ff.), but these seem to have had little or no support, and the grammarians and commentators continue to quote and expound him as the unquestioned master of language and learning. He figures largely in the philological discussions in Aulus Gellius' *Attic Nights* (second century) and we can gather from the latter and other sources, especially the commentary by Servius, much of the Virgilian scholarship of grammarians and commentators whose works are now lost, such as Hyginus, Probus, Asper, and Aelius Donatus (whose commentary on Terence, second to Virgil in educational popularity, still survives). The extant life of Virgil already referred to is attributed by some to Suetonius but was more probably the introduction to Donatus' lost commentary on Virgil. There also survives a rhetorical commentary on Virgil by Tiberius Claudius Donatus (late fourth century) which paraphrases the *Aeneid* in a very pedestrian way.

By far our most valuable source of information about Virgil in antiquity is the commentary of Servius (*c.* 420 AD; this also survives in an expanded form, supplemented by later commentators and generally called Servius *auctus* or Servius Danielis (after the first editor of the longer version, 1600 AD). For Servius Virgil is not merely the supreme authority on diction and grammar (in its widest sense), not merely the outstanding mouthpiece of the greatness of Rome's traditions, not merely the master of all the techniques of the highest form of poetry (the epic), but also a repository of learning of every kind, religious, philosophical, mythological, historical, antiquarian, geographical and so on. All the branches of scholarly knowledge known to the ancient world were to be found embodied in the work of the master. Virgil has become not merely the master poet, but a complete encyclopaedia of the Roman world. Servius was not what we would now regard as a penetrating literary critic, but he was determined to explain his author to the best of his ability, and to defend him against any accusations of incorrectness; he did battle with any critics of Virgil who had alleged that there were flaws (even if minute ones) in the master's perfection. Servius defended him in every area, sometimes tortuously but always with total devotion.

Roughly contemporary with Servius was Macrobius, whose *Saturnalia* contains in seven books an account of discussions held among a group of scholars (including Servius) at the festival of *Saturnalia*. These ranged over various topics, but are predominantly

(Books 3 – 6) concerned with Virgil. Much of the time is taken up with the citation of passages from Virgil in which he has imitated Homer or the Greek tragedians, or earlier Roman writers such as Ennius and Lucretius; often the conclusion is drawn that Virgil has improved on his original. Throughout there is insistence that Virgil was 'expert in all branches of knowledge' (*omnium disciplinarum peritus, Saturnalia,* 1. 16. 12), and most specifically at the start of the fifth book one of the participants in the discussion says that in the art of the best use of words and expressions Virgil surpasses everyone including Cicero, because he commands all types of diction and rhetoric – *facundia Mantuani multiplex et multiformis est et dicendi genus omne complectitur.* There are, he says, four types of style: the ample, in which Cicero excels, the brief (Sallust), the dry (Fronto), the florid (Pliny the Younger); but Virgil has all four, and he proceeds to give examples.

These are some of the chief indications of the nature and extent of Virgil's influence on literature and education up to the time of the collapse of the Roman Empire in the West. Much more could be said – about Virgil's influence on the style and thought of early Christian prose writers such as Augustine and Jerome; on the versification of Christian poets such as Juvencus, Paulinus and especially Prudentius, whose allegorical poetry had so great an impact on subsequent literature; on the pagan poet Claudian, who wrote (at a time when the barbarians were closing in on Rome) as if he were living in the Augustan age; on Ausonius, whose many poetic endeavours included a Virgilian cento (*Cento Nuptialis*), i.e. a poem made up entirely of Virgilian lines and phrases adapted to a new context (a melancholy practice which had originated earlier and was to continue into medieval times). The idea of Virgil as a magical prophet, which was to become dominant in the later Middle Ages, had already begun with the practice (said to have been used by the Emperor Hadrian) of consulting the *sortes Vergilianae,* that is of opening a text of Virgil at random to seek guidance for the future.

This enormous admiration for Virgil, still undiminished in the fourth and fifth centuries AD, is perhaps most powerfully illustrated by the manuscripts of his poems which have survived. By far the greater number of Latin authors do not survive in manuscripts earlier than the ninth or tenth century, and in some cases the earliest manuscript is from the fourteenth or fifteenth century. No other author has more than one manuscript from as early as the fifth century, but Virgil has three almost complete as well as long fragments from several others of this early date. And Virgil's popularity, as we shall see, was destined to continue unabated, well ahead of all other Classical Latin authors, up to the present time.

(ii) THE MIDDLE AGES

During the thousand years between the downfall of the Roman Empire and the beginning of the Renaissance the preservation of western culture and learning depended to a large extent upon the monks in Christian monasteries. Their attention was concentrated rather on Christian religious writings and ritual than on pagan Classical authors, but the latter continued to be read and studied, and Virgil still remained by far the most popular of them. This was above all because he traditionally supplied a very large part of the grammatical and rhetorical training necessary to sustain the Latin language as a main instrument of cultural and religious expression. But there were other powerful reasons too, connected with Christian beliefs.

Virgil's fourth *Eclogue* (40 BC) is a short poem foretelling the birth of a child destined to inaugurate a new golden age when all sin and strife will have passed away. It is a poem of hope and optimism, connected with the mystic Sibylline prophecies of the East, and the medieval interpretation of this poem (already proclaimed by Constantine and Lactantius) led to Virgil's being widely regarded as a pre-Christian prophet, in some ways comparable with Isaiah. It is still disputed for what particular occasion, if any, the poem was written, but very widely in the Middle Ages and indeed often afterwards it was thought to be a vision of the coming birth of Christ, and it is frequently referred to as the Messianic *Eclogue*. The legend arose that St Paul, looking upon the tomb of Virgil, exclaimed:

> *quem te, inquit, reddidissem*
> *si te vivum invenissem*
> *poetarum maxime.*

What would I have made of you, he said, if I had found you alive, greatest of poets.   (Comparetti, p. 98)

Here are some lines from the fourth *Eclogue*:
> *tu modo nascenti puero, quo ferrea primum*
> *desinet et toto surget gens aurea mundo,*
> *casta fave, Lucina . . .*   (8 – 10)

Do you, chaste Lucina, goddess of childbirth smile upon the child because of whom the iron race shall disappear and a golden race will grow up through all the world . . .

and

> *si qua manent sceleris vestigia nostri*
> *inrita perpetua solvent formidine terras.*
>
> (13 – 14)

Any traces of our sin which remain shall be made void and thus free the earth from fear for ever.

and

> *aspice venturo laetentur ut omnia saeclo!*   (52)

See how everything rejoices at the age that is to come.

A second reason for special Christian interest in Virgil was that Aeneas' quest to found Rome was seen as a kind of Pilgrim's Progress, with the hero passing through various stages and various temptations in his determination to reach the promised land. There are indeed many aspects of Aeneas which suggest the Christian soldier: he has dedicated his life to the divine purpose, subduing his own personal inclinations in order to follow the greater goal; he is scrupulous in prayer and religious rites and he is frequently given divine help at times when it seems that his own human strength is too frail; in a very real sense he has accepted a mission to become a man of God. It is possible to press this point too far: Aeneas differs from the Christian hero in that his divine revelation does not convert him to a state of absolute confidence; it is a dim and faintly grasped concept which only gradually and partially is revealed to him throughout the poem. Nevertheless the parallel is close enough for the pious scholars of the Middle Ages to have accepted that Virgil, in addition to providing the most valuable training available in the use of the Latin language, was closer to Christian beliefs than any other pagan author.

Thirdly, the mission which Aeneas had to fulfil was to bring about the foundation not of some half-forgotten city of antiquity but of Rome itself, of the city which was the centre of the Holy Roman Empire, the seat of the popes, God's chosen rulers of western Christendom.

One of the outstanding features of medieval approaches to the *Aeneid* was interpretation of the poem by means of highly elaborate allegory. There had been a certain amount of allegorization in Classical times, especially of Homer by the Stoics, but the length to which this was now carried in the case of Virgil may be illustrated from Fulgentius, who in the sixth century wrote a work, which survives, entitled *De Continentia Vergilii*. This makes much play with the most unlikely etymological derivations in order to allegorize the characters – for example, Turnus is from the Greek *thuros nous* ('frenzied mind'), and Lavinia from *laborum via* ('the way of toil'). The whole work purports to show how the successive books of the *Aeneid* represent the stages of a man's pilgrimage through life. The stormy scenes of Book 1 represent the storms of infancy, the adventures of Books 2 and 3 the delights of the young in excitement, the love-story of Book 4 the growing man, the games of Book 5 the exercise of the body, the descent to the underworld in Book 6 the introduction to the mysteries of religious knowledge – and so on to the end.

This kind of allegorization persisted throughout the period, for example by Bernardus Silvestris, and is powerfully expressed again by John of Salisbury in the twelfth century, this time with reference only to the first six books of the *Aeneid*, and with greater emphasis on the philosophical content of the poem.

Side by side with the literary tradition of Virgil during the Middle Ages there grew up in popular folk-lore a series of stories about Virgil's magical powers. These originated in Naples (where Virgil was buried) and became more and more widespread, producing a cult of the poet in which he was regarded as a wizard: he invented a magic mirror which could reveal events happening far away; he built a butcher's block which could keep meat fresh indefinitely; he made a bronze fly to keep away the plagues of ordinary flies from Naples. These and many other similar fantastic stories are recounted and discussed by Comparetti and Spargo.

A different slant to the literary influence of Virgil began to be evident from the twelfth and thirteenth centuries onwards, with the increasing popularization of the Troy legend, as transmitted in prose by Dictys and Dares and later by William of Malmesbury and Geoffrey of Monmouth. This version was greatly expanded from Homer and Virgil, and in particular was given added love interest. Thus the section of the *Aeneid* which particularly appealed was the story of Aeneas and Dido, and this was transplanted (especially in France and Germany) into romances of chivalrous court poetry; and it was this aspect of the *Aeneid* which greatly influenced Chaucer.

Chaucer certainly knew the *Aeneid* in the original: there are references to it in the *Canterbury Tales*, and the first book of the *House of Fame* is an account of paintings seen in a dream in the temple of Venus, which are illustrations of the story of the *Aeneid* with special emphasis on Dido. It is introduced with a translation of the beginning of the *Aeneid*:

'I wol now singen, yif I kan,
The armes, and also the man
That first cam, thurgh his destinee,
Fugityf of Troy contree,
In Itayle, with ful moche pyne
Unto the strondes of Lavyne.'

(*House of Fame*, 1. 143 – 8)

Chaucer pursued his interest in the Dido story, as he could adapt it for his quite different romantic treatment, by writing a complete poem about her – the *Legend of Dido*. In this, typically of the times, Aeneas is seen as a false lover, a traitor, and Dido as a gentle and beautiful heroine of romance.

The greatest literary figure of all Virgil's disciples lived a century before Chaucer, but his appreciation of Virgil, though medieval in many ways, was of a less restricted kind and looks forward in certain respects to the Renaissance. More than any of his predecessors Dante recognized in Virgil a fellow-poet with a view of the world which expressed a wide-ranging appreciation of universal aspirations and ideals, a kind of combination of the spiritual and the rational, expressed in a severely disciplined art form. Virgil for him was not so much a source from which to draw but rather a kindred spirit whose poetical insight into the deepest of human problems was an inspiration, based as it was upon a profound understanding which corresponded with Dante's own passionate desire for learning. Dante does not have a very considerable number of verbal or episodic similarities with the *Aeneid* (with the exception of *Aeneid* 6); the debt he owes is larger and less definable.

The *Divine Comedy* is an account of Dante's journey through Hell and Purgatory to Paradise, and for his guide he chose the pagan Virgil, who conducts him all the way to the very gate of Paradise, where he gives way to Statius, whom Dante regarded (erroneously) as a Christian. When Dante says to Virgil, 'You alone are he from whom I took that beautiful style which has brought me honour' (*Inferno*, I. 85 – 7), he does not mean 'style' in its narrower technical sense: Dante's style is far less elevated than Virgil's. He means that Virgil's way of expressing by means of poetry the fundamental issues of human behaviour in relation both to worldly affairs and to spiritual ideals has deeply influenced him to do the same thing in a different way.

There are other more specific, though not more important, reasons which must have led Dante to choose Virgil as his 'master' and his 'guide'. First, as we have seen, Virgil was regarded (because of the Messianic *Eclogue* and the religious and moral values of the

Aeneid) as a prophet of Christ, as the pagan who was nearest of all to Christianity. This view had prevailed throughout the Middle Ages in the allegorization of Aeneas' pilgrimage through life in search of fuller communication with the divine; and Dante was sufficiently a child of his time to be influenced by this interpretation.

Secondly Virgil's poem was a national one about the glory of Rome and its Empire, about the ultimate suppression of civil war and opposition to ordered authority, under a stable government such as Dante longed for in his own time. It is of course true that the *Aeneid* shows many doubts about how justified Aeneas was in his actions, and about how glorious the predicted golden age would be, and that it is full of pity for those who suffer because they do not, or will not, fit into the scheme (with Dante, indignation rather than pity rules). But nevertheless Dante could read the *Aeneid* as the optimistic presentation of how the Romans (symbolized by Aeneas) had gradually learned to govern and, through imperial rule, to civilize. What is more, the *Aeneid* was about Dante's own country; and the pagan period of which Virgil wrote led directly to the Holy Roman Empire about whose present and future organization Dante was so deeply concerned. The *Aeneid* therefore, as a prefiguration of the Roman Empire, shed light for Dante both on the spiritual qualities which had prepared the way for Christianity and on the conditions of enlightened temporal authority which could make the true spiritual life possible.

(iii) FROM THE RENAISSANCE TO MILTON

With the beginning of the Renaissance and the rediscovery in the West of Greek literature and of many more Latin authors whose work had been neglected or lost, Virgil's position of eminence among the ancients did not change. Petrarch quotes him in his prose works more often than any other Latin poet, and his unfinished Latin epic about Scipio (the *Africa*) closely follows Virgilian techniques and diction. Boccaccio's epic in Italian, the *Theseid*, is said to have been started in the shadow of Virgil's tomb. Much later, in the sixteenth century, Vida's *Christiad* aimed to use Virgilian epic techniques (as he had strongly advocated in his *Ars Poetica*), and Ronsard's *Franciad* set out to be a second *Aeneid*. Much more successful adaptations of the *Aeneid's* methods came about this time from Camoens (the *Lusiads*) and Tasso (*Liberation of Jerusalem*). But from the beginning of the Renaissance in the fourteenth century it was not until Milton, in the seventeenth, and never again since, that the Classical epic of Homer and Virgil was rivalled in a modern language.

Translations of the *Aeneid* into various modern languages began to appear in the fifteenth century, and the first complete British verse translation to appear was by the Scot Gavin Douglas (1553), a vigorous rendering which is highly thought of by modern Virgilians. This was followed by a number of English versions of varying merit (Phaer, Stanyhurst, Surrey), and Virgil was now available to English readers who could not or would not read him in Latin. For those who could, it is said that there were more than ninety printed editions before 1580.

Edmund Spenser had no need of translations as he set out to adapt, as Ariosto had in Italian, some of the techniques and episodes of the *Aeneid* to his romantic 'epic', the *Faerie Queene* (1579 – 96). The poem shows many of the aspects of later medieval literature – fondness for allegory and moralizing, courtly chivalry and romance – so that in some respects it recalls Chaucer's (much more limited) use of Virgil in the *House of Fame* and the *Legend of Dido*. Spenser had already shown his fondness for Virgil's *Eclogues* in the *Shepheardes Calendar*, and a few examples of the attraction which Virgil's imaginative and descriptive passages had upon him in the *Faerie Queene* will suffice. The story of the Red Cross Knight (1. 2. 30 ff.) is based extremely closely on that of Polydorus (*Aen*. 3. 24 ff.); the meeting of Belphoebe and Trompart (2. 3. 32 ff.) recalls verbally the meeting of Aeneas and Venus (*Aen*. 1. 314 ff.); the description of the Rock of Vile Reproach and the Gulf of Greediness (2. 12. 3 ff.) is based on Virgil's Scylla and Charybdis (*Aen*. 3. 420 ff.).

Among the dramatists of the sixteenth century Christopher Marlowe wrote plays which (like his poetry) are soaked in Classical imagery, and one of them, *Dido Queen of Carthage*, follows the structure of Virgil's story very closely, with frequent Latin quotations from *Aeneid* 4. The play itself is as far removed from Virgil in spirit and ethos as could well be imagined.

It is well known that Shakespeare had 'small Latin and less Greek', but equally well known that the world of Greece and Rome made a tremendous impact on his imagination. His knowledge was partly derived from the all-pervasive impact of the Classical world and its history and mythology on his environment, on his friends, on his fellow authors, on the works of visual art around him, quite apart from the direct influence of the techniques of Greek drama reaching the Elizabethans through Seneca. But he also used at first hand translations of his favourite authors, such as Plutarch in North's translation or Ovid in Golding's, or sometimes the original (for it was Ovid whose poetry most captured his imagination and there is no doubt that he sometimes used his 'small Latin' as well as Golding's translation in order to read his favourite Latin poet).

There are some clear traces in the plays of a knowledge of the *Aeneid*, probably almost always through translations: a very famous one is

> In such a night
> Stood Dido with a willow in her hand
> Upon the wild sea-banks, and waft her love
> To come again to Carthage.
>
> (*Merchant of Venice*, 5. 1. 9 – 12)

Another is

> . . . conflict such as was suppos'd
> The wandering prince and Dido once enjoy'd
> When with a happy storm they were surpris'd
> And curtain'd with a counsel-keeping cave . . .
>
> (*Titus Andronicus*, 2. 3. 21 – 4)

But it would not be true to claim that Virgil was a major contributor to Shakespeare's love of the Graeco-Roman world.

Two generations later English literature was enriched by the last great writer of the traditional Classical epic. Milton ranks with Homer and Virgil both in the artistic use of the genre and in the high seriousness and sublimity of the theme. Prior to him the influence of the *Aeneid* on English literature had been mainly centred upon the imaginative, romantic and pictorial impact of parts of the poem. But in Milton's *Paradise Lost* Virgil is behind the language (indeed the very syntax), the structure, and most especially the intention to use epic poetry in order to explore at the highest possible level the nature of man's place in God's universe and the problems of right behaviour imposed by man's frailty. Of course much is new – Milton's focus is theological where Virgil's had been imperial and Homer's 'heroic'; and of course there had to be some different techniques (particularly because of the absence from Milton's poem of large numbers of human characters, and because of the difficulty of portraying religious figures so different from Homer's and Virgil's Olympian gods). The note of confident religious assertion in Milton (redemption in spite of sin) gave a new dimension in contrast with Homer's pessimism about the world after death and Virgil's tentative groping for some solution of man's spiritual destiny. But there is no question that Virgil shaped Milton's ultimate poetic ambition to be a great epic poet (there is ample evidence that all through his life he was preparing himself for this) and taught him many of the techniques by which the grandeur of his theme could be expressed.

To begin with small-scale imitation: examples of Milton's adaptation of Virgil's phraseology are very numerous, and it will suffice to cite three short ones:

> . . . *facilis descensus Averno:*
>
> (*Aen.* 6. 126)

Easy is the descent to Hell.

> . . . from hence a passage broad
> Smooth, easy, inoffensive down to Hell.
>
> (*Paradise Lost*, 10. 304 – 5)

> *ei mihi, qualis erat, quantum mutatus ab illo*
> *Hectore . . .*
>
> (*Aen.* 2. 274 – 5)

Alas, how he looked, how changed from that other Hector . . .

> If thou beest he – but oh how fallen, how changed
> From him . . .
>
> (*Paradise Lost*, 1. 84 – 5)

> *quam multa in silvis autumni frigore primo*
> *lapsa cadunt folia . . .*
>
> (*Aen.* 6. 309 – 10)

As many as in the woods at the first cold of autumn are the leaves which glide and fall . . .

> His legions, angel forms, who lay entranced,
> Thick as autumnal leaves that strow the brooks
> In Vallombrosa . . .   (*Paradise Lost*, 1. 301 – 3)

Longer passages include among many others the description of Sin (*Paradise Lost*, 2. 650 – 4; cf. *Aen.* 3. 426 – 8); the sports of the fallen angels (*Paradise Lost*, 2. 528 ff.; cf. *Aen.* 6. 642 ff., 653 ff.); the simile of the bees (*Paradise Lost*, 1. 768 ff.; cf. *Aen.* 1. 430 ff.).

More striking than these imitations of phraseology is the over-all aspect of Milton's style and use of language. In all sorts of ways he set about moving the English language, both in diction and in syntax, towards the Latin which he loved so well, and in which he wrote many of his shorter poems. Words are used in their Latin meaning (for example, *Paradise Lost*, 2. 706, 'more dreadful and deform' – *deformis* = ugly; *Paradise Lost*, 2. 51, 'my sentence is for open war' – *sententia* = vote). Latin participial constructions occur (for example, *Paradise Lost*,1. 573 'never since created man' = *post homines creatos*); there are often long sequences of elaborate subordinate clauses, and highly artificial word order is used, as if English too were an inflected language. All these combined to produce a unique kind of diction which not all critics have thought to be successful; it was at all events unique. F. R. Leavis, with some justification, said, 'The mind that invented Milton's grand style had renounced the English language', and T. S. Eliot very truthfully commented, 'In Milton there is always the maximal, never the minimal alteration in ordinary language'.

One very special feature of Milton's style, and one which he owed in large measure to Virgil, was the Latin nature of his versification. He very frequently used enjambement and mid-line stops in order to make the verse paragraph his unit rather than the single line (this is a feature in which Virgil had differed most markedly from his predecessors in hexameter verse, such as Ennuis, Catullus and Lucretius). Milton paid extreme attention, as the subject-matter might require, to the speed or slowness of the rhythm, and to the assonance and alliteration of vowels and consonants, so that Helen Darbishire has said of him: 'Never has poet known better than he that sound expresses sense'. But one poet did know this just as well, and perhaps better, and that was Milton's model, Virgil. Let us consider a passage from each: I take the pupil first, and then the master.

> From his slack hand the Garland wreathed for Eve
> Down drop'd, and all the faded Roses shed;
> Speechless he stood and pale, till thus at length
> First to himself he inward silence broke.
>   (*Paradise Lost*, 9. 892 ff.)

We notice first the preponderance of monosyllables, slowing the movement at this terrible moment when Eve tells Adam that she has eaten of the tree. The slow emphasis is stressed by assonance of *a* ('slack hand'), remarkable assonance of *e* ('wreathed for Eve'), and alliteration of the heavy consonant *d* ('down drop'd') echoed again in 'faded' and 'shed'. Notice too the way that the words struggle against the metre: in the first line the iambic rhythm does not emerge until the third foot – 'fróm his/sláck hánd/the Gár/land wreáthed/for Éve'. Similarly the second line opens with tremendous emphasis on the non-accented part of the foot, 'Dówn drop'd'; and in the third and fourth line the iambic rhythm is reversed in the first-foot trochees 'Speéchless he stood' and 'fírst to himself'. Both words gain great emphasis in this way and both significantly express Adam's utter consternation – at first he cannot speak at all, and then when he can it is 'fírst to himself' before he can bring himself to address Eve.

Now let us take a passage from Virgil: I have chosen it mainly to illustrate what I have just called in the Milton passage 'the words struggling against the metre'. It is part of Dido's speech to Aeneas when she realizes that he will not stay and in bitter anger curses him, rejecting his excuse of divine compulsion for his departure.

> *scilicet is superis labor est, ea cura quietos*
> *sollicitat. neque te teneo neque dicta refello:*
> *i, sequere Italiam ventis, pete regna per undas.*
>
> (Aen. 4. 379 ff.)

Oh yes of course that is work for the gods, care for such things disturbs their peace. I don't hold you back or refute your words – away, make for Italy on the winds, look for your kingdom over the waves.

We notice here of course the scornful hissing of *s* – *scilicet is superis labor est, ea cura quietos sollicitat* (Dido is being highly ironical), and the harsh consonants of the next phrase *neque te teneo neque dicta refello*; but what I want to draw attention to is the conflict between the pattern of the metre and the pronunciation of the words. Here Virgil had a great advantage over Milton. Milton's verse pattern is based, like all English poetry, on word accent, and so is the pronunciation of our words; but Virgil's verse pattern was based on the quantity of vowels (or syllables), while the pronunciation of the Latin words was based on accent. Thus Milton had to violate the pattern of iambic metre when he began a line with 'Speéchless', and clearly to do this through a large part of the line would destroy the pattern altogether. But Virgil had two rhythms available, the metrical pattern based on one thing (quantity) and the word pronunciation based on another (accent), and he could make them coincide or not according to his poetic requirement. Thus Dido begins with coincidence, *scílicet*, the ironical word introducing her anger, and then her words conflict with the metrical pattern to a very unusual degree:

> *Ís súpe/ris lábor / est éa/ . . .*
> *Sollíci/tat néque / te téne/o néque/ . . .*
> *Í séque/re Itáli/am vén/tis péte/ . . .*

It is the exploitation of this double rhythm which perhaps more than anything else makes the Virgilian hexameter a measure of such amazing musical variety. Milton appreciated it, and responded to it, and as far as – or even further than – English allowed he tried to imitate it.

Apart from the aspects of diction which have been illustrated, Milton was able to use and adapt many of the epic techniques, or 'machinery', which Virgil had used, often taken over by him from Homer. One example is the frequent employment by the characters of long and formally expressed speeches in order to clarify action or motivation and add variety to narrative. Another is the use of the elaborate simile, with its development beyond the actual point of comparison which Virgil had taken from Homer; this is often used by Milton in the way in which Virgil had used it, to link thematically both backwards and forwards with the movement of events as well as to give a vivid illustration from a different world of the specific situation. Again, as Homer had given a long catalogue of the Greek naval forces (end of *Iliad* 2) and Virgil one of the Italian contingents (end of *Aen.* 7), so Milton has a long catalogue of the fallen angels (*Paradise Lost*, 1. 376 ff.) introduced, as Homer's and Virgil's were, by a new invocation to the Muse.

An outstanding example of similarity of technique is the manipulation of the time-scale of the epic to extend both before and after the actual narrative. Milton begins his poem, as Virgil had done, by plunging *in media res*; and just as Virgil had a flashback (*Aen.* 2 and 3) in which events prior to the beginning of the poem were narrated, so Milton has Raphael expound to Adam (*Paradise Lost* 5, 6 and 7) the events which led to the expulsion of the fallen angels with whose plotting in Hell the poem began. Again, Virgil extends his time-scale forward to his own times by means of prophecy (*Aen.* 1 and 6) as well as by other devices; in Milton (*Paradise Lost* 11 and 12) Michael prophesies the events from the fall of Adam and Eve to the flood, and then beyond the flood to the coming of Christ, and beyond that again to the second coming.

One of Milton's problems was that the tradition of Homeric and Virgilian epic required the conflicts in the poem to be largely represented by means of heroic battle scenes. The *Iliad* is very much concerned with the readiness of the heroes to fight and to die for the ideals dear to them, and prowess on the battlefield is a pre-eminent status symbol. The last four books of the *Aeneid* represent both the Trojans and the Italians bravely and tragically fighting for their causes. Although Milton's theme did not require battle scenes as a necessary part of the plot, he so far conformed to the tradition of ancient epic as to introduce (*Paradise Lost* 6) a large-scale description of the battles in heaven.

But it was not primarily in any of these things (which I have categorized as verbal and structural) that Virgil's influence on Milton was greatest. It was greatest in convincing Milton that the highest work of literary art to which anyone could aspire was to convey in the traditional epic form matters of the highest moment concerned with the nature of man's moral behaviour and responsibility. For Homer the responsibility centred almost entirely on right and courageous action in this world for its own sake; for Virgil it extended gropingly into right action as a preparation for another world (only dimly imagined); for Milton it was something totally different, a confident proclamation of the eventual triumph of good over evil in a divinely ordered universe in which the goodness of God and the redemption of man's sin through his Redeemer was an unquestioned article of religious faith.

(iv) DRYDEN TO THE PRESENT DAY

In the late seventeenth and the eighteenth centuries idolization and imitation of the literature of the Greeks and Romans reached its highest point in England, as elsewhere in Europe (most notably France, where Boileau's *Art poétique* insisted on the supremacy of the ancient writers). The Roman authors exercised generally the greater influence, as the Greeks were destined to in the nineteenth century, and among the Romans Virgil (followed closely by Horace) was still pre-eminent. The *Eclogues*, 'the sweetest poems in the world', were beloved by Pope and many more. The *Georgics* produced a plethora of imitative didactic pieces on country life (Thomson's *Seasons*, Cowper's *The Task*); indeed they gave rise to a whole literary genre, indulged in by many minor poets, which can be called the English Georgic. Dryden, in an extravagant moment, classed the *Georgics* as 'the best poem of the best poet'. But the *Aeneid* was seen as the vaster work, and was endlessly discussed in comparison with Homer's poems, and its characteristics and moral messages preoccupied the great critics.

In 1697 Dryden published his translation of the *Aeneid*, a masterly work based on his conviction that a successful translation does not reflect the original (for it cannot), but seeks to recreate something as near as possible to the spirit and intention of the original. 'I have endeavoured', he said, 'to make Virgil speak such English as he would himself have spoken, if he had been born in England, and in this present age' (Ker, *Essays*, vol. 2, p. 228); and again, 'Lay by

Virgil . . . when you take my version' (Ker, *Essays*, vol. 2, p. 233).
He prefaced his translation with a long dedication in which he
analysed the literary qualities of the poem and found them fully to
correspond with those at which the greatest of poetry should aim.
First and basically he praised Virgil's techniques and judgement,
whether on the small scale ('the sweetness of the sound') or on the
larger scale, the structure of the various parts, the proper use of the
divine machinery, the characterization, the maintenance of the true
epic tone throughout, so that all things were 'grave, majestical, and
sublime'. In other words Virgil was a complete master of the 'rules'
of the genre (better indeed even than Homer).

But even more significant for Dryden than its technical perfection
was the great ethical and moral message which the *Aeneid* offered,
thereby fulfilling the proper aim of the epic ('the greatest work
which the soul of man is capable to perform'), namely 'to form the
mind to heroic virtue by example'. There were many ways in which
the political situation in England at this time resembled the
'restored' Rome under Augustus following the chaos of the civil
wars at the end of the republic. In the *Aeneid* Dryden saw Aeneas
as the perfect prince, a prototype of Augustus, who ruled his people
with benign authority and instilled into them a respect for him
which was able to 'confirm their obedience to him, and by that
obedience to make them happy'. For Dryden therefore the *Aeneid*
was essentially about patriotism and leadership and dedication to
the ideal of responsible exercise of authority. He was not unaware
of the pathos and sorrow of the poem, but he responded more to its
vigour, its robust portrayal of Roman leadership, its depiction of a
Trojan prince who for the benefit of his people and of all mankind
endured hardships and setbacks, but finally triumphed because of
unselfish devotion to his divinely appointed mission.

Dryden's view of the *Aeneid*, and his admiration of it because of
its stylistic perfection and its moral lessons, continued to hold the
field for several generations. This adulation of the critics and of the
leading authors of the time did not produce any new epic poetry of
the highest qualities, but it is reflected in countless translations,
complete or in part (Addison, Trapp, Pitt), and in imitation in poetry
of other genres, including by Dryden himself (perhaps especially in
Annus Mirabilis). It is also illustrated by the mock-epic burlesque
parodies of the *Aeneid* which were much in vogue at the time, such
as Cambridge's *Scribleriad*. Comparisons of Virgil with Homer
continued to be made, generally conceding to Homer a greater
power of invention and grandeur, but insisting on the more
controlled nature of Virgil's art, on his dignity and propriety in
maintaining at all times the required epic sublimity of style and

subject-matter. These points are elaborated in Pope's introduction to his translation of the *Iliad*: Homer is like the Nile in its overflow, Virgil like a river within its banks; Homer is the greater genius, Virgil the better artist. The nature of neo-Classical admiration is very well summed up in the adjectives chosen by Pope in his lines about Virgil in the *Temple of Fame*:

> The Mantuan there in sober triumph sate,
> Composed his posture and his look sedate.
>
> (200 – 1)

This neo-Classical passion for correctness of form and for a moral message in the poetry which they placed in the highest category was not shared by the literary revolutionaries of the Romantic movement. Towards the end of the eighteenth century voices began to be raised in strong criticism of the imitation of Classical models, and increasingly the concept of what poetry should aim at underwent change. Many writers thought that much of the poetry of the previous few generations had been stiffly imitative and dull, and as far as the Classical authors were concerned the Romans were the chief target of disapproval. Greek literature was felt to have been fresh, vivid, near to the springtime of the world; the Romans on the other hand were formal, prosaic, unexciting, and themselves imitators of the Greeks as neo-Classical English literature had been imitative of both.

In this climate of opinion Virgil came in for more sustained criticism than ever before or since. The most famous expression of disapprobation was Coleridge's question: 'If you take from Virgil his diction and metre, what do you leave him?' (*Specimens of the Table Talk*, 1851). Shelley preferred Lucan (a more revolutionary poet) to Virgil, while Byron called Virgil a 'harmonious plagiary and miserable flatterer', summing up in two rhetorical phrases the main Romantic objections to Virgil: that he was an imitator not an originator, and that he wrote not for himself but for Augustus. The hero of the *Aeneid* came in for very harsh criticism: Charles James Fox said that he 'sometimes excites interest against him, and never for him', and Dryden's admiration of the 'perfect prince' is countered by Thomas Green's comment, 'Aeneas exhibits few traits which either conciliate our affection or command our respect'. It is not hard to see why many of the Romantics disapproved of Aeneas as a hero: in their eyes he lacked grandeur and sparkle; he seemed a kind of depersonalized symbol, without individuality; he was a generalized character without vitality, indeed a kind of anti-hero, lacking 'heroics', and not in any way exciting the imagination.

These are some examples of a sharpness of criticism that was new in attitudes towards the *Aeneid*; but of course it should not be thought that Virgilian influence suddenly ceased or that his poetry was wholly out of favour. It continued to play a large part in the educational system, and to affect the way of thinking both of his severest critics and of those who continued to admire him. Wordsworth knew him very well, imitated him often, greatly appreciated the idea of Nature in the *Georgics*, and translated parts of the *Aeneid*. Keats's overpowering love of the ancient Greek world did not lead him to exclude the Roman authors, and he too translated some of the *Aeneid*. Landor was steeped in the *Aeneid*, imitated it on occasion and constantly discussed it, sometimes with blame, often with high praise.

A new direction was given to Virgilian appreciation in the middle of the nineteenth century when Sainte-Beuve delivered a series of lectures on the *Aeneid* (published as *Etude sur Virgile* in 1857). In these he placed the emphasis on the universality of Virgil's portrayal of the human condition and particularly on the tenderness and sensitivity of his sympathies. From that time until the present day Virgil has been seen predominantly as the poet of the world's sorrows, and probably the most frequently quoted line in the *Aeneid* has been *sunt lacrimae rerum et mentem mortalia tangunt* ('there are tears for what happens and mortal sufferings move men's hearts', *Aen.* 1. 462). This is a long way from Dryden's attitude of admiration for perfection of technique and rigour of characterization.

Throughout the Victorian period it was on the whole the pathos of the poem which appealed predominantly. Matthew Arnold, who was influenced by Greek authors rather more than by Latin, nevertheless was deeply moved by Virgil and speaks of 'an ineffable melancholy', 'a sweet, a touching sadness' ('On the Modern Element in Literature', 1857), and Myers coined the phrase which is nowadays much in favour: 'that accent of brooding sorrow' (*Essays Classical*, 1883). More than any other Victorian it was Tennyson who was profoundly influenced by Virgil.

Tennyson was sometimes called 'the English Virgil', an overstatement which is somewhat paradoxical as Tennyson wrote nothing that had any close similarity in its literary form and structure with Virgil's poetry (as did, for example, Pope with the *Eclogues*, Thomson with the *Georgics*, Milton with the *Aeneid*). But he was steeped in Virgil's poetry, he used phrases from Virgil again and again, and above all he found in Virgil a magical descriptive power in a world of poetic imagination, and his own poetry aimed at and sometimes achieved word-music of a haunting quality comparable with that of Virgil. His poem 'To Virgil', written at the request of the Mantuans to commemorate the nineteenth centenary of Virgil's death, not only expresses a most sincere and heart-felt admiration for the greatest of Mantua's sons but contains phrases which superbly describe the most essential qualities of Virgil's work: the mysterious spell of his diction and versification , and the basic conflict in the *Aeneid* between pathos ('sadness at the doubtful doom of human kind') and patriotic optimism ('. . . sound for ever of Imperial Rome'). Here is the poem:

Roman Virgil, thou that singest
   Ilion's lofty temples robed in fire,
Ilion falling, Rome arising,
   Wars, and filial faith, and Dido's pyre;

Landscape-lover, lord of language
   More than he that sang the Works and Days,
All the chosen coin of fancy
   Flashing out from many a golden phrase;

Thou that singest wheat and woodland,
   Tilth and vineyard, hive and horse and herd;
All the charm of all the Muses
   Often flowering in a lonely word;

Poet of the happy Tityrus
   Piping underneath his beechen bowers;
Poet of the poet-satyr
   Whom the laughing shepherd bound with flowers;

Chanter of the Pollio, glorying
   In the blissful years again to be,
Summers of the snakeless meadow,
   Unlaborious earth and oarless sea;

Thou that seest Universal
   Nature moved by Universal Mind;
Thou majestic in thy sadness
   At the doubtful doom of human kind;

Light among the vanished ages;
   Star that gildest yet this phantom shore;
Golden branch amid the shadows,
   Kings and realms that pass to rise no more;

> Now thy Forum roars no longer,
>   Fallen every purple Caesar's dome –
> Though thine ocean-roll of rhythm
>   Sound for ever of Imperial Rome –
>
> Now the Rome of slaves hath perished,
>   And the Rome of freemen holds her place,
> I, from out the Northern Island
>   Sundered once from all the human race,
>
> I salute thee, Mantovano,
>   I that loved thee since my day began,
> Wielder of the stateliest measure
>   Ever moulded by the lips of man.

(v) EPILOGUE

During the twentieth century, especially the second half of it, the place of the Classical languages in the educational system has rapidly become less dominant, and therefore the direct influence of Virgil less pervasive. But this trend has been accompanied by a widespread interest in Greek and Latin literature, acquired by means of translations and explanatory books, and strengthened by original works based on material from Classical authors. Hermann Broch's psychological study, *The Death of Virgil* (1945), and Cyril Connolly's *The Unquiet Grave* (1944) are two Virgilian examples of the latter category. Translations of Virgil into English have appeared in very large numbers, including a masterly version by the then Poet Laureate, C. Day Lewis; works of critical appreciation have proliferated, especially in the last twenty or thirty years, and it is a very safe guess that far more published material has appeared during this time about Virgil than about any other Roman author. There is a Virgil Society in England and a Vergilian Society in America, both of which produce important journals. There were congresses and ceremonial occasions in many countries to mark the bimillenary of Virgil's death, and the exhibition at the British Library was accompanied by a commemorative book entitled *Virgil: His Poetry through the Ages* (1982). The *Aeneid* now, as it was two thousand years ago, is the most thumbed Latin text in the schools.

The reasons why this should have been so have been discussed at length in the earlier chapters; they may be summed up by saying that the *Aeneid* has a most remarkable multiplicity of literary qualities, and that its values and its sympathies are presented with extraordinary sensitivity and insight into man's problems, both as an individual and as a member of society. Nothing is falsified in the interest of a *parti pris*; we are led one way and another in our thoughts; we are studying a poem of honest and honourable ambivalence. In T. R. Glover's fine phrase, 'There is a wavering about the whole poem' (*Virgil*, 1923). In many ways indeed, as the Victorians insisted and as many modern commentators maintain, it is a poem of sorrow; but in many ways too it is a poem of the glory of the Roman vision of a golden age for the world. It deals indeed with the plight of the human condition, but it proclaims the aspirations and achievements upon which modern civilization is founded. In the words of T. S. Eliot, who was president of the Classical Association in 1942 and of the Virgil Society in 1944, Virgil's work represents 'central European values', and 'led Europe towards the Christian culture which he could never know' ('What is a Classic?'' [1944] 1957); and again, Virgil's 'concept of destiny leaves us with a mystery, but it is a mystery not contrary to reason, for it implies that the world, and the course of human history, have meaning' ('*Virgil and the Christian World*', 1957).

BIBLIOGRAPHY AND BRIEF CRITICAL SURVEY

The following is a selective bibliography taken from the mass of material on the *Aeneid* which has appeared in recent years. Some additional references with comments may be found in my *Greece and Rome, New Surveys in the Classics*, no. 1, *Virgil* (Oxford, 1967; 2nd edn with addenda, 1979). For fuller information, see E. J. Kenney and W. V. Clausen (eds) *The Cambridge History of Classical Literature*, vol. 2 (Cambridge, 1982), pp. 846 ff., and the yearly lists in *L'Année philologique* and *Vergilius*.

1 TEXTS

Broadly speaking the text of the *Aeneid* is in an excellent state of preservation. We possess a number of manuscripts from the fourth and fifth centuries along with many citations in early authors and the commentary of Servius. The work of collating and reporting the MSS has been most thoroughly done, especially by Ribbeck, Goelzer and Sabbadini: and the points of difficulty are mainly concerned with a choice between two well-attested readings.

The standard modern text is the Oxford Classical Text edited by Sir Roger Mynors (Oxford, 1969; 2nd edn 1972), which replaces the previous OCT edition by Hirtzel (1900). The Loeb edition (with facing English translation) is by H. R. Fairclough (2nd edn, London and Cambridge, Mass., 1934 – 5). The most detailed modern edition (with very full *apparatus criticus* and ancient *testimonia*) is by M. Geymonat (Corpus Paravianum, Turin, 1973), which is based on Sabbadini's Rome edition of 1930 and 1937 revised by Castiglioni.

2 COMMENTARIES

The extensive and learned fourth-century commentary by Servius is available in modern editions. Important and detailed editions of individual books have appeared in the last twenty years, especially from the Clarendon Press, Oxford. Commentaries on the whole *Aeneid* are: Servius, ed. Thilo and Hagen (Leipzig, 1878 – 1902), and *edit. Harvard.* (*Aen* i – v, American Philological Association, Lancaster, Penn., 1946 – 65); J. Henry, *Aeneidea* (London and Edinburgh, 1873); Conington and Nettleship (London, 1858 – 81); T. E. Page (London, 1894 – 1900); J. W. Mackail (Oxford, 1930); R. D. Williams (London, 1972 – 3).

3 TRANSLATIONS

The last twenty years have seen a number of excellent translations: in verse, attempts have been made to make Virgil speak the kind of English he would have spoken had he been a mid-twentieth-century Englishman or American. In prose Jackson Knight's Penguin translation renders faithfully and accurately the meaning of Virgil in a more modern idiom than Mackail or Fairclough.

Verse: Dryden: (1697); R. Humphries (New York, 1951); C. Day Lewis (London, 1952); A. Mandelbaum (Berkeley, Calif., 1971); R. Fitzgerald (London, 1984).

Prose: J. W. Mackail (London, 1908); H. R. Fairclough (Loeb, 1934–5); W. F. Jackson Knight (Harmondsworth, 1955).

Of the moderns C. Day Lewis seems to me the best. For an account of early translations into English see J. Conington, *Miscellaneous Writings*, vol. 1, *The English Translators of Virgil* (1872).

4 LITERARY CRITICISM

Sainte-Beuve's *Etude sur Virgile* has proved to be the model and foundation for literary criticism of Virgil in the past hundred years. In response to the feeling of nineteenth-century critics that the ideals of the Augustan age were prosaic, he insisted on the universal aspect of Virgil's work, putting the emphasis on Virgil's sensitivity of feeling, his pity, his universal humanity. Sellar's book followed this line of approach and, being more complete, gained a very influential position outside England. Glover's *Virgil* is in the same tradition, more discursive but with the same warm approach: Mackail's writings have the same spirit. The emphasis has been on the tenderness of the poetry, and the most quoted line since the time of Sainte-Beuve – but not before – has been *sunt lacrimae rerum et mentem mortalia tangunt* (*Aen.* 1. 462).

One of the most fruitful of modern approaches to the *Aeneid* examines the conflict in the poem between this sensitivity and the sterner theme of Roman destiny and world-rule. This is an approach which has been developed with differing emphases by Bowra and Tillyard and, with particular reference to the tension and conflict within Aeneas himself, by Perret. Pöschl explores these tensions especially in terms of imagery: he sees the poem as an exploration of conflict between cosmos (order) on the one hand and daemonic power and lawless violence on the other; and this conflict is symbolized in storm and peace, darkness and light, harsh or friendly landscape. Putnam also lays great stress on recurrent imagery and diction, on the interwoven threads which make the poem look backwards and forwards; and his interpretation of the last book is noteworthy for what Putnam sees as its pessimistic tone – he sees Aeneas finally engulfed by the waves of violence which he has fought so hard to subdue. 'It is Aeneas who loses at the end of Book XII, leaving Turnus victorious in his tragedy.' For Putnam, Book 12 negates any view of the *Aeneid* as an ideal vision of the greatness of Augustan Rome (*Poetry*, p. 123).

Otis examines Virgil's narrative technique, the essence of which is his personal involvement in the narrative by means of sympathy or empathy, by psychological continuity of tone and feeling achieved by recurrent imagery, metaphor, simile, moral phraseology. In contrast with the bright perpetual foreground of Homeric narrative we find in Virgil a penumbra of implication, a perpetual presence of oblique overtones, a preoccupied attitude. Otis also emphasizes the moral values of the poem rather than the sympathy for suffering, and he presents a sympathetic picture of Aeneas as representative of Roman values set against the *violentia* and *furor* of those who stand in his way. 'Virgil pities Turnus, gives him his full heroic due, but recognizes also that his fury can lead nowhere but to death (*Virgil*, p. 393).' Otis's evaluation of the tensions of the poem is an excellent counterblast against those who have thought that *Aeneid* 4 ran away with Virgil, or that Turnus is the true hero of the poem. Quinn sticks more closely to the text, aiming to reveal the uncomfortable and disquieting elements in Virgil's presentation without glossing over incongruous aspects in the interests of a coherent individual theory as to Virgil's intentions. The great merit of Camps's book is its admirable balance in presenting a synthesis of modern views on characters, themes, sources, and Virgil's art.

A marked feature of recent studies of the *Aeneid* has been the investigation of pattern and structure, of poetic architecture. Seminal work on this aspect was done by Heinze and Conway. Conway developed the idea of the intense books (the even numbers) separated by books which diminish the tension. Duckworth views the *Aeneid* as a trilogy, with the tragedies of Dido and Turnus flanking the central Roman section: this is complementary to the concept of two halves, the Iliadic and the Odyssean. Different schemes are propounded by Camps, Perret and Otis. In his 'structural patterns' Duckworth goes further, and from an idea by Le Grelle elaborates a scheme by mathematical analysis which presents the *Aeneid* as a series of patterns based on the golden section.

Detailed stylistic amd metrical analysis of the *Aeneid* is to be found in the modern commentaries, and special contributions to this aspect of the poem have been made by Marouzeau, Quinn, Wilkinson and especially Jackson Knight. The latter's studies of the interplay of rhythms associated with metrical ictus and word-accent – their coincidence or conflict, which he terms homodyne and heterodyne – have greatly advanced our understanding of the music of Virgil's hexameter.

On Virgil's use of source-material, the late nineteenth and early twentieth century concentrated on the painstaking collection of parallel material: more recently Knauer has listed the Homeric material in complete and formidable indexes, and has illustrated how it can be used to analyse Virgil's poetic and structural intentions. One of the main themes of Otis's book is Virgil's relationship with Homer, and his comparison of their narrative styles should be read alongside the first chapter of Eric Auerbach's *Mimesis* (Berne, 1946; trans. 1953), in which the difference between the externalized, distanced style of Homer and Virgil's 'inner' style is brilliantly explored.

Bowra, C. M., *From Virgil to Milton* (London, 1945).

Boyle, A. J., *The Meaning of the Aeneid: A Critical Inquiry*, Ramus I (Victoria, Aus., 1972).

Camps, W. A., *An Introduction to Virgil's Aeneid* (Oxford, 1969).

Conway, R. S., *The Architecture of the Epic* (Cambridge, Mass., 1928).

Duckworth, G. E., *Structural Patterns and Proportions in Vergil's Aeneid* (Ann Arbor, Mich., 1962).

Eliot, T. S., 'Virgil and the Christian World', in *On Poetry and Poets* (London, 1957).

Eliot, T. S., *What is a Classic?*, presidential address to the Virgil society, 1944, reprinted in *On Poetry and Poets* (London, 1957).

Glover, T. R., *Virgil* (London, 1912, 1923).

Gransden, K. W., *Virgil's Iliad: An Essay in Epic Narrative* (Cambridge, 1984).

Hardie, C. (ed.), *Vitae Virgilianae Antiquae* (Oxford, 1966).

Heinze, R., *Virgils epische Technik* (Leipzig, 1903; 3rd edn., 1928).

Jackson Knight, W. F., *Roman Vergil* (London, 1944, 2nd edn, Harmondsworth, 1966).

Johnson, W. R., *Darkness Visible* (Berkeley, Calif., 1976).

Klingner, F., *Virgil: Bucolica, Georgica, Aeneis* (Zurich, 1967).

Knauer, G. N., *Die Aeneis und Homer* (Göttingen, 1964).

Mackail, J. W., *The Aeneid of Virgil* (Oxford, 1930).

Marouzeau J., *L'orde des mots dans la phrase latine*, 3 vols (Paris, 1922–49).

Marouzeau, J., *Traité de stylistique latine* (Paris, 1954).

McKay, A. G., *Vergil's Italy* (New York, 1970).

Otis, B., *Virgil: A Study in Civilised Poetry* (Oxford, 1963).

Perret, J., *Virgile, l'homme et l'oeuvre* (Paris, 1952; 2nd edn, 1965).

Pöschl, V., *Die Dichtkunst Virgils: Bild und Symbol in der Aeneis* (Innsbruck, 1950; trans. Seligson, Mich., 1962).

Putnam, M. C. J., *The Poetry of the Aeneid* (Cambridge, Mass., 1965).

Quinn, K., *Virgil's Aeneid: A Critical Description* (London, 1968).

Sainte-Beuve, C. A., *Etude sur Virgile* (Paris, 1857).

Sellar, W. Y., *The Roman Poets of the Augustan Age: Virgil* (Oxford, 1877; 3rd edn, 1897).

Wight Duff, J., *A Literary History of Rome; From the Origins to the Close of the Golden Age* (London, 1960).

Wilkinson, L. P., *Golden Latin Artistry* (Cambridge, 1963).

Williams, G., *Technique and Ideas in the Aeneid* (New Haven, Conn., 1983).

Williams, R. D., *Greece and Rome, New Surveys in the Classics*, no. 1 *Virgil* (Oxford, 1967; 2nd edn with addenda, 1979).

Williams, R. D., 'The Aeneid', in E. J. Kenney and W. V. Clausen (eds), *The Cambridge History of Classical Literature*, vol. 2 (Cambridge, 1982), pp. 333 – 69.

5 VIRGIL'S INFLUENCE

Bolgar, R. R., *The Classical Heritage and its Beneficiaries* (Cambridge, 1954).

Comparetti, D., *Vergil in the Middle Ages*, trans. Benecke (London, 1895).

Dudley, D. R. (ed.), *Studies in Latin Literature and its Influence: Virgil* (London, 1969).

Foerster, D. M., *The Fortunes of Epic Poetry* (Washington, DC, 1962).

Harding, D. P., *The Club of Hercules* (Urbana, Ill., 1962).

Highet, G., *The Classical Tradition* (Oxford, 1949)

Kenney, E. J. and Clausen, W. V. (eds), *The Cambridge History of Classical Literature*, vol. 2 (Cambridge, 1982), index s.v. Virgil, influence.

Ker, W. P. (ed.), *Essays of John Dryden* (Oxford, 1900).

Lewis, C. S., *A Preface to Paradise Lost* (London, 1942).

Mackail, J. W., 'Virgil and Virgilianism,' in *Lectures on Poetry* (London, 1914).

Martindale, C. (ed.), *Virgil and his Influence* (Bristol, 1984).

Nitchie, E., *Vergil and the English Poets* (New York, 1919).

Quinn, K., *Latin Explorations* (London, 1963).

Sandys, J. E., *A History of Classical Scholarship* (Cambridge, 1903 – 8).

Spargo, J. W., *Virgil the Necromancer* (Cambridge, Mass., 1934).

Thomson, J. A. K., *Classical Influences on English Poetry* (London, 1951).

Tillyard, E. M. W., *The English Epic and its Background* (Oxford, 1954).

Whitfield, J. H., *Dante and Virgil* (Oxford, 1949).

Williams, R. D., and Pattie, T. S., *Virgil: His Poetry through the Ages* (London, 1982).

INDEX

verse form 13, 152; *Eclogues* 3; hexameter 13, 21–3
Vida: *Christiad* 148
Virgil: life 1–2; works 2–3; fame of 137; influence of 137–61; cult of 146
Virgil Society 160

war: battle scenes 15, 17, 18, 56–77, 95–6, 99–100; Aeneas' attitude towards 97, 119; Turnus' attitude towards 119
Wight Duff, J. 78
William of Malmesbury 146
Wordsworth, William 158